MW00640383

The Stockton and Darlington Railway, the first public railway to be empowered to convey goods and passengers by steam traction, has been dismissed by historians as fulfilling little more than a precursory role in the inauguration of the 'Railway Age'. This book establishes its claim to recognition as a significant element in the maturing phase of Britain's industrialisation after 1830, through an examination of its critical role in the contemporary national debate on the merits of steam power and its direct effect on the economic growth of south Durham and north-east Yorkshire, a region which became the most important iron-producing centre in the world partly as a result of the Stockton and Darlington Railway's role as a 'fuel artery'. The experience of the company is of direct relevance to economic historians concerned with the regional basis of Britain's industrialisation, and also to business historians seeking to evaluate the sources of entrepreneurial success.

The origins of railway enterprise: the Stockton and
Darlington Railway, 1821–1863

The origins of railway enterprise: the Stockton and Darlington Railway, 1821–1863

Maurice W. Kirby

Reader in Economic History at Lancaster University

Published by the Press Syndicate of the University of Cambridge
The Pitt Building, Trumpington Street, Cambridge CB2 1RP
40 West 20th Street, New York, NY 10011–4211, USA
10 Stamford Road, Oakleigh, Melbourne 3166, Australia

First published 1993

Printed in Great Britain at the University Press, Cambridge

A catalogue record for this book is available from the British Library

Library of Congress cataloguing in publication data

Kirby, M. W.
The origins of railway enterprise: the Stockton and Darlington Railway,
1821–1863 / Maurice W. Kirby.
    p.   cm.
Includes bibliographical references and index.
ISBN 0 521 38445–1 (hc)
1. Stockton and Darlington Railway – History. 2. Railroads – Great Britain –
History. I. Title.
HE3020.S8K57   1993
385'.06'542851 – dc20   92–41856 CIP
ISBN 0 521 38445 1 hardback

To Alexa and David

Contents

Illustrations

Maps and plans

Tables

Acknowledgements

I have incurred many debts in writing this book. My parents assisted greatly in identifying primary sources in the north-east of England. In transcribing innumerable documents they also facilitated the process of research and eased the task of writing. My colleagues, Mary Rose and Oliver Westall, provided much intellectual stimulus and Dr Rose in particular, with her extensive knowledge of sources, kept me abreast of developments in the relevant literature. I should also like to thank Tom Eden of the Darlington Railway Preservation Society for his early encouragement of my work. We share a common interest in the local history of north-east England and Tom has laboured extensively to sustain and popularise the visual legacy of a rich industrial heritage. Special thanks are due to Tom Pearce. An engineer by training and inclination, he possesses an unrivalled knowledge of the engineering history of the Stockton and Darlington Railway. He has given liberally of his advice and has provided me with invaluable primary documentation. Readers will notice that the present work comments sparingly on technical issues. This is, in large measure, the result of my acquaintance with Tom Pearce. Unwittingly, perhaps, he has persuaded me that to comment accurately and with authority on such matters as locomotive and rolling stock design demands the kind of insight that can only be forthcoming from professional expertise and long deliberation of the minutiae of technological change. The staff of libraries and record offices have been unfailingly helpful in responding to queries and in directing me to archive material. I should like to thank, in particular, staff at the Public Record Office, Kew, at the Newcastle City Library, and at the Durham and Darlington branches of the Durham County Record Office. The opportunity to consult archive deposits was provided by the Economic and Social Research Council which provided a grant in aid of my research. Finally, I should like to thank my wife and children for their support and encouragement of this project. I have dedicated the result to my daughter and son.

MAURICE W. KIRBY

1 The Stockton and Darlington Railway in economic and business history

Every fifty years since it opened in 1825 the Stockton and Darlington Railway has been celebrated publicly as the pioneer of all subsequent railway development – 'the starting point of the vast network of lines which covered a considerable portion of the globe,'[1] and as the harbinger of a technological revolution by virtue of its employment of locomotive haulage. The sesquicentenary in 1975 was marked by extensive local celebrations, exhibitions, the issue of special postage stamps, and, most impressive of all, the inauguration of the National Railway Museum at York as a fitting memorial to the event. It is true that commercial considerations loomed large on these occasions – the desire for advertisement and preferment on the part of the sponsoring North Eastern Railway in 1875 and the succeeding London and North Eastern Railway in 1925, and the expectation of enhanced revenues from tourism in 1975. Yet it was obvious that all three events were marked by considerable feelings of local pride in what was regarded as an outstanding commercial and technological achievement sufficiently impressive to have given south Durham, and Darlington and Shildon in particular, an established place in the history of human progress.

In stark contrast to popular perceptions have been the views of economic historians, ever mindful of the need to clothe their accounts of transport development with restraint and objectivity. In the sober light of historical analysis the Stockton and Darlington Railway has been accorded little more than a precursory role in the inauguration of the 'Railway Age'.[2] Contrary to popular belief it was not the first railway to receive parliamentary sanction.[3] It was not even the first public railway[4] or, indeed, the first to employ steam locomotives commercially.[5] More specifically, in comparison with the Liverpool and Manchester Railway which opted from the outset of operations in 1830 for complete mechanical traction under the control of a board of directors, the Stockton and Darlington Company's combination of horses and stationary engines, with an apparently minimal commitment to locomotives, together with the leasing of the line to contractors for the conveyance of passengers (until 1833), lends further support to its detractors. It is also the case that the founders of the earlier company had strictly

1

1   Corporate seal of the Stockton and Darlington Railway Company. The literal translation of the motto means 'At Private Risk for Public Service'.

limited objectives: the Stockton and Darlington Railway was to be a coal line serving a small number of landsale collieries in the south-west of County Durham with the shipment of other minerals such as limestone, and the carriage of passengers in particular, very much as afterthoughts.

This book modifies the scholarly consensus in several important respects. In the first instance, although the Quaker founders of the company possessed a shrewd sense of immediate *possibility* and little sense of *direction* the latter developed rapidly once the construction phase had begun. By 1823 the company's management committee had perceived the desirability of locomitive traction and in the following year its leading members provided the bulk of the finance for the establishment of the world's first locomotive building enterprise – Robert Stephenson and Co. of Newcastle upon Tyne. Contemporaneous with this was the creation of George Stephenson and Co. as a surveying organisation, initially under Stockton and Darlington auspices, for the planning of railways elsewhere in the UK. After the opening of its line in 1825 the Stockton and Darlington Company provided an invaluable testing ground for the technical development of locomotives such that by 1828 the company's own engineering staff, led by the highly talented Timothy Hackworth, had produced a powerful short-haul engine which was to resolve the management committee's doubts as to the reliability of locomotive haulage, and in the immediate setting its cost effectiveness. This is not to suggest that Hackworth's endeavours proved decisive in the contemporary national debate on the merits of locomotive power. The Liverpool and Manchester Company's decision to convene the Rainhill Trials in 1829 was symptomatic of a continuing concern with the weight of locomotives in relation to the available materials for the construction of the permanent way and their steaming capacity in differing traffic conditions. It is not coincidental, however, that a Stephenson-designed engine, drawing on the accumulated experience of the Stockton and Darlington Company, proved to be the successful entrant. In the Stockton and Darlington context, moreover, the decision to phase out horse haulage after 1828 was to prove critical in ensuring the company's subsequent commercial success.

Although the early progress of railway technology must be an important ingredient in the study of an innovatory company in a new sector of the economy the principal object of this study is to establish the Stockton and Darlington Company's claim to recognition as a significant element in the maturing phase of British industrialisation after 1830. Small though the company may have been in relation to the trunk lines constructed in the later 1830s and 1840s, its evolving network came to occupy a position of vital strategic importance in the development of a new and highly concentrated industrial district. By the time of the opening of the railway in 1825 the Stockton and Darlington management committee had begun to broaden its original self-limiting conception of a landsale mineral line to include a coastal trade in coal via the Tees in direct competition with long-established interests on the Tyne and Wear. During the final stages of construction of their line the Stockton and Darlington proprietors had come to appreciate that the innovation of the public joint stock railway, in resolving the problem of wayleaves and in offering a potentially cheap and efficient means of bulk mineral transport, would lower the costs of entry for new firms into the colliery business. Their expectations proved correct: the railway precipitated the expansion of the Auckland coalfield after 1825 and provided local colliery entrepreneurs with a competitive edge over their northern rivals in the coastal trade thereby destabilising the Tyne and Wear 'Limitation of the Vend' agreement for the supply of coal to the London market. By the end of the 1830s the Stockton and Darlington Railway was firmly established as the 'fuel artery' for south Durham and north-east Yorkshire: the Tees coal trade was booming and with it the newly established urban settlement of Middlesbrough – founded in 1831 as a deep-water coaling port by leading financial interests in the Stockton and Darlington Company. In 1841 the same interests opened the extensive Middlesbrough Docks as a major addition to the already considerable infrastructure investment in coal drops and Tees navigation facilities. The Docks were absorbed formally by the Stockton and Darlington Company in 1849, a date which marks the onset of a renewed upsurge in the rate of economic development of the Tees and upper Wear valley districts. After 1850 Teesside rapidly outgrew the limits set by exclusive concentration on the coal trade as a result of the exploitation of the recently discovered iron ore deposits of Cleveland. By 1870 the district was the most important iron-producing centre in the world, an achievement which had been facilitated in large measure by a Stockton and Darlington rail network which was deliberately designed for the bulk transhipment of coal, coke, limestone, and ironstone. The point to be made in this context is that the district of south Durham and north-east Yorkshire, poorly endowed with navigable rivers and with a terrain inimical to the construction of canals, gained immense advantages from investment in railways. As such, the Stockton and Darlington Company provides a classic example in the UK context of the concept of innovational 'indispensibility' in an area where waterways were not a feasible alternative to rail transport.[6] The railway widened markets, changed the structure of costs and prices for commodity inputs and outputs and in so doing made a largely autonomous contribution to regional economic growth. Economic historians should therefore bear in mind that the experience of north-east England as a distinctive region is highly untypical of the rest of the UK in terms of the applications of social savings analysis to transport innovation.[7]

The industrial development of the Tees and upper Wear valleys under the impetus of railway expansion serves also to illuminate the ongoing debate among economic historians between those who have espoused the need for a regional perspective on Britain's early industrialisation in the face of the aggregative approach adopted by the new macro-economic school of quantitative historians.[8] Industrialisation during the first half of the nineteenth century was a distinctly regional phenomenon. As E. A. Wrigley commented in the early 1960s, 'industrial growth [before 1850] was essentially a local rather than a national affair. In this regard it is perhaps unnecessarily inexact to talk of England and the continent rather than, say, of Lancashire and the Valley of the Sambre-Meuse. Each country was made up of a number of regional economies.'[9] This disaggregated approach was subsequently adopted by Sidney Pollard in his penetrating analysis of European industrialisation, with an explanatory framework grounded in regions reaching across geographical borders. On the specific subject of railways Pollard observed that in marked contrast to the Continental European experience railway development in Britain did not lead to significant changes in the country's economic geography.

That had been fixed by coal, and while the railways here and there extended the workable parts of coalfields as in South-West Durham, the East Midlands, or the Scottish Lowlands ... they did not call into being a major industrial region that had not existed before. Only in the second half [of the nineteenth century] were they instrumental in developing mineral areas, such as Tees-side and Furness, and in locating ports and seaside holiday resorts.[10]

The fact remains that as a distinctive region the north-east of England had emerged as 'a powerful force in the British economy' long before the end of the seventeenth century. As Neil Evans has pointed out, 'By the reign of Charles I one Tyneside pit could probably have produced the entire output of Henry VIII's reign. Coal was increasingly mined in response to the phenomenal growth of London, and the gentry of the north-east flourished as a particularly market-oriented group in an increasingly commercialised society.'[11] The coal-based development of the north-east economy has received insufficient attention in the historiography of British industrialisation. At the regional level the main focus of attention has been on Lancashire, hardly surprising in the light of the explosive market growth of the cotton textile industry and accompanying supply-side changes.[12] Yet it is salutary to remember that the north-east coal industry experienced substantial growth of output during the eighteenth and early nineteenth centuries. Between 1700 and 1830 production quintupled from an overwhelmingly dominant base figure at the same time as the industry experienced ongoing technological change. Diminishing returns which followed in the wake of the deepening of mines were contained by steam pumping and winding. Coalmining, moreover, is as much a 'transport' as a productive industry[13] and well before the end of the eighteenth century the banks of the Tyne and Wear had given birth to a network of waggonways – the forerunners of nineteenth-century railway technology. As Professor Flinn remarked, the Durham sea-coal industry, 'Despite its antiquity was ... still vigorous enough to trigger off both a mining and a transport revolution.'[14] It is therefore this regional dimension which provides the broad contextual framework for analysing the economic significance of the Stockton and Darlington Railway.

The experience of the Stockton and Darlington Company thus serves to illuminate some recent and ongoing debates in economic history. It also sheds considerable light on issues of direct relevance to business historians. Modern transaction costs theory, for example, insofar as it relates to the coordination and allocation of resources, suggests that the efficiency of firms can be enhanced by internalising such costs.[15] As the history of the Stockton and Darlington Company reveals, however, transaction costs arising from

market uncertainties can be reduced by external networks. This is exemplified in the case of the Stockton and Darlington Company by its record of
capital formation. In this respect the company was unique in the history of
UK railway enterprise as a public joint stock concern which was, in effect, a
close family partnership. Throughout its existence as an independent entity
the company relied heavily upon the Society of Friends for its capital and
borrowing requirements. This had been a notable feature of the enterprise
at the time of its inaguration in 1821, but by the mid-1840s the pattern of
share ownership had come to be concentrated in the hands of the Quaker
Pease family of Darlington which by virtue of its extensive intermarriage
with a number of Britain's leading Quaker business dynasties was able to tap
a private, nation-wide capital market. This aspect of the history of the
Stockton and Darlington Railway has been touched upon by other economic
historians and in an earlier monograph by the present writer.[16] What it
reveals is that the company's investment strategy came to be dominated
increasingly after 1830 by the brothers Joseph and Henry Pease, both of
whom epitomised the thrusting urban–manufacturing–industrial interest
which was to transform the economy and society of Britain during the
course of the nineteenth century. The ascendancy of the Peases and their
immediate Quaker associates was assured as they became major traffic
senders on the Stockton and Darlington network following their own extensive investment in local mineral development and the docking and associated urban facilities of Middlesbrough. It would be true to say that the
expansion of the Stockton and Darlington Company was never at any time
constrained by lack of financial resources. It is impossible, therefore, to
examine the capital structure and investment strategy of the company
without taking account of kinship ties of unusual strength and geographical
dispersion.[17]

In terms of business organisation the Stockton and Darlington Company
provides some pointed contrasts to the managerial structures adopted by
later trunk line companies founded in the 1840s and 1850s. To the end of its
independent existence the company's management committee remained
committed to the principle of subcontracting in numerous aspects of
operations. The subcontracting of locomotive repairs and servicing, and the
maintenance of the permanent way, for example, rendered the boundaries of
the firm indistinct. In this respect the Stockton and Darlington Company
occupies an unusual position in British business history. It was innovative
and profitable and helped to propel regional economic growth in the maturing phase of Britain's industrialisation. Yet in its managerial procedures it
was antediluvian, looking back to precedents set in the canal era of the
eighteenth century.

Subcontracting may have set the Stockton and Darlington Company apart from the internalising strategies of larger contemporary enterprises. It did, however, conform to practice elsewhere in floating nominally independent concerns as a means of reinforcing its hold on the mineral traffic of south-west Durham and north-east Yorkshire. A cursory examination of this structure would suggest excessive fragmentation of control leading to increasing inefficiency rather than sophistication in the managerial process. It is important to note, however, that there was, in reality, a substantial degree of overlap between the directorates of associated companies, with a central core drawn from the Pease family. This ensured continuity of decision-making throughout the Stockton and Darlington Company's independent existence. The disadvantage of such a structure was that the fortunes of the company were subject to the Peases' overwhelming determination to exert a form of autocratic control over localised mineral traffic movements. In their anxiety to destroy, or at least limit the threat of, competition, the Pease brothers led the Stockton and Darlington Company into a series of unsound speculations in the early 1840s which were to endanger its financial solvency during the commercial crisis of 1847–8.

The importance of this book lies in the fact that comparatively little is known about British industrial enterprise in the first half of the nineteenth century. As far as the Stockton and Darlington Company is concerned its experience indicates that in the immediate context of railway development it provided two invaluable sources of inspiration and guidance for subsequent railway promoters. In the first instance, it demonstrated the efficacy of steam locomotion *per se* but in so doing highlighted the need for high-quality construction techiques in the laying of the permanent way when the available materials were of poor or inconsistent quality. Secondly, its early commercial success encouraged other promoters, not least the merchants of Liverpool and Manchester, to proceed with their own schemes. In this respect, however, the Stockton and Darlington Company's experience was misleading. It was conceived and operated as a mineral line in a district where a cost-reducing transport innovation would have maximum impact. It therefore provided few lessons for the promoters of trunk lines whose primary interest was in the carriage of light freight and passengers.

Similar considerations apply to the analyses of modern economic historians: in giving birth to a new industrial district based upon the exploitation of bulk raw materials the Stockton and Darlington Railway underlines the fact that in the context of the ongoing social savings controversy, the disputed 'axiom of indispensibility' holds fast for the growth-inducing effects of an innovation in a region where there was no effective substitute in the form of navigable waterways. As a contribution to business history the book provides a case study of the role of the individual entrepreneur in determining commercial strategy. As the dominant managerial element the

Peases were undoubtedly advantaged by the network of Quaker financial relationships that they were able to exploit. As entrepreneurs they were also lucky, as evidenced by the timely discovery of ironstone deposits which were fortuitously located in relation to other key industrial raw materials. But whilst it is true that luck can be as important as sound commercial judgement in determining the fortunes of business enterprise the Peases consistently revealed themselves as dynamic, forceful, and innovative Schumpeterian-style entrepreneurs. Nowhere was this more evident than in their investment strategy after 1850 when they took the lead in projecting a succession of strategically located new lines. The effect was to lay the basis for the emergence of Teesside as an outstanding centre for the production of iron manufactures and also to pave the way for a most lucrative merger with the North Eastern Railway Company in 1863.

2   The prelude to railways

The origins of the public steam railway are firmly located in the expanding coal industry of the eighteenth century. Between 1700 and 1830 national coal output grew tenfold, from approximately 3 million tons to 30 million tons per annum, in response to the growth in home demand for household coals, and more especially to the evolving raw material and energy requirements of other industrial sectors.[1] With the demise of charcoal burning in the iron industry after 1770, for example, coke was required for smelting and puddling, whilst in textiles the gradual abandonment of the water wheel after 1810 gave rise to a new demand for coal as primary fuel in the generation of steam power. In confronting these market pressures the industry refined and developed the techniques of mining coal, as shafts were deepened, faces extended, and rudimentary ventilation methods improved. The efficiency of underground haulage rose dramatically following the substitution of horse for human power, and also as a result of the introduction of the metal-surface railway for the movement of tubs between coal face and shaft. Coal seams liable to the ingress of water were rendered accessible by the diffusion of Newcomen's steam pump after 1712, while in the final quarter of the eighteenth century the application of the same technology in rotary form revolutionised the business of colliery winding. Together, these innovations enabled the industry to fulfil the needs of newly emergent coal-based activities elsewhere, and to that extent coalmining had a critical role to play in facilitating the secular expansion of the industrial sector as a whole.[2] Even more importantly, the industry contributed to an acceleration in the overall rate of economic growth. This was achieved in two main ways, first of all by promoting greater technical sophistication in the design and operating efficiency of the stationary steam engine, and secondly by encouraging technological innovation in the transport sector of the economy.

Whilst an established tradition of improving the quality of river navigation should warn against overestimating the revolutionary impact of the canal era in the history of British transport, there can be little doubt that canals fulfilled a crucial role in expanding the volume of internal trade after

2   Coal waggon on a four-foot waggonway in Co. Durham, 1765 (not to
scale).

1760.[3] In lowering distribution costs for a wide range of commodities
canals, like improved river navigations, could be justified without reference
to the needs of the coal trade, yet it was in this sphere of economic activity
that their cost effectiveness was first displayed, most notably in the south
Lancashire coalfield after 1760. The Sankey Brook Navigation and the
Duke of Bridgewater's Worsley Canal dramatically lowered the supply price
of coal at their respective terminal points in Liverpool and Manchester, and
their commercial success in an area of great economic potential encouraged
a host of imitators in other coalfields ill-served by coastal or river navigation.[4]

   The same can be said of the coal industry's contribution to the development of railway technology, culminating in the innovation of the steam
locomotive after 1800, running on specialised track, and open to public use
for the carriage of passengers and goods of all kinds. Probably originating in
the Wollaton district of Nottinghamshire at the beginning of the seventeenth century, the colliery railway was first constructed of wooden rails,
usually of oak or fir, laid directly on the ground. The consequent reduction
of friction, in combination with very moderate gradients, greatly facilitated
the passage of coal waggons, resulting in marked productivity gains over the
conventional means of overland transport – the pack-horse and wain-cart.[5]
Thus, the innovation of the colliery waggonway long pre-dated the canal era
in transport development. The process of diffusion, however, was slow and
it was only in the north-east of England that the waggonway was introduced

on a significant scale and with a degree of technical sophistication hitherto unknown. The much-famed 'Newcastle waggonways', for example, were built for vehicles with flanged wheels and considerable attention was paid to the preparation of the track bed in order to facilitate drainage and the use of sleepers. Even in the north-east, however, extensive waggonway development was delayed until the final quarter of the seventeenth century. The precipitating factor was the need to reduce transport costs as the area of colliery working was extended away from the banks of the Tyne and Wear. This occurred when the most accessible seams had either been worked out or where the deepening of shafts was rendered difficult or impossible because of flooding. The banks of the Tyne and Wear, moreover, were ideally suited to waggonway operations. The journey from the pit head to the river-side coal staithes was rarely more than ten miles in length and downhill gradients offered the advantages of gravity so that the productivity of horses was greatly enhanced.[6] It has been estimated that a single horse and railway waggon could displace twenty-four pack-horses and up to three four-horse wain-carts.[7] In these circumstances it is hardly surprising that in 1711 the owners of the Tanfield Moor Colliery, responsible for the construction of the most elaborate waggonway in the north-east, could look forward to a threefold increase in profits following the abandonment of wain-carts.[8] Nevertheless, waggonways were a costly addition to the fixed capital of colliery enterprises with average construction costs for much of the eighteenth century well in excess of £750 per mile. In some cases it seems likely that the cost of construction equalled or even exceeded the sum invested in the pit to be served by the waggonway. Information on maintenance charges is sparse, but in view of the fact that wooden rails rarely survived for more than three years, renewal expenses must have been a significant recurring item of fixed expenditure for colliery proprietors. Indeed, the practice developed at an early stage of laying extra strips of hard-wearing beech on top of the original track to produce a 'double way', a mode of strengthening which was supplemented by wrought-iron plates for points of maximum wear after 1760. Successively modified the wooden waggonway was 'a fully-fledged horse-and-gravity operated mineral railway of great capacity and considerable flexibility'. Some time after 1780 the practice was introduced of coupling waggons to form trains, a development facilitated by the invention of the overshot brake and the local innovation of the rope-operated balanced incline whereby descending sets of waggons hauled up an equivalent number of empties. The latter innovation was, indeed, 'the first step towards both the disappearance of the horse, and the full introduction of the iron rail from the 1790s onwards'.[9]

A continuous cast-iron plated track was first laid down at the works of the Coalbrookdale Iron Company in 1767,[10] but the widespread adoption of the cast-iron rail had to await the 1790s when the canal construction boom of that decade led to a considerable expansion in the feeder network for inland waterways in those areas of the country – south Wales, and Notting-hamshire and Derbyshire in particular – where the iron industry was developing most rapidly. A further precipitating factor was the outbreak of the Napoleonic Wars which served to raise the price of wood and at the same time placed a premium on increasing the productivity of draft-horses in view of their growing scarcity and the rising cost of fodder.[11]

A majority of the new canal feeders were constructed of plate-rails, flanged on the inside edge thus enabling ordinary road carts to be used without adaptation. Their principal advocate was Benjamin Outram of the Butterley Ironworks in Derbyshire, and it was due to his influence that the plate or tramway spread throughout the Midlands from the mid-1790s, penetrating rapidly into south Wales after 1799.[12] In addressing the British Association in 1863 Sir William Armstrong offered the plausible observa-tion that the plateway was a distinctive and evolutionary step in the devel-opment of the edge-railway, before the guiding flange was transferred from the rail to the wheel.[13] It was, however, a separate development in its own right, ideally suited to the flexible traffic needs of the canal era but con-demned to ultimate obsolescence as a result of its technical and engineering limitations. The retaining flange, for example, was an impediment to smooth running, harbouring dirt and stones, whilst the limited strength of the plate-rail itself effectively precluded the use of heavy and specialised rolling stock. In these respects the iron edge-rail was superior, especially in the 'fish-bellied' form first introduced by William Jessop on the Forest line of the Leicester Navigation in 1793–4.[14] It is of considerable significance that at the very time when the plateway was being rapidly diffused as a canal feeder throughout the Midlands and south Wales, the colliery owners of the north-east and Cumberland, with their established tradition of waggonway operations, remained committed to the edge-rail. In 1807 the great north-east viewer, John Buddle, drew attention to the advantages of metal track when he stated that 'a horse on the average will do more work by 30 per cent on an iron way than a wooden way; but frequently he will do 50 and even 100 per cent more'.[15] Although important iron-founding capacity in the north-east was as yet confined to the Bedlington Iron Company and the Tyne Iron-works at Leamington, Buddle's comments marked the beginnings of a general movement from wooden to iron edge-rails in the colliery districts of County Durham and Northumberland. Elsewhere, however, the acknowl-edged primacy of the edge-rail had to await the construction of the Stockton and Darlington line after 1821.

The development of waggonways in the Tyne and Wear districts cannot be divorced from the evolving structure of the coal industry. Restrictive practices among colliery owners can be traced back to the latter part of the sixteenth century when a tradition of collusive activity for the control of prices in the London market was initiated.[16] Early producers' associations rarely lasted for more than one year, but by the end of the seventeenth century conditions in the trade were encouraging the search for a more permanent regulation. Competition had intensified as the number of independent producers expanded, whilst profit margins were being eroded in response to the growth of restrictive practices among numerous categories of merchant-middlemen and shippers. These factors were probably sufficient in themselves to justify costly investment in improved methods of overland transport on the part of colliery owners whose pits were not immediately adjacent to the shipping staithes. There was, however, one major impediment in the way of achieving cost reductions by means of transport innovation. This took the form of the annual rent, or surface wayleaves, payable to the owners of land traversed by a waggonway. Wayleaves were unavoidable and their contentious nature frequently resulted in bitter conflict which on occasion proceeded to the point of litigation. Indeed, where the wayleave owner was himself a colliery proprietor there was a powerful incentive to deny transport facilities to competitors.[17] One obvious solution to these difficulties was a private Act of Parliament which would have endowed colliery owners with statutory powers to purchase the land necessary for the construction of a waggonway. This practice was, after all, the accepted procedure for the projectors of turnpike roads and canals, even though compulsory powers were only rarely invoked. But as Professor Flinn has remarked, the construction of waggonways was an established practice long before it had become customary to secure private legislation for transport improvements.[18] More to the point, the great majority of colliery proprietors were intent upon reserving waggonways for their own exclusive use, either individually or collectively. There is little, if any, indication in the eighteenth century that waggonways were perceived as anything other than an industry-specific form of transport – in effect part of the essential infrastructure of the coal trade. This is well illustrated by the activities of the most powerful combine of colliery owners to appear in the coal industry of the eighteenth century. In 1726 the Montagu family of Wortley, the Liddells of Ravensworth, and George Bowes of Gibside agreed 'to join some of their collieries and to enter into a friendship and partnership for the purchase or taking other collieries, and for winning and working of coals thereout, and to exchange benefits and kindnesses with each other, upon a lasting foundation'.[19] This partnership, subsequently known as the Grand Allies, engaged in an ambitious and effective policy of output regulation by the control of wayleaves. After 1726 further mines were acquired by leasing or licensing, wayleaves purchased,

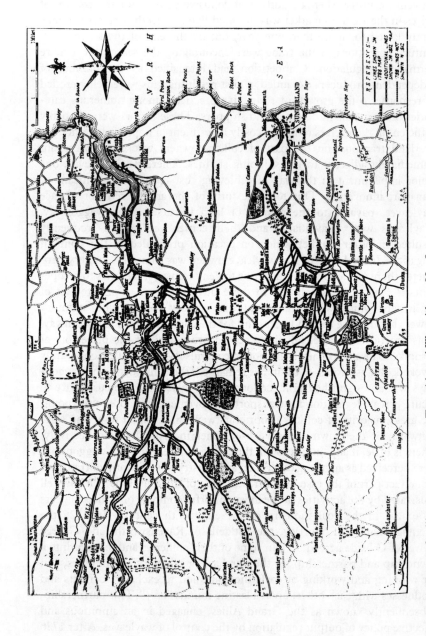

1 The development of colliery waggonways on Tyneside and Wearside, 1788–1812.
Source: the details of the lines in 1788 are taken from a 'Plan of the Collieries on the River Tyne and Wear, taken from actual surveys

and on occasion dead rents paid for land in order to deny potential competitors the right of way to a point of shipment. By 1739 the Allies controlled 'so large a share of all lands adjoining to the river Tyne that they have almost totally debarred all other persons from access to it with coals, especially on the south side where the best coals lie, and the like has been done with respect to the River Wear'.[20] The influence of the Allies began to decline after 1750 as new entrants to the coal trade were able to take advantage of technical progress, easier access to credit facilities, and a regime of higher prices in the London market. The most that could be accomplished thereafter in terms of the regulation of output was a succession of 'Agreements of Limitations of the Vend' beginning in 1771. The Vend, however, proved to be an unstable cartel, weakened periodically by new competitors and volatility of prices, until its demise in the 1840s.[21] The introduction of the Vend may well have signalled the end of 'the Golden Age of the Tyne Coalowner', but for the Grand Allies the enduring and visible legacy of their association was the extensive waggonway system – amounting to forty-two miles on Tyneside alone in 1739 – and representing a capital investment of £50,000.[22]

Shared waggonways of the kind inaugurated by the Grand Allies were a common feature in the north-east coalfield by the end of the eighteenth century. By this time too the practice had begun to develop of throwing waggonways open to common use on the part of any interested colliery proprietor. These were, in effect, 'public' ways, resembling in their mode of operation canal companies, although in the north-east, unlike in the Forest of Dean coalfield, the practice never developed of incorporating colliery waggonways by Act of Parliament.[23]

By the end of the eighteenth century waggonways were firmly established as part of Britain's transport system. Their contribution to the growth of the coal industry – in facilitating the extension of coal working by containing rising marginal costs – had been an important one. In their absence river navigations and canals would have been forced to rely upon a feeder network of roads which even in improved form could not have sustained the kind of traffic density and haulage weights which had long been the norm in the north-east coalfield. Yet it is important to note that after more than a century of operating experience, the waggonway was still regarded as an appendage of a single, albeit critically important, sector of the economy. It is true that in the two decades after 1800 the notion that waggonways could justify an independent existence began to gain ground. The Surrey Iron Railway, for example, was incorporated in 1801, for the carriage of agricultural produce, lime, chalk, and coal between Wandsworth and Croydon, whilst the Oystermouth Railway was incorporated three years later to carry minerals and subsequently passengers between Swansea and Oystermouth.[24]

3   Richard Trevithick (1771–1833), designer of the first high-pressure locomotive engine.

In the period to 1821 sixteen horse-drawn tramways were incorporated by Act of Parliament, but they were conceived on such a small scale and with objectives so limited that they failed to establish worthwhile precedents. Visionary schemes for the construction of a national railway system can be traced back at least as far as the late 1760s when Richard Lovell Edgeworth envisaged laying 'railways for baggage waggons on the great roads of England', an idea to which he returned in 1802 with his suggested scheme for an iron railway stretching forth from London with traffic being hauled by stationary steam engines.[25] Inspired in part by Adam Smith's assertion that transport improvements had a vital role to play in extending the market, thereby facilitating economic growth, Edgeworth was far in advance of his time in appreciating the potential impact of the railway on the economy as a whole. Even as late as 1821, when Thomas Grey achieved some publishing success with his *Observations on a General Iron Railway*,[26] with horses being entirely superseded by steam traction, railways were still viewed primarily as subordinate feeders to navigable water, and reliant for their motive power on the dependable and ubiquitous horse.

If the essence of railway economics was greater fixed investment in order to reduce working costs then the transition from wooden- to metal-surface track was clearly an important factor in improving the efficiency of waggon-way operations. But the technological innovation which paved the way for the widespread use of the railway as an independent transport facility was the steam locomotive, vastly superior to the horse in tractive effort, and offering the economic advantages of greater fuel efficiency and labour productivity. Not that these attributes could be achieved instantaneously. Steam locomotives only attained sufficient speed and reliability in performance to begin the process of revolutionising the transport system as a whole in the 1830s, and even then locomotive development was dependent upon parallel improvements in the quality of the permanent way, both in terms of the manufacture of the rails themselves and the engineering techniques of construction. The breakthrough to the application of steam power to mechanical traction came in two stages, the first in 1787 with James Watt's development of rotary motion, and the second in 1804 when the brilliant Cornish engineer, Richard Trevithick, produced his first high-pressure locomotive engine.[27] The latter was the product of a wager between Samuel Homfray, owner of the Pen-y-Daren Ironworks in south Wales, and his neighbour, Anthony Hill of the Plymouth Ironworks, that ten tons of iron could be hauled along the Pen-y-Daren tramway from the ironworks to Abercynon Wharf utilising steam power.[28] That this task was amply accomplished was a tribute to Trevithick's engineering abilities, in particular his invention of the return-flue boiler with a rudimentary steam blast to enhance the tractive effort. The 'Achilles' heel' of Trevithick's engine – and one which was to plague all of the early locomotive builders – was its excessive weight in relation to the available track. The cast-iron plates of the Pen-y-Daren tramway were only 3 feet in length and far too brittle to sustain the crushing weight of an unsprung locomotive with 1¼ tons resting on each wheel. It was this defect which caused Christopher Blackett, the owner of Wylam Colliery in Northumberland, to refuse delivery of a Trevithick-type locomotive which was built for him at John Whinfield's foundry in Gateshead in 1805. The Wylam waggonway was of traditional wood construction and Blackett immediately recognised that it would be irreparably damaged by locomotive haulage. Even in this very early phase of locomotive development Trevithick's endeavours had highlighted one of the most critical factors in railway economics, namely the interrelatedness of a specialised capital stock. It was simply not possible to employ locomotives to advantage without incurring additional and proportionately much greater expenditure on a purpose-built metal track, and this acted as a powerful deterrent to further experiments in locomotive haulage. Not that Trevithick was especially concerned to resolve this problem. As his biographer has pointed out, he lacked the necessary persistence, and in any event his high-pressure steam engines were capable of adaptation to a variety of uses. The Pen-y-Daren engine was eventually used to drive a tilt hammer in Homfray's ironworks, whilst its Gateshead counterpart was used to blow a cupola in Whinfield's foundry.[29]

The obvious solution was the introduction of heavier and better designed track, preferably of wrought-iron construction. But to the extent that this would have entailed the scrapping of an existing investment giving an adequate return with horse haulage, it was financially unattractive. It is significant that when north-east colliery owners began to convert their wooden waggonways to metal track after 1807 the practice developed of making them 'piece by piece keeping up the old waggons and running them partly on wood and partly on iron'.[30] This practice was dictated by the high replacement cost of iron for wood and it provided a further impediment to locomotive haulage.

An interim solution to the problem of achieving a reasonable tractive effort in a locomotive sufficiently light to operate on a flimsy track was provided by John Blenkinsop, agent to Charles Brandling, the owner of Middleton Colliery near Leeds.[31] In 1811 Blenkinsop patented a Trevithick-type engine with a cogged driving wheel. At the same time an existing wooden tramway was replaced by a cast-iron track with one of the two edge-rails carrying a projecting rack. This 'cog and rack' transmission enabled the locomotive to exert a tractive effort five times greater than Trevithick's Pen-y-Daren engine even though it was no heavier. By 1813 three engines – all of them built by Matthew Murray – were at work at Middleton and it is a tribute to Blenkinsop's reputation that others were to be found at Orell Colliery in Lancashire and at the Coxlodge and Fawdon waggonway near the Tyne. According to contemporary accounts these locomotives proved reliable in service, at least as employed on the Middleton line where they operated until the early 1830s only to be replaced by horses.[32] In a longer term perspective this was a retrograde step since the locomotive had by then reached a state of operating efficiency far superior to that provided by horse haulage. But in the short term it was a rational response to the falling cost of fodder which fully outweighed the advantages of cheap coal at the Middleton Colliery pit head.[33] This did not apply, of course, in 1813 when the price relationships were reversed due to the effects of war. Indeed, the high cost of horse feed was an important factor under-pinning Blenkinsop's calculations of the projected savings arising from the transition to locomotives. On the Coxlodge and Fawdon line, for example, he estimated that the cost of hauling a chaldron waggon of coal along the 5½ mile track would fall from 3s 1¾d to 5¾d after the introduction of locomotives. Against this would have to be set the capital cost of installation amounting to £6,247, but after allowing for the sale of horses and other redundant equipment, the colliery owners would experience a net capital gain of £1,911 10s.[34] Blenkinsop's claim of an overall 24 per cent cost reduction in operating costs seems exaggerated in the light of subsequent experience, but by the mid-1820s a consensus had emerged that the Middleton line marked 'the first useful introduction of locomotive engines'.[35]

Whether Blenkinsop's achievement inspired other engineers to greater efforts is questionable since several exercises in locomotive building, notably in the north-east coalfield, were also taking place in 1812–13 at the time of the early Middleton Colliery experiments. These included the self-hauling 'chain engine' of William Chapman, patented in December 1813 and placed on the Heaton waggonway in 1813, and William Brunton's 'mechanical traveller', first patented in May 1813 and commencing work on the Newbottle waggonway in the final months of 1814. Both of these engines were of eccentric design, mechanically unreliable, and expensive in operation.[36] A more orthodox approach to locomotive development, in conformity with the practice of Trevithick and Blenkinsop, was adopted by William Hedley and George Stephenson. The former, a colliery viewer in the employment of Christopher Blackett's Wylam Colliery, was effectively prevented from adopting Blenkinsop's rack-rail system by the fact that the Wylam waggonway had only recently been relaid as a metal plateway. He therefore designed and built his own Trevithick-type locomotive, ultimately resolving the problem of excessive weight by doubling the number of axles to four. As with Blenkinsop's Middleton locomotives, the 'Wylam Dilly' type of engine proved reliable in service, although it did suffer from the prevailing defect of an inadequate supply of steam, and initially, at least, relied upon a clumsy arrangement of teeth or flanges attached to the wheels and entering the ground on either side of the rails in order to increase the tractive effort.[37]

In the case of George Stephenson a clear distinction must be drawn between his misplaced reputation as 'the father of the locomotive', as portrayed by Samuel Smiles,[38] ably assisted by Stephenson himself, and his very real achievement in advancing the design and construction of the locomotive to its modern form in essential details. When Blenkinsop began his experiments on the Middleton waggonway Stephenson was employed as enginewright by the Grand Allies at Killingworth Colliery in Northumberland.[39] He was certainly familiar with the work of Chapman and Hedley, and it seems likely that he had observed at close quarters the Blenkinsop rack-rail locomotive at work on the Coxlodge and Fawdon waggonway. Indeed, Stephenson's own engine, the *Blucher*, constructed at the West Moor colliery workshop during the first half of 1814, followed Blenkinsop's design in detail. But since the Killingworth waggonway was laid with wooden edge-rails with a metal strip surface this meant that the *Blucher* had two critical operational weaknesses. In the first instance its single straight-flue boiler offered limited steam-raising powers when compared with the Trevithick-type return-flue installed in the Wylam engines, and in the absence of the rack-rail transmission its tractive effort was relatively poor. It also proved too heavy for the wooden track, although this aspect can hardly have been a fatal one in view of the construction of a second locomotive early in 1815. It was perhaps the fortuitous combination of these defects with Stephenson's abilities and personality – his remarkable engineering talents and qualities of dogged persistence – which transformed the Killingworth waggonway into the focal point of railway experiment and design after 1815. The problem of poor tractive effort was soon alleviated, but by no means solved, by the simple expedient of increasing the diameter of the boiler flue and applying the power directly to the wheels by connecting rods, thus reducing the need for crudely manufactured gearing, whilst further developments were directed towards increasing the longevity of the track. One approach was to reduce the damage inflicted by the engine itself and to this end Stephenson collaborated with William Losh, the senior partner in the iron-making firm of Losh, Wilson and Bell of Newcastle, to produce the so-called 'steam spring', an arrangement of pistons on each axle bearing the weight of the boiler and its attachments. Far more effective were his patent improvements to the track, involving a new method of jointing and more sophisticated rail chairs. These too were produced in association with Losh and by the end of 1818 the Killingworth waggonway had been relaid with cast-iron edge-rails bearing the Losh–Stephenson patent.[40]

It was Stephenson's outstanding achievement that he alone of the early locomotive builders proved capable of viewing railway development as an entity. In perceiving the vital link between locomotive and track he succeeded in demonstrating the economic and practical advantages of mechanical traction. The smooth edge-rail was superior in the engineering and technical sense both to the tram plate and Blenkinsop's rack-rail, and the Stephenson–Losh design improvements practically reconfirmed the principle first established by Trevithick that the weight of a locomotive was sufficient to provide the necessary adhesion on the rails. The *Blucher* may have been far less sophisticated in its boiler design to the Pen-y-Daren and Wylam engines, but in its mode of operation it ranks as the first 'modern' locomotive, reliant upon the force of adhesion via flanged wheels.[41] When it was put to work on the Killingworth waggonway the number of horses was reduced from fifty to thirty and by 1820, when the cast-iron track was relaid with wrought-iron edge-rails, haulage by horses had all but disappeared.[42]

It was appropriate that the major advances in early railway technology should have taken place predominantly in the Great Northern Coalfield, Britain's leading mining region. Here, the technical practice of mining had advanced furthest and the industry's comparative maturity was reflected in its sophisticated commercial organisation focusing on the coastal trade in coal to the London market. Yet although the link between mining operations and transport development was pressed furthest in the north-east, the breakthrough to the public railway employing locomotive power was to come not from the banks of the Tyne and Wear with their extensive network of colliery waggonways, but from the southernmost limit of the coalfield in south-west Durham. Here, the coal measures outcropped and from the medieval period onwards bell-pits in the localities of Copley, Etherley, Railey Fell, Spennymoor, and Ferryhill had been sunk into coal measures leased from the Bishop of Durham residing at Auckland Castle.[43] Unlike their northern counterparts these southern pits were wholly dependent for their markets upon the surrounding districts. Not only were mining techniques comparatively primitive, so too was the mode of distribution. According to Robert Galloway, as late as 1800 at one colliery near Witton-le-Wear 'the coals were drawn by an ass, and banked out and sold by an old woman, while the western dales of Yorkshire were supplied with coals from Butterknowle Colliery, carried on the backs of droves of mules'.[44] Attempts to modify this 'medieval simplicity' began in the 1740s when seven local roads were turnpiked, initially to facilitate the trade in 'Scotch cattle', but ultimately to reduce the delivered price of coal from the pit head.[45] The 'coal road' between West Auckland, Darlington, and Piercebridge was turnpiked in 1751 and from the outset differential tolls were levied in favour of the coal trade.[46] It was, however, a sign of continuing local dissatisfaction with the price of coal, as well as a tribute to current perceptions of the utility of canals, that in November 1767 the leading merchants of Darlington and its surrounding district agreed to commission a survey for a canal from the Auckland coalfield to navigable water on the River Tees at Stockton.[47] James Brindley, the foremost canal engineer of the day, was approached for his services, and in the summer of 1768 his son-in-law and subordinate, Robert Whitworth, began work on the survey. Whitworth's report was presented in the following October and it recommended the construction of a canal from Winston to the west of Darlington to Stockton-on-Tees, together with attendant branches into the North Riding of Yorkshire. The total length was 33½ miles at an estimated construction cost of £64,000.

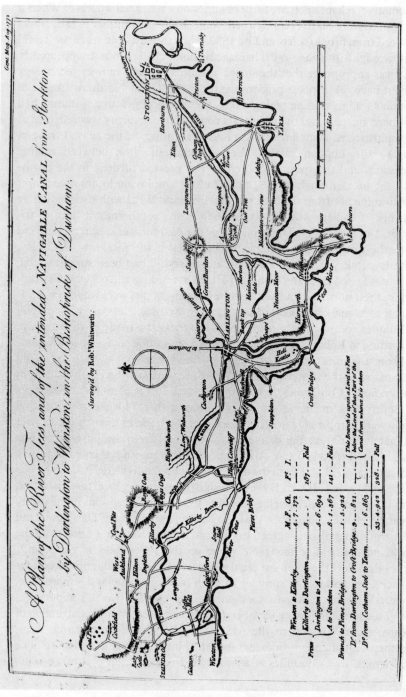

2 Plan of a navigable canal from Stockton to Winston, 1772.

4   James Brindley, canal engineer. Brindley confirmed the first canal route from Stockton to the edge of the Auckland coalfield.

Brindley subsequently verified the feasibility of Whitworth's route and their joint report was considered by the aspiring promoters in Darlington in July 1769. By that time local opinion had moved in favour of further extensions of the canal towards the edge of the coalfield itself, with waggon-ways linking the pits to terminal points on the canal. These additions were estimated to cost £8,000 and a map of the original scheme with embellishments was published in 1770. At first it appears that some scepticism was expressed concerning the likely rate of return on the capital invested in relation to the prospective toll revenue, but by August 1772 the *Gentleman's Magazine* was reporting that these initial worries were 'pretty well over'.[48] In 1773, however, the north-east viewer, William Brown, wrote to the Earl of Darlington stating that the proposed canal 'will not cost half the expense of a waggonway and when once made needs no repair and the expense of conveyance by water is not ¼th the expense by waggons',[49] suggesting that apprehensions still existed about the financial rationale of a canal project. This was confirmed by the eventual outcome as the scheme was allowed to lapse.

The Duke of Bridgewater is reported to have stated that 'every canal must have coals at the heel of it', an aphorism whose accuracy can be justified by the fact that by 1803, of the 165 canal Acts obtained since 1758, 90 of them were linked directly to the interests of the coal trade with the remainder serving iron, lead, and copper mines and works.[50] The Duke might well have added that a further requirement was for the existence of a sufficiently large market for the commodities conveyed. In south Lancashire, Manchester and Salford had a combined population of 20,000 in 1757, and Liverpool a population of 25,000 in 1760. By the standards of the time these were large urban settlements giving rise to substantial toll revenues, as the Duke correctly anticipated when constructing the Worsley Canal.[51] In south Durham, however, the two largest towns – Stockton and Darlington – had populations of less than 4,000 in 1760 and their rate of expansion, on the basis of the woollen and linen industries in the latter case, was comparatively slow. It was therefore in all likelihood the low density of population in the upper Wear and Tees valleys which gave the Darlington canal promoters pause for thought. This consideration continued to apply as late as the 1790s when, in the midst of a flurry of canal projects in the north-east, the Brindley scheme was revived by Ralph Dodd with a connection to the proposed Durham canal, and a branch penetrating as far south as Boroughbridge in the North Riding of Yorkshire.[52] In 1800 another route was surveyed by George Atkinson, stretching from Boroughbridge to Piercebridge and the Tees in County Durham, and to Bedale and Richmond in the North Riding. The cost was estimated at £107,353 and it was presented as 'a substitute for the canal so much wished for by the gentlemen of the counties of Durham and York about the year 1768'.[53] But these schemes were also allowed to lapse, as were several others in the north-east at the time. Clearly, the north-east provided an unfruitful environment for canal promoters: the locally available pools of capital and consumer demand were probably too small to sustain such large-scale infrastructure projects, whilst the geographical isolation of the region meant that it was irrelevant to the construction of trunk canal routes. Nevertheless, as W. W. Tomlinson emphasised, the abortive canal schemes of the eighteenth century were to fulfil an important and useful role after 1800 in informing railway promoters of likely routes and the attendant engineering problems, as well as the probable sources of revenue.[54]

3   The foundation of the Stockton and Darlington Railway Company, 1818–1825

In the first three decades of the nineteenth century the area of the lower Tees valley was still rural in character. Agriculture was the dominant industry and this was reflected in a settlement pattern consisting mainly of small villages and hamlets. There were three urban centres. The largest was Darlington, with a population of 5,750 in 1821. As well as serving as a market outlet for the local agricultural economy the town was also the manufacturing centre of the district with well-established interests in the textile industry. The woollen and worsted trades were well represented and these branches of the industry had overtaken the business of flax dressing and linen production in importance after 1800.[1] By contemporary standards the town possessed a quite sophisticated financial structure as reflected in the private banking concerns of Pease and Partners and J. and J. Back-house.[2] The former was essentially an appendage of the Pease family's woollen business in that it facilitated the advancing of credit to customers and its receipt from suppliers, a highly desirable transactions mechanism in an industry with several separate but dependent stages of production. Backhouses' bank was a more complex concern. It too was an outgrowth from the textile trades, having been founded in 1774 as an accompaniment to the family linen and worsted business. By the early 1820s, following the decline of the linen industry, the Backhouses had easily made the transition to full banking with their own note issue and branch network. These two Quaker families were connected by marriage both between themselves and with other Quaker business dynasties, notably the Gurneys of Norwich. The Gurneys also possessed banking and textile interests with the result that these marital relationships replicated in the world of Quakerism a 'web of credit' not unlike that which played an important role in financing the early development of the Yorkshire woollen and Lancashire cotton industries.[3]

The second urban centre was Stockton, located twelve miles to the east of Darlington on the banks of the Tees estuary. In 1821 the town's population numbered 5,184 and it had experienced modest growth after 1770 following the bridging of the Tees which had opened up a line of communications with the Cleveland district of north Yorkshire to the south. By the end of the century it too was a market centre. It also served as a port, exporting lead and agricultural products in some quantity to other north-east ports as well as to the London market. The town's commercial prosperity was reflected in the 'quays, granaries, warehouses, breweries, roperies, sail-cloth work-shops, lead works, shipbuilding and timber yards' lining the river bank. Stockton itself had grown at the expense of the third urban centre, Yarm, in north Yorkshire. Formerly an inland port, by the end of the eighteenth century Yarm had reverted to its original status as a market town for the surrounding district. In 1821 its population numbered 1,504.[4]

One impediment to Stockton's maritime functions was the unsuitability of the Tees as a navigable river. Its outlet was excessively meandering and susceptible to choking by silt, with the result that larger sea-going vessels were loaded and unloaded at the small outports of Newport and Cargo Fleet further downstream. It was in reaction to these circumstances that the Tees Navigation Company was founded in 1805 as the sponsoring body for river improvements. Attention was immediately focused on a scheme first mooted in 1769 for the cutting of a straight channel of 220 yards across a large loop in the river at Mandale Bottoms. In 1809 the company purchased for £2,000 a portion of the estate of Lord Harewood and on 10 September in the following year the Mandale Cut, constructed at a cost of £12,000, was opened thereby shortening the distance between Stockton and the river mouth by 2½ miles.[5] The opening was celebrated by a dinner in the town hall when Leonard Raisbeck, the recorder of Stockton and solicitor to the Navigation Company, seconded by Benjamin Flounders of Yarm, moved a successful motion for the appointment of a committee 'to inquire into the practicability and advantage of a Railway or Canal from Stockton and Darlington to Winston, for the more easy and expeditious carriage of coals, lead, etc.'.[6] This reference to a railway was unusual since there were no precedents in the north-east for the construction of such a line over an extended distance. It is hardly surprising, therefore, that when the inter-ested parties met in Darlington on 17 January 1812, attention should be concentrated on the long-standing canal project. This was confirmed in the decision to engage the distinguished canal engineer, John Rennie, to make a survey of the intended route.[7]

The cost of Rennie's survey was met principally by the merchant and trading community of the Tees valley, including the Backhouses and Peases.[8] It was submitted on 13 August 1813 when the engineer confirmed the validity of the Whitworth–Brindley route of 1768 and recommended the construction of a canal, with branches to Yarm, Croft, and Piercebridge, at an estimated cost of £205,618.[9] Even allowing for some price inflation this was far in excess of the cost of the earlier scheme. The estimate for the

5   John Rennie (1761–1821), civil engineer. Rennie, like Brindley before him, recommended the construction of a canal from Stockton to the Auckland coalfield.

Stockton to Darlington section alone amounted to £95,600 and there can be little doubt that the aspiring promoters were taken aback at the magnitude of the task in raising the necessary funds. Their pessimism could only have been deepened by the subsequent failure of several local banks which followed in the wake of the collapse of Mowbray, Hollingsworth and Co. in 1815.[10] There was a brief revival of interest in the following year when a suggestion emerged for a railway to form that part of the communicating link between Darlington and Winston. On Rennie's advice this reduced the cost of the direct route between Stockton and Winston (later amended to West Auckland) from £179,578 to £141,460, a 22 per cent saving, but capital funding was still not forthcoming. The fact remains that these years marked the beginning of a transitional phase in railway development. Waggonways may have established themselves in short-distance haulage on Tyneside and in south Wales, but they had yet to convince investors, let alone landowners, of their utility over long distances. The longer the line the greater the need for a broad base of support, and as in the bulk of canal enterprise this inevitably entailed a formal company structure, if only to share the costs of construction. In the depressed commercial climate of the later Napoleonic War period and the postwar depression after 1815, investors were unlikely to be attracted into such a speculative venture.[11]

An entirely new development, reflecting the onset of economic recovery and stemming from a different perspective on transport improvements in south Durham, occurred in 1818 when Christopher Tennant, a merchant of Stockton with interests in the lime trade at Thickley, funded at his own expense a canal survey by the engineer George Leather, with the instruction that the route to be followed should be 'the *lowest*, least expensive, and shortest practicable line for a canal from the river Tees into the present working coal-field'.[12] From Portrack near Stockton Leather's route moved north-westwards, crossing the River Skerne at Bradbury: it then progressed south-westwards via Rushyford on the Great North Road to enter the eastern edge of the Auckland coalfield at Windlestone near Ferryhill. Thus, in meeting Tennant's requirements the route veered well to the north of Darlington. Nearly thirty miles long, with fifty locks, Leather's canal scheme presented significant engineering problems and this was reflected in the estimated construction cost of £205,283, virtually the same as for the route recommended by Rennie. Tennant, however, was in no way deterred because the rationale of his project rested on the assumption that a direct route from the coalfield to the mouth of the Tees would afford the Auckland collieries an excellent opportunity to compete successfully with their counterparts on the Tyne and Wear for a portion of the coastal trade in coal with London. At a crowded public meeting held in Stockton town hall on 31 July 1818 Tennant's scheme for a Stockton and Auckland canal was received with acclamation and a vote taken to proceed with it. In the following November, therefore, Tennant led a deputation to London to raise the necessary four-fifths of the cost of construction so that parliamentary authorisation could be obtained.[13]

The new initiative from Stockton was greeted with dismay in Yarm and Darlington and the response was swift. Even before Tennant had departed for London a rival scheme designed to confirm Darlington as the focal point of the line of communication had been initiated. The leading instigator was Jonathan Backhouse, senior partner in Backhouses' bank. Little more than a week after the public acceptance of Tennant's scheme he wrote first to his fellow Quaker, Richard Miles of Yarm, a lead agent with interests in the timber and slate trades, and then to Leonard Raisbeck calling for a meeting of potential subscribers to the scheme last discussed in 1816. According to Backhouse a route via Darlington was 'undoubtedly the best line', preferably with a canal from Stockton to Darlington and a railway from the latter to the coalfield. As for Tennant's intention of entering the coastal trade in coal Backhouse was adamant that

the prospect of *Stockton* becoming a port for the export of coals is hopeless at least for a century to come – that our profits must therefore come from *land sale*, that the old line will embrace *double* the tonnage of coals for home consumption that the new one can possibly do – besides all the merchandise traffic from a Manufacturing District – the number of locks will be one third less – and that even when the export of coals may become practicable, the additional expense of bringing them by Darlington will be so trifling as such to effect it.[14]

These views were subsequently confirmed in a letter to Richard Miles from Matthew Plummer, a Newcastle shipping agent.[15] Plummer was hardly a disinterested party, but in responding to a query from Miles concerning Tennant's calculations on the likely return on his canal scheme he offered the valid observation that the Tees in its present navigable state could not hope to carry on an extensive coal trade in competition with the Tyne and Wear. In addition to the cost of a canal Tennant's scheme would necessitate simultaneous and costly investments in port and river improvements, not to mention the extra capital which would have to be sunk in keels and ships. The implication, therefore, was that a Stockton and Auckland canal would not be remunerative.

By the end of August the Darlington and Yarm interests had divided into two groups. United in their opposition to Tennant in the belief that his intended route would 'end in total miscarriage and prove a Public injury by creating disgust to all future improvements for perhaps a century to come',[16] they had drawn apart with respect to the mode of transport to be employed. One group, led by Jonathan Backhouse, favoured a combined canal and railway (as in the proposal of 1816), whilst another group, dominated by Thomas Meynell, the squire of Yarm, the Darlington builder Robert Botcherby, Richard Miles, and Edward Pease, were equally insistent in their advocacy of an unbroken line of communication by rail or tramway on the grounds of technical feasibility and, more especially, lower operating costs.[17] An unbroken line, moreover, would enhance the value of any coal transported since it would not be broken in on-and-off loading.[18] It was a sign, perhaps, of the dominance of the latter group that it was decided to authorise a new route survey to be carried out by George Overton of Lanthelly near Brecon, an engineer with considerable experience in laying down tramways in the colliery districts of south Wales.[19] It is just as likely, however, that Overton owed his appointment to the fact that he was a relative by marriage to Meynell's land steward, Jeremiah Cairns. In any event the division of opinion was fully reflected in the wording of a successful resolution moved by Leonard Raisbeck at a meeting in Darlington on 4 September 1818 directing 'estimates to be made for a line from Stockton by Darlington to the collieries, with branches to Yarm, Croft and Piercebridge, as well as by the joint mode of having a canal and railway as by railway the whole distance'.[20]

Overton's report was in readiness by the end of September 1818. Although it was stated that savings could be made in constructing the canal section between Stockton and Darlington by a slight deviation in the line followed by Brindley and Rennie, Overton's recommendation was for a tramway traversing the entire route. From Stockton to its terminus near Etherley Colliery this was to be thirty-five miles in length. Branches to other collieries and to Yarm, Croft, and Piercebridge increased the length by sixteen miles. A single way with passing places was costed at £2,000 per mile with an extra £400 per mile for twenty miles of double way on the main line. The total cost, therefore, was £92,000, with the addition of £32,000 for the branch lines. Estimates of revenue were also given, with Overton suggesting the possibility of a 15 per cent rate of return on the main line expenditure.[21]

The recommendation for a railway was presented, with slight modification, to a meeting of potential subscribers held at Darlington on 13 November. A 15 per cent rate of return was projected on an expenditure of £100,000 for the main line and three of the branches. This was calculated on an annual coal shipment of 90,000 tons – 10,000 tons less than that allowed for in Tennant's scheme, and including an allowance of only one cargo a week for the coastal trade. The meeting was also furnished with a new pronouncement from Rennie setting out the following principles:

first, ... a Canal will convey goods with the same facility upwards as downwards, whereas a Railway conveys them with more facility downwards than upwards: secondly, ... when the descending and the ascending trade is equal in quantity, a canal is preferable to a railway; but, where the descending trade very much *exceeds* the ascending, a Railway is preferable to a Canal.[22]

In view of the anticipated traffic movements on the line this was a ringing endorsement of a continuous line of railway, thus vindicating the views of Meynell and his associates. That there was no rancour on Backhouse's part was confirmed by his address to the meeting when he spoke impressively in favour of a railway, citing 'fact and figures which he used with sledge-hammer effect to demolish the arguments and calculations' of those who were inclined to support Tennant's Stockton and Auckland canal scheme. More specifically, he argued that Tennant had underestimated both the cost of transferring coal from the pit head to canal barges and the screening out of dirt and stones preparatory to sale.[23] Force was lent to this view by William Stobart Jr, managing partner of Etherley Colliery, when he stated that Tennant had underestimated by 3s 3d the cost of placing a chaldron of his coals into barges.[24] In holding out the prospect of a 25 per cent return on a capital investment of £120,000, Backhouse seems to have been carried away by his own enthusiasm and it was left to the woollen manufacturer, Edward Pease, to instil a greater sense of reality into the meeting. Backhouse had cleverly derived his calculations from a pessimistic interpretation of Tennant's own estimates. Pease, however, was equally astute in referring to the annual toll revenue from coal transported on the existing turnpike road from Darlington to the Auckland coalfield. Pease argued bluntly that a railway was assured of a certain 5 per cent return from this traffic alone:

You need not go any further. This quite satisfies me. That revenue on this short piece of road yields me 5 per cent, on the outlay, and this is enough … Some perhaps can make it out to be 6 or 8 or 10 or 12 per cent. I do not know how much – but there is ample room for calculation; but I am quite satisfied with my 5 per cent; and I have only made this statement to show that by one single article we can make a sufficient rate of interest by this undertaking, and all the rest may be taken as profit over and above 5 per cent.[25]

These arguments, coming from two of Darlington's most sober and respected inhabitants, with well-established reputations for commercial acumen, proved highly persuasive and the meeting concluded by appointing a forty-strong management committee to be chaired by William Chaytor Jr, and composed of all those prepared to subscribe a minimum of £500 to the project. Its principal task was to draw up a prospectus preparatory to making an application to Parliament for an Act 'for a tramway, on the plan and estimates given by Mr. Overton'.

The prospectus, which was devised in large measure by Pease's second son, Joseph, then aged nineteen, was issued on 15 November 1818,[26] and within five days £20,000 had been subscribed 'without exertion by the promotors'.[27] From the correspondence of management committee members, however, it appears that all did not go smoothly. The problem lay in the fact that the locally available pool of capital could not sustain two large and competing infrastructure investments. As Richard Miles stated to George Overton, the Darlington scheme was 'unlikely to press ahead forcefully' until the demise of Tennant's canal project.[28] The standing orders of the House of Commons stipulated that four-fifths of the estimated cost of a project had to be raised by a specific date if a subscription was to remain valid. For the Tennant scheme the due date was 1 January 1819, but it had become obvious by mid-December that subscriptions were going to fall short of the necessary £160,000. It was entirely natural, therefore, for the Darlington committee to hope that some of the canal promoters would transfer their subscriptions to their own scheme.[29] In this they were to be disappointed. Despite an open appeal to the canal subscribers to unite in effecting the Darlington-based railway link on the grounds that the two parties had no separate interest,[30] Tennant and his fellow promoters stood firm in their belief that Stockton's prosperity could only be guaranteed by a direct northern route to the coalfield. Why, indeed, should Stockton have 'to pay dues on its coals for thirty miles when there were working collieries within fourteen miles of its doors'?[31] The logical response was for Tennant to launch his own 'northern' railway project and this was accomplished before the end of the year.

It was in anticipation of a shortfall in subscriptions that some of the Darlington and Yarm promoters, such as Edward Pease and Thomas Meynell, made additional subscriptions. These proved insufficient and the problem was only resolved by making extensive use of the Quaker chain of credit alluded to earlier. It was this which enabled the subscription list to be closed on 26 December 1818. Of the 1,209 shares of £100 each the majority were subscribed locally. The Backhouse family was prepared to invest £20,000 and the Peases £6,200. Other large subscriptions came from the Quaker Benjamin Flounders of Yarm (£5,000), William Chaytor Jr of Croft (£5,000), Thomas Meynell (£3,000), and Leonard Raisbeck (£1,000), one of the few subscribers from Stockton. Two-thirds of the subscriptions were from local sources and in this respect the project was typical both of canals and other railway companies.[32] The remaining third was derived from extra-regional sources, principally from within the Society of Friends. Thus, the Gurneys of Norwich were committed to the extent of £20,000, and Thomas Richardson of London, bill-broker and cousin of Edward Pease, to £10,000. Other large subscriptions were forthcoming from the Quaker community at Whitby, some of whose members enjoyed filial ties with their co-religionists in Darlington.[33] As Joseph Pease stated to Quaker 'cousins' in Leeds on the day the subscription list closed, the scheme for a 'Darlington Railway' was 'so popular amongst Friends that about £80,000 stands in the names of members of our society'.[34]

That the railway promoters of Darlington and Yarm could not rely on local sources of finance alone was recognised formally in the prospectus which provided for the appointment of a separate committee of bankers and financiers (mostly Quakers) in London charged with the task of obtaining subscriptions. But extensive use of the Quaker chain of credit meant that in the context of subsequent railway development the scheme for a Stockton and Darlington Railway was a special case.[35] As with other railway enterprises the bulk of the subscriptions were obtained from interests in trade, commerce, and banking, yet this was a project for a public joint stock company with a capital of £100,000, which in important respects replicated a close family partnership. Even if Tennant's canal scheme had been practicable he could not have competed with a personalised capital market bound together by ties of mutual trust and kinship.[36]

After the necessary subscriptions had been obtained the next hurdle confronting the projectors was the passage of a parliamentary bill of incorporation. Although the company form of organisation in manufacturing industry was virtually prohibited after the Bubble Act of 1720, public utilities, principally canals, had been able to avail themselves of the benefits of incorporation, namely, the raising of capital publicly and the receipt of compulsory powers to purchase land. There had, of course, been numerous canal Acts in the eighteenth century but the negotiation of rights of way remained a sensitive issue.[37] Landowners who objected to a canal traversing their property could create severe difficulties for canal promotors in Parliament and unless they had a direct pecuniary interest their opposition had to be bought off, often at considerable expense. Waggonways for the transport of coal were potentially subject to the same disability and, as noted in the previous chapter, it was fortunate that the relatively short waggonways of the Tyne and Wear invariably ran over the property of landowners, such as the Grand Allies, who were themselves colliery proprietors. Because of its length, however, the Stockton and Darlington line was exceptionally vulnerable, all the more so because Overton's chosen route cut deeply into the estates of the two most influential landowners in the district – the Earl of Darlington (later first Duke of Cleveland) and the Earl of Eldon, at that time Lord Chancellor in the Liverpool administration. The latter was eventually bought off, but Lord Darlington remained implacable in his opposition to a scheme which in his view was 'harsh and oppressive to the interest of the country through which it is intended the railway shall pass'.[38] Unlike Eldon, who had interests in the coal trade, Lord Darlington was not involved in industrial activities and his real concern, almost to the point of obsession, was the damage that the railway would inflict on his fox coverts. That the projectors were uneasy as to the likelihood of aristocratic opposition to their scheme in Parliament was confirmed by their attempt to re-engage Rennie to pass judgement on Overton's line, and the invitation extended to Robert Stevenson, the engineer of the Bell Rock lighthouse and several railway projects in Scotland, to participate in any new survey. The former refused the invitation, however, on the grounds of professional jealousy,[39] and whilst Stevenson's services were secured he spent much time and effort in the last weeks of 1819 in examining waggonway operations on Tyneside, paying particular attention to the use of stationary engines and inclined planes. The result of this activity was that the bill went forward with Overton's original route intact.[40]

The first Stockton and Darlington Railway Bill was defeated by 106 votes to 93 on 5 April 1819. An unidentified member of the House of Lords subsequently commented: 'Well if the Quakers in these times, when nobody knows anything about railways, can raise up such a phalanx as they have on this occasion, I should recommend the country gentlemen to be very wary how they oppose them.'[41] To put it another way, the closeness of the vote was not so much the product of a new awareness among 93 members of the House of Commons of the virtues of railways. It was far more the result of the highly effective lobbying carried out by the promoters in February 1819 when a group of them, led by Charles Hamilton, the Archdeacon of Cleveland, descended on London to canvass the support of MPs, calling in pairs at their homes. They were considerably aided in their task by the network of Quaker financial connections in the capital, but even so the first solicitor to the Stockton and Darlington Railway, Francis Mewburn, was moved to remark in later years that 'The difficulties, pain and anguish which I endured during my sojourn in London while soliciting the Bill can scarcely be imagined.'[42] Mewburn was a rather sensitive individual, but his legal responsibilities to the promoters cannot have been eased by the failure of Lord Eldon, in his capacity as Lord Chancellor, to comprehend some of the technical and legalistic details in the Stockton and Darlington Railway Bill. This was particularly evident in his confusion over the need for the compulsory purchase of land, as opposed to the customary practise in the north-east coalfield of negotiating wayleaves.

The promoters were far from discouraged by their experiences, ascribing their lack of success to 'a want of money, time and talent'.[43] In future they would be better prepared. As Robert Stevenson stated, citing expert opinion within the private bill office of the House of Commons, it was essential for the promoters to 'forthwith adopt the most perfect line – and if possible the least objectionable track'[44] to Lord Darlington, whose continuing antipathy to their plans extended as far as a crude attempt to bankrupt Backhouses' Bank.[45] In July 1819, therefore, Overton's offer to undertake a new survey was gladly accepted and the promoters felt sufficiently confident to reject the overtures from Christopher Tennant and his associates for a union of their respective schemes 'by making branches from the intended main Northern line to Yarm and to Darlington'.[46]

By the end of the year the promoters were ready to renew their application to Parliament. Lord Eldon had accepted the compulsory purchase of land and Overton had succeeded in drawing a new route to avoid Lord Darlington's estates. This was nine miles shorter than the original line but carried with it the disadvantage of abandoning any projected link with north Yorkshire via Piercebridge. A temporary truce had also been negotiated with Tennant whereby he agreed to lay aside his own scheme on the understanding that it would be revived immediately if there was significant parliamentary opposition to the Stockton and Darlington bill.[47] Yet even at this stage further delay was to be forced on the promoters by the death of George IV in January 1820. With no hope of the bill passing before the dissolution, and considerable uncertainty as to the prospects of success in the new Parliament, they were advised by the parliamentary agents to renew their application for an Act of Incorporation in the session of 1820–1. As Tomlinson observed, however, these circumstances were hardly detrimental to the promoters for in avoiding the estates of Lord Darlington, Overton had delivered them into the hands of Lord Barrington thus raising the prospect of renewed aristocratic opposition to their scheme.[48] A further source of local acrimony which had yet to be appeased emanated from the Misses Hale, joint lessees of the Coxhoe and Quarrington Collieries who enjoyed the support of Lord Harewood and claimed, with justification, that their interests would be adversely affected by the enhanced competitiveness of those collieries more closely positioned to the line of railway. Noting these difficulties Tennant and his supporters threatened to resuscitate their own scheme, with the added observation that there was a considerable difference between the current subscription list, amounting to no more than £24,700 and the estimate for the Stockton and Darlington scheme of £92,000 lodged with the private bill office of the House of Commons.[49] As events were to prove the prospect of a shortfall in subscriptions was a real one, despite the existence of the Quaker chain of credit.

Clearly, more time was needed to overcome these obstacles involving as they did the possibility of changes to the route of the intended line. Overton was approached yet again and it was a sign, perhaps, of his frustration, and also his limitations as an engineer and surveyor, that he came forward with a revised and still shorter route which, in reintroducing the link with Piercebridge to the south, failed to reach some of the more prominent collieries in the coalfield. Not surprisingly, this was rejected so that in the event the promoters were obliged to resort to the time-honoured expedient of compensation, with generous offers to Lord Barrington and the Misses Hale.[50]

Leaving nothing to chance the promoters once more engaged in lobbying support for their scheme, even more intensively than in 1819. J. S. Jeans, the 'Jubilee' historian of the Stockton and Darlington Railway, was guilty of only slight exaggeration in his claim that 'Every member of Parliament that could be influenced, directly or indirectly, was pressed into the service of the promoters. Every peer that was known to have any doubt or hesitation was seized upon and interviewed until he became a convert, while those who looked upon the measure with favour were confirmed in the faith.'[51] But despite these efforts, which even included attempts to influence the selection of parliamentary candidates in the north of England, the bill was nearly lost due to a failure to comply with parliamentary standing orders which required the subscription of four-fifths of the share capital of a projected public company before a bill could pass to the committee stage. Mewburn, who was once again responsible for soliciting the bill, panicked when he found that no more funds were forthcoming from Norwich or London and in desperation he contacted his colleague, Leonard Raisbeck, in Stockton. With only a few days to spare, Raisbeck was able to obtain the extra subscription, amounting to £7,000, from Edward Pease.[52] It was this gesture of confidence in the enterprise at a critical moment which marked the beginning of the ascendancy of the Pease family over the conduct of the Stockton and Darlington Railway. Henceforth, it was known as 'the Quaker line', much to the disgust of William Chaytor who had earlier resigned as chairman of the management committee in protest at the growing domination exercised by the Pease–Backhouse alliance.[53]

By the end of March 1821 the bill had passed the committee stage 'in high style',[54] and with only one hostile petition presented, it received the Royal Assent on 19 April. The provisions of the Act, extending to sixty-seven pages and incorporating the whole of the law on railways up to that time, had been devised in large measure by Francis Mewburn who had borrowed freely from the Berwick and Kelso Act of 1811.[55] It provided for the construction of 'a railway or tramroad from the River Tees at Stockton to Witton Park Colliery with several branches therefrom, all in the County of Durham' with 'men and horses' as the sole means of conveyance. The sum of £82,000 was to be raised in shares and a further £20,000 by loan to facilitate the construction of the thirty-seven miles of track, inclusive of branches to Yarm, Darlington, and the collieries, and all within a stipulated period of five years. Restrictions were also to be placed on the number of operating hours on a daily basis, an antediluvian clause which in conjunction with the schedule of tolls incorporated in the Act betrayed the extent to which the promoters had borrowed from established canal company practice. Thus, the Stockton and Darlington line was to be open to all users (although the Act made no reference to the carriage of passengers) on payment of the stated tolls and as long as the vehicle employed conformed to the specifications laid down in the Act.

A further noteworthy feature of the Act, highlighted in the company prospectus, was that it laid great stress on the potential contribution of the line to the development of internal trade. As the prospectus stated:

Local circumstances entitle this undertaking to the support of the Public. The line passes through a populous district in which an extensive Trade already exists (this maintains Trade and Capital in their wonted channel without detriment to old establishments). General merchandise will be carried from the coast *upwards* and coal, lime, lead, Blue Stone for repair of Roads and agricultural purposes from the interior of the county *downwards*. Coal and Lime abound in the western parts of the

6   Edward Pease (1767–1858), Quaker woollen manufacturer of Darlington. Pease was the Stockton and Darlington Railway's leading promoter after 1821.

county of Durham, from which the South East and North Riding of Yorkshire are supplied. By the facilities thus given the carriage will be reduced nearly *one-half* the present charge and that over a district containing not less than 40,000 inhabitants.[56]

Such emphasis provides confirmation of the promoters' belief that a coastal trade in coal via Stockton would not be remunerative. In the Act itself further attention was drawn to this belief in the published list of tolls. At

½d per ton per mile the toll payable on 'all coal which shall be shipped on board of any vessel or vessels in the port of Stockton-upon-Tees for the purpose of exportation' was the lowest and it conveyed the impression that the promoters, far from wishing to give the Auckland collieries a competitive advantage in the coastal trade, regarded the likely revenue to be derived from this category of traffic as slight. As experience was to show this was a gross misconception, but in the circumstances of 1821 it greatly facilitated the passage of the bill. As one sympathetic MP with interests in the Tyne and Wear coastal trade subsequently stated, 'if he thought any export would ever have taken place by the Darlington Railway they should never have had an Act'.[57] Such a view would, of course, have led to the rejection of any bill introduced by Christopher Tennant which had as its main rationale the development of a coastal trade.

Having obtained their Act the promoters were then faced with the business of bringing their scheme to fruition. This task was entrusted to a new and smaller management committee composed of fourteen of the principal local subscribers and chaired by Thomas Meynell, with Jonathan Backhouse acting as treasurer. Edward Pease and his son Joseph were elected on to this committee and also onto a sub-committee of seven members responsible for the detailed execution of the project.[58] If there were any doubts as to the true locus of power they were soon dispelled by the manner of appointment of the engineer to the line. All students of railway history know that George Stephenson was offered the position even though Overton had expected to be recalled. Less well known is the fact that Stephenson's claims were pressed on a somewhat reluctant management committee by Edward Pease. On the day that the Stockton and Darlington bill had received its third reading Pease and Stephenson had met by appointment in Darlington when the latter argued the case not only for an edge-railway as opposed to the tramway recommended by Overton, but also advocated with persuasive lucidity the introduction of locomotives onto the line as a complement to stationary winding engines and horses. By this time, Stephenson's reputation as a railway engineer was well established on Tyneside and it had been further enhanced in the late spring of 1821 when he had experimented successfully at Killingworth Colliery with a new locomotive capable of hauling twenty loaded coal waggons up a gradient of 1 in 288 'with an amazing degree of rapidity which beggars description'.[59] Pease subsequently accepted Stephenson's invitation to visit Killingworth and to say that he was impressed by the experience is an understatement. As he commented, in truly visionary terms to Thomas Richardson,

Don't be surprised if I should tell thee there seems to us after careful examination no difficulty of laying a railroad from London to Edinburgh on which waggons would travel and take the mail at the rate of 20 miles per hour, when this is accomplished steam vessels may be laid aside! We went along a road upon one of these engines conveying about 50 tons at the rate of 7 or 8 miles per hour, and if the same power had been applied to speed which was applied to drag the waggons we should have gone 50 miles per hour – previous to seeing this locomotive engine I was at a loss to conceive how the engine could draw such a weight, without having a rack to work into the same or something like legs – but in this engine there is no such thing.[60]

Heavily influenced by Pease the management committee took the critical decision to opt for a railway on 23 July, at the same time authorising the sub-committee to ascertain Stephenson's willingness to undertake a new survey.[61] As if to emphasise the degree of scepticism which still existed about the application of steam power the management committee had earlier incorporated an image of a horse drawing four waggons in its corporate seal, whilst Pease's instructions to Stephenson emphasised that the construction of the railway 'must be solid, and as little machinery introduced as possible'. More specifically, Stephenson was asked to consider any improvements to Overton's line and in the event of recommending deviations outside the authorised limits (100 yards on either side of the approved parliamentary line) he was to submit comparative estimates of the construction costs. To an engineer endowed with Stephenson's immense practical abilities and missionary zeal for the employment of locomotives these instructions could not have been more suitably devised. Realising that Stephenson was being given an effective *carte blanche* Thomas Meynell protested about the cost of a new survey and stated his opposition to any deviations in the line which would require a renewed application to Parliament.[62] He was, however, too late. Stephenson had already agreed to undertake the task for a fee of £140 and Meynell's criticisms were easily deflected by the sub-committee's response that Overton's survey was insufficiently specific to proceed with the purchase of land or the awarding of construction contracts.

Stephenson's plans, estimate, and report were presented to the management committee on 18 January 1822. At the hillier western end of the line, in the final stages of the route to Witton Park Colliery, he recommended a more direct line than Overton with four inclined planes to surmount the two hill ridges flanking the River Gaunless. Three of them were to be worked by winding engines to be located on the ridges at Etherley and Brusselton. Travelling eastwards the line was designed for the employment of horses up to New Shildon, but from there to Stockton, over a distance of twenty-five miles, where the gradients were comparatively easy, the Overton route was straightened to facilitate the use of locomotives.[63] Together with a shorter branch line to Darlington, these alterations reduced the length of the parliamentary line by four miles and produced a more than proportionate fall in the estimated construction cost from £77,341 18s 8d to £60,987, 13s 3d.

7 George Stephenson (1781–1848), first engineer to the Stockton and Darlington Railway Company, 1821–5.

On this basis Stephenson was appointed engineer of the line at a salary of £660 per annum (to include the salaries of assistants), and was authorised to begin construction of those sections conforming to Overton's route pending an application to Parliament for a second Act to take account of the deviations.[64]

Prior to this, at the end of 1821, the sub-committee had made a critical decision concerning one of the most significant items of expenditure. This involved the type of rail to be used, a controversial issue in view of the recent innovation by John Birkinshaw of the Bedlington Iron Company of the malleable or wrought-iron rail offering a number of alleged advantages over its cast-iron counterpart. In a joint report issued in February 1821

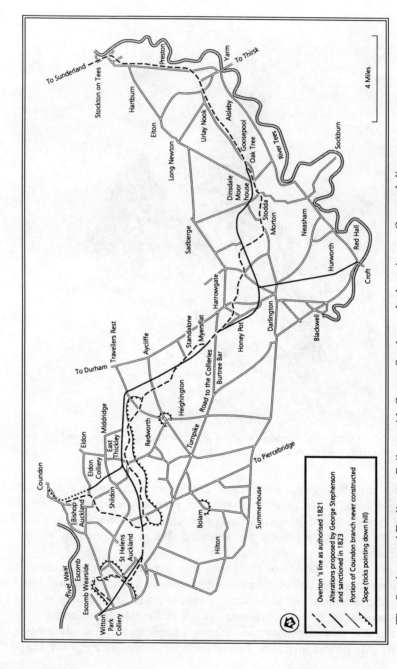

3 The Stockton and Darlington Railway with George Stephenson's alterations to Overton's line.

Birkinshaw and his employer, Michael Longridge, had claimed that the former was superior on several counts:

1. The original cost of a Malleable Iron Rail-Way is less than that of a Cast Iron Rail-Way of equal strength.
2. As the rails can be made in lengths of 9, 12, 15 or 18 feet each, and even longer when required, the number of joints is reduced; and thus is removed, in a great measure, the liability to which the short [cast-iron] rails now in use are exposed, of receiving blows and shocks from the carriages which move over them.
3. In order to remedy the evil arising from the Rails being imperfectly joined, the plan of *welding* the ends of the Rails together has been adopted; by this means making one continued Rail the whole length of the road without any joint whatever.
4. It hence follows, that on the Iron Rail-Ways, the loss of coals, caused by the jolting of the Waggons at the joints of the Rails, and the injury done to the Wheels, the Carriages, and Engines, from the same cause, are, if not entirely prevented, at least considerably diminished.

   The chief objection argued against malleable rails is that they are more subject to waste, by *rust* or *oxydation*, than cast iron rails. Yet the Agent at the Earl of Carlisle's Colliery at Tindal Fell states in a letter received in May 1819:– 'Our Rail-Way carries four tons weight and it has never cost us anything yet, as to the expense of the Malleable Iron, except creasing. The Iron I cannot see the least alteration with, although it has now been laid eight years. The Cast Iron is a daily expense: it is breaking every day.[65]

These arguments persuaded George Stephenson of the efficacy of wrought-iron rails, not least because a reduction in the number of joints would greatly facilitate the use of locomotives. It was on his recommendation that the sub-committee decided to form the line with two-thirds malleable iron rails with the remaining third of cast-iron.[66] Stephenson clearly had an eye for the future since in the short term he suffered a severe financial loss as a result of this decision. If the line had been laid wholly with cast-iron rails then it is likely that the contract would have been awarded to Messrs Losh, Wilson and Bell of Newcastle, a firm with which Stephenson had a close association. Not only had the firm manufactured locomotives and stationary engines to his designs at the Walker Ironworks, Stephenson also possessed a joint patent for the manufacture of cast-iron rails with the owner, William Losh. Not unnaturally, the latter regarded Stephenson's recommendation as a breach of faith and as a result their relationship was ended.[67]

As Tomlinson observed, with the engagement of Stephenson as engineer to the line 'The master-mind had appeared to direct and control its future development.'[68] With the backing of Pease and Thomas Richardson he persuaded the management committee to opt for mechanical traction, ignoring in effect the original injunction to avoid, as far as possible, the use of machinery. In this he was aided by the timely success of the Hetton

Colliery Railway which came into operation in November 1822. This had been engineered by Stephenson and it provided practical confirmation of the utility of a haulage system employing self-acting planes, stationary engines, and locomotives.[69] These factors in combination explain why the bill to give effect to Stephenson's route deviations (including a branch to Croft-on-Tees) also contained a clause permitting the use of 'locomotive or moveable engines for the purpose of facilitating the transport, conveyance and carriage of goods, merchandise and other articles and things upon and along the same roads, and for the conveyance of passengers upon and along the same roads'. The bill, which received its third reading in May 1823, also permitted the company to reduce its capital from £82,000 to £74,300, in accordance with the reduced track mileage.[70]

By the summer of 1823, with twenty-two miles of the main line laid down, construction of the railway was well advanced. All of the track and rail chairs had been delivered, the contracts having been awarded to Longridge's Bedlington Iron Company for the malleable iron rails, and to the Neath Abbey Ironworks of south Wales for the cast-iron rails and all of the chairs.[71] Contracts had also been issued for the stone and wood blocks to act as foundations for the chairs, the former being obtained locally at Brusselton, and the latter imported via the Tees from Portsea in Hampshire.[72] To facilitate the construction of the line itself the route had been divided into one-mile sections open to individual contract with the contract price varying according to the degree of difficulty in preparing the earthworks.[73] Although the bulk of the unskilled labour was obtained locally, numbers were augmented by Tyneside keelmen made redundant after the great strike of 1822. Most of the contractors, specialist blasters, and tunnel makers were recruited by Stephenson himself from the Northumberland coalfield.[74]

As for the supply of steam engines, moveable and stationary, the break in Stephenson's relations with William Losh presented both a problem and an opportunity. His established supplier having withdrawn from the market, and the Bedlington Iron Company devoid of manufacturing facilities, Stephenson had the option of coming to some arrangement with one or more of the colliery engineering workshops on Tyneside. Instead, he chose the radical solution of establishing his own manufacturing business. These were the origins of Robert Stephenson and Co., formed as a specialist engineering concern in June 1823, only two months after the Stockton and Darlington sub-committee had directed Stephenson 'to give estimates for Steam Engines on the Main Line of Railway'.[75] The business was carried on at the Forth Street works in Newcastle and it was founded as a co-partnership between Stephenson and his son Robert, together with Thomas Richardson, Michael Longridge, and Edward Pease.[76] As the principal supplier of rails to the Stockton and Darlington line Longridge clearly had a vested interest in Stephenson's success, and in later years the Bedlington Iron Company certainly derived much advantage from direct and subcontracted business. However, the largest portion of the modest initial capital of £4,000 was subscribed by Pease. His share amounted to £1,600 but he also loaned Robert Stephenson £500 towards his own subscription.[77] Whatever Pease's motivation – a romanticised vision of a communications system transformed by steam traction (see above, pp. 39–40), or the more likely and immediate concern of obtaining an assured supply of reliable stationary engines and locomotives for the Stockton and Darlington line itself – this was the beginning of a long and fruitful business partnership between the Pease and Stephenson families until the onset of managerial difficulties in the firm after 1880.[78] In the immediate setting, however, commercial and personal relationships were hardly conducive to the ultimate success of the firm, or indeed of the Stockton and Darlington Company itself. From the outset of their acquaintance in 1821 Pease had entertained a glowing opinion of Stephenson's abilities. As he stated to Thomas Richardson after Stephenson's appointment as engineer, 'The more we see of Stephenson . . . the more we are pleased with him . . . he is altogether a self-taught genius . . . there is such a scale of sound ability.'[79] The engineer's genius was never doubted,[80] but as Stephenson became increasingly embroiled in other public railway projects during the 'mini mania' of 1824 his fellow partners' irritation at his prolonged absences from Forth Street could scarcely be concealed. By the end of the year Stephenson was acting as surveyor and engineer to four projected railways – the Liverpool and Manchester, the Liverpool and Birmingham, the London and Northern and the London and South Wales. Not unnaturally, he came to believe that he was 'a railway engineering supremo destined to survey, engineer and equip every line'.[81] To make matters worse Robert Stephenson, who had shown both talent and interest in developing the business 'through the discipline of design engineering rather than by piecemeal evolution', as favoured by his father, had accepted an offer to act as an expeditionary engineer for the Columbian Mining Association, and had departed for South America for what was to prove to be an indefinite period in June 1824.[82]

Lacking firm engineering and managerial direction the Forth Street works were subject to labour problems and the poor scheduling of contracts. Noting George Stephenson's growing fame Pease again commented to Thomas Richardson that 'whilst his talent and ingenuity is great, his execution is torpid, defective and languid as to promptings'.[83] The four winding engines (two of thirty horsepower each and two of fifteen horsepower) ordered for the Brusselton and Etherley inclines in November 1823[84] had not been completed by the beginning of 1825 and work had yet to begin on the two 'travelling engines' ordered in the previous September.[85]

8   Robert Stephenson (1803–59), co-partner in the locomotive building company bearing his name. His absence in Venezuela was to cause anxiety to the Stockton and Darlington Company in the early phases of locomotive operations after 1825.

With other important contracts seriously delayed and confidence in the firm at a low ebb, a management crisis was precipitated. In December 1824 Pease recommended to Longridge and Richardson that 'we really ought some way or other, to engraft ourselves on to GS emoluments so far as to indemnify us from loss . . . he [Stephenson] should not place our property at risque by the application of his time and talent to other objects . . . to be selfish is unaccountable, but self preservation, that first law, must I think . . . be kept in view'.[86] 'Self preservation' in this instance resulted in Stephenson's acquiescence in the formation of a new partnership agreement to establish 'an office for Engineering and Railway Surveying' to be known as George Stephenson and Son.[87] The expectation was that Stephenson would use the new concern as an effective means of delegation for contract work to his assistants, in particular John Dixon and Richard Storey, and to his son Robert on his return from South America. A further development was the appointment of a reluctant Longridge as executive partner in Robert Stephenson and Co. with the clear objective of infusing the management with greater vigour and efficiency.[88] It is an indication, however, of the limited success of these measures that despite Stephenson's return to Forth Street after the failure of the Liverpool and Manchester Railway Bill in April 1825, the Stockton and Darlington management committee in the succeeding November invited Fenton and Murray of Leeds to contract for the supply of locomotives to the newly opened railway. It was fortunate for the Stephensons that the firm declined the invitation on the grounds that 'High Pressure or Locomotive Engines' were not 'a regular article of sale'.[89]

Pease's well-founded anxieties concerning the mismanagement of Robert Stephenson and Co. are placed in their true perspective in the light of the deteriorating financial condition of the Stockton and Darlington Railway Company in 1824–5. By the end of 1822 the company had sixty-nine proprietors who, collectively, owned 463 of the individual shares valued at £100.[90] The leading shareholders, owning 5 or more shares were as follows:

Proprietor	No. of shares
*Jonathan Backhouse (banker, Darlington)	50
*John Backhouse (banker, Darlington)	20
John Baxter (Darlington)	10
*Henry Birkbeck (banker, Lymm, Norfolk)	20
Richard Blanchard (Esquire, Northallerton)	10
Robert Chaloner (Esquire, York)	10
*Joseph Gurney (banker, Norwich)	50
*Joseph John Gurney (banker, Norwich)	20
*John Kitching (merchant, Stamford Hill, Middlesex)	16
*William Leather (banker, Wakefield)	15
Thomas Meynell (Esquire, Yarm)	20
Richard Miles (timber merchant, Yarm)	5
Annie Peacock (spinster, Danby Hill, York)	10
*Edward Pease (merchant, Darlington)	30
*Joseph Pease Jr (merchant, Darlington)	5
Leonard Raisbeck (Esquire, Stockton)	15
*Thomas Richardson (bill-broker, Stamford Hill)	50
*William Skinner (banker, Stockton)	5
*William Skinner Jr (banker, Stockton)	5

*denotes Quakers

The Quaker and banking influence is unmistakable and this feature of the shareholding list was reinforced in subsequent years. By July 1823, when the number of shares had risen to 537, Edward Pease had increased his holding to 35 shares, Thomas Richardson to 55, and John Kitching to 22. There were also several substantial new holdings:[91]

*Edward Backhouse (banker, Sunderland)	
*Robert Barclay (banker, Lombard Street)	20 (collective
*Joseph John Gurney (banker, Norwich)	holding)
*Robert Barclay (banker, Lombard Street)	10
*Simon Martin and family (banker's clerk, Norwich)	5
*George Newman (leather seller, Godalming)	10
*Henry Newman (leather seller, Bermondsey)	26
*John Newman (leather seller, Worcester)	6
Josiah Newman (leather seller, Ross, Hertfordshire)	5
*Thomas Newman (leather seller, Bermondsey)	10
*denotes Quakers	

After this date there were few new shareholdings of note before the opening of the line in September 1825, the exceptions being those of David Bevan, Quaker banker of Lombard Street (10 shares), George Stacey, chemist of London (8 shares), and most significant of all, in view of an impending marital alliance with the Gurneys, the acquisition of a further 45 shares by members of the Pease family.[92]

By the date of opening, with 656 shares taken up, the company was approaching the limit of its authorised capital under the Act of 1823. Considerable reliance was therefore being placed on borrowing powers, far more so than had been originally anticipated. The summary statement of the company's financial position in September 1825, as illustrated in table 1, indicates why. Under the heading of expenditure the amount payable for land and damages had been grossly underestimated by £18,000. From the outset of construction the forming of the way had proved to be far more difficult and costly than Stephenson had anticipated due to adverse terrain.[93] Contingencies, such as the installation of a temporary self-acting plane at Brusselton Quarry for the sum of £2,000, and the allocation of funds to oppose a rival 'Tees and Weardale' railway project in 1824 (see below, pp. 71–2), had also been unexpectedly large, whilst a 20 per cent rise in the price of bar-iron during the course of 1824 led to the revision of several contract prices.[94] With these unforseen expenditures the Stockton and Darlington Company set a precedent which virtually all succeeding railway enterprises were to follow: there was an inexorable tendency for the

Table 1. *Abstract of expenditure and receipts up to 25 July 1825*

	£	s	d
Total expenditure: £133,539 10s 3d of which:			
Forming the way, excavations, and embankments	19,078		
Laying the rails and preparing the way with stones	9,773		
Smith and wright work (including waggons, barrows etc.)	9,821		
Malleable rails	22,367		
Land and damages	24,976		
Engineers, surveyors, clerks, etc.	5,542		
Committee expenses	184		
Total receipts: £133,539 10s 3d of which:			
To cash received from the several subscriptions for and on account of their respective shares	65,603	4	0
To cash received at sundry times from Messrs Gurney and Co. as per the company's promissory notes	60,000		
To cash received for interest from different subscribers in arrears	6	2	6
To sundry rents for small detached parcels of land	24	6	0
To cash received for dividends insurance	88	4	10
To cash received from the Earl of Strathmore's trustees towards defraying the expenses of obtaining an Act of Parliament for the Hagger Leases branch	300		
To balance due to treasurer:	7,517	12	11

Source: PRO RAIL 667/8, Stockton and Darlington management committee minutes, 9 September 1825 (abstract of expenditure and receipts).

expenses in construction to exceed those allowed for in the original parliamentary estimates.[95] It was the inflation in costs which forced the company to borrow extensively on the basis of its promissory notes. Indeed, the company's third Act of Parliament, obtained on 17 May 1824 with the ostensible purpose of replacing the Evenwood branch line by one to Hagger Leases,[96] contained a clause permitting the company to increase its borrowing powers by a further £50,000. During the course of 1824, therefore, £40,000 was obtained from the Gurney banking partnership, and £20,000 from the bill-brokers Richardson, Overend and Co.[97] These were legitimate transactions but they were entered into on the expectation that the main line of railway would be open for traffic by the end of the year. Unfortunately, this was not accomplished due to a variety of circumstances, including adverse weather conditions, the supply of defective waggon wheels, and vexatious litigation on the part of local landowners.[98] In this setting the additional delays caused by the failure of Robert Stephenson and Co. to meet their contractual obligations had serious and adverse implications for the proprietors. By the beginning of 1825 the acute need of the company was for traffic revenues to help meet the cost of servicing outstanding loans. In July 1825, when George Stephenson announced that the main line of railway would be completed within two months, the management committee acted immediately to set 27 September as the date of official opening.[99] This could not have been more timely for on 9 September the company solicitor, Francis Mewburn, was informed by Richardson, Overend and Co. acting on behalf of the Gurneys, that notwithstanding their large shareholding in the company they required repayment within six months of the whole of their outstanding loan.[100] In these circumstances there was more than a hint of anxiety in the management committee's decision 'to borrow the amount due to Messrs Gurney and Co. upon the best terms they can effect, and either upon the Promissory notes of the Company or by Mortgage of the Toles'.[101] Even more revealing as to the desperation of some of the leading proprietors was the decision of Thomas Richardson in the summer of 1825, with active encouragement from Jonathan Backhouse, to explore the possibilities of developing a coastal trade in coal in competition with the Tyne and Wear.[102] Backhouse, of course, had long been adamant in his belief that such a trade would be unremunerative (see above, p. 30) and it may be assumed that in his capacity as treasurer of the company he, more than most, was aware of the immediate financial prospects.

Financial difficulties notwithstanding, one of the main themes of this chapter has been the critical role played by members of the Society of Friends in mobilising capital for the Stockton and Darlington project. It has also been shown that in the years after 1819 Quakers fulfilled leading entrepreneurial roles in bringing the project to fruition. In both respects the history of the Stockton and Darlington Company provides a valuable addition to the corpus of knowledge on the sources of business leadership at a formative stage of Britain's industrialisation. The fact remains that although Quakers are overrepresented in the ranks of the most successful entrepreneurs in the eighteenth and early nineteenth centuries, credible business histories of individual Quaker, or Quaker-dominated, enterprises are regrettably few. Moreover, of those that are available the absence of specific reference to Quakerism *per se* is even more apparent. One notable reason for this has undoubtedly been the reluctance of business historians to offer informed comment on the debate inaugurated by Max Weber on the supposed causal link between the Protestant religion and the rise of capitalism.[103] That the relevant literature is in part dense and impenetrable can serve as some excuse for this scholarly apartheid, as can the fact that in its later stages the debate was informed by concepts such as 'high achievement motivation' more fitted to the realm of psychology than business history.[104] It is also the case that credible interpretations of the rise of capitalism can be advanced without reference to independent theological forces. An alternative interpretation would be to suggest that a growing emphasis on material reward and enhanced status for entrepreneurs in the wider society were all part of a general process of secular economic growth. In these circumstances 'businessmen were gradually recognised as creators of opportunity and wealth as they put men in touch with new products and with new and expanding markets'.[105] The accumulation of wealth became acceptable as a means to social mobility so that wealth seeking itself stimulated further economic growth. The point is well taken, therefore, that religious beliefs provide only one possible route to economic growth, and even in this context the prevailing creed or ethic need not necessarily have been founded upon Protestantism. Nevertheless, the fact remains that what little empirical information is available does point to a causal link between religious 'activism' and economic success, or as David Pratt has put it in his study of Quakers and industrialisation in England, 'between enthroning work and preaching a morality which prevents the dissipation of talent and resources elsewhere'.[106] Pratt concludes, reasonably, that such values could stand alone and be a force for change without doctrinal or theological impulses. 'However, it is not surprising that ready acceptance was not forthcoming in a traditionalistic society until the ethic was embraced as a counter value by the one factor which was sufficiently all-encompassing and was endangered most by the established order: reforming religion.'[107] That said, the strong suspicion remains that the explanation for the overrepresentation of Nonconformists in general and Quakers in particular among the ranks of Britain's successful entrepreneurs is multifaceted. Distinctive religious precepts, an approach to education which stressed both spiritual and practical needs, and a system of internal government designed to promote a national and international consciousness of community without stifling local initiative are all part of the story. So too is the Quakers' well-founded sense of exclusion from the wider society in response to the Test and Corporation Acts which barred them from traditional areas of advancement such as the ancient universities, government service, and the armed forces. It is entirely plausible, therefore, that more ambitious and assertive Quakers were propelled into the politically neutral world of business and commerce, if only to sustain living standards.[108] As Voltaire commented in his *Letters on England*, 'They are reduced to the necessity of earning money through commerce.'[109] Simple geographic determinism must also be a relevant factor in explaining overrepresentation in view of the relative numerical strength of the Society of Friends in the north of England where sustained industrialisation was concentrated in the eighteenth and nineteenth centuries. It is true that in the current state of knowledge these explanations for overrepresentation lend themselves more to 'heroic generalisations about the Quakers as businessmen'[110] than to firmly based hypotheses about the sources of business success, but their cumulative effect is to suggest that of all the dissenting sects of the seventeenth- and eighteenth-centuries Quakers appear to have been 'the most favourably disposed ... towards economic endeavours'.[111]

As the experience of the Stockton and Darlington Railway reveals, the distinctive structure and organisation of the Society of Friends had major consequences for business strategy and confidence. In a pioneering work, Arthur Raistrick suggested that as a close-knit sect the Society of Friends represented an extended family group in which personal contacts reaching over unusually wide geographical areas were facilitated by peripatetic ministers and the regular monthly, quarterly and yearly meetings of the Society.[112] At these meetings, many of which involved considerable travel and lengthy periods away from home, it was not unusual for Friends with commercial and business interests to discuss the state of trade and also the possibility of partnership in joint ventures. In the absence of institutional capital markets it was the ability to exploit geographically dispersed pools of capital which helped to sustain the Stockton and Darlington project at critical junctures. In this respect there could be no greater contrast with the experience of the 'northern' canal party in general and Christopher Tennant in particular.

The existence of personalised financial networks should not, of course, be taken as *prima facie* evidence that all members of the Society of Friends were single-minded capitalists dedicated to the pursuit of commercial advantage. On the contrary, the bulk of the membership continued to be dominated throughout the eighteenth century by small farmers, shopkeepers and craftsmen – manufacturers who remained committed to the original Quaker code with its insistence on spiritual priorities. Neither should it be thought that Quaker marital alliances were the product of narrow business calculation, merely that in the restricted world of the Society of Friends, and when 'marrying out' led to immediate disownment, the pressure to contract marriages with those from similar backgrounds sharing common perceptions and beliefs could prove irresistible.[113]

The institutional structure of the Society of Friends, insofar as it impinged upon business practice, can be related directly to the ongoing debate on the nature of the firm in terms of goals and organisation. Recent work on the theory of the firm, building upon an original paper by R. H. Coase,[114] has highlighted the concepts of transaction costs and internalisation.[115] As Coase emphasised, the coordination and allocation of resources via competitive markets imposes costs on a business. But these so-called transaction costs may be reduced as a result of internalisation, that is the supercession of market functions by the individual firm. Perhaps the most striking example of the benefits of internalisation is provided by the motives for vertical integration. Historically, technological imperatives have undoubtedly played a role in stimulating the growth of vertically integrated enterprise. However, 'emphasis on transaction costs stresses the importance of internalising long term contracts, the advantages of holding a monopoly of supply in intermediate markets, quality control, and transfer pricing. The firm, must, therefore, have both a technological and contractual rationale but with pride of place being held by the latter.'[116] The focus on internalisation as a cost-reducing strategy has loomed large in the literature of business history in recent years, no more so than in Alfred Chandler's empirical work on the rise of the modern business corporation.[117] However, in the context of the Stockton and Darlington Railway it seems clear that the Coase–Chandlerian perspective on the theory of the firm should be complemented by the concept of personalised external networks. As this chapter has indicated such networks are an alternative means of reducing transaction costs arising from uncertainty and deficient knowledge.[118] When trust between economic agents is weak transaction costs will be relatively high and economic performance retarded. The Society of Friends, however, was infused with a strong moral culture which redounded to the advantage of the Quaker businessman in terms of confidence and expectations. The Society was by no means unique in this respect during the formative stages of Britain's industrialisation, but its unusual cohesion and extensive family linkages, well illustrated in the case of Backhouses and Peases, render it the most impressive of external networks conducive to the formation and subsequent growth of the firm.

4   Hopes fulfilled, 1825–1833

The formal opening of the Stockton and Darlington Railway took place on 27 September 1825. The proprietors were determined to mark the opening with a grand display, beginning with the formation of a train headed by the company's first locomotive and hauling coal, merchandise and passengers from Brusselton to the Stockton terminus. A contemporary account in the *Newcastle Courant* recorded the day's events in glowing terms:

To give eclat to the public opening of the road, a programme was issued, stating that the proprietors would assemble at the permanent steam-engine below Brusselton Tower, about nine miles west of Darlington, at eight o'clock. Accordingly, the committee, after inspecting the Etherley Engine Plane, assembled at the bottom of Brusselton Engine Plane, near West Auckland, and here the carriages, loaded with coals and merchandise, were drawn up the eastern ridge by the Brusselton Engine, a distance of 1960 yards in seven and a half minutes, and then lowered down the plane on the east side of the hill 880 yards in five minutes. At the foot of the plane the locomotive engine was ready to receive the carriages; and here the novelty of the scene and the fineness of the day had attracted an immense concourse of spectators – the fields on each side of the Railway being literally covered with ladies and gentlemen on horseback, and pedestrians of all kinds. The track of carriages was then attached to a locomotive engine of the most improved construction, and built by Mr George Stephenson.[1]

As the train approached Stockton the permanent way ran parallel to the turnpike road from Yarm and it was at this point that the revolutionary import of steam locomotive transport was demonstrated in spectacular fashion. As the *Courant* commented,

Numerous horses, carriages, gigs, carts and other vehicles travelled along with the engine, and her immense train of carriages, in some places within a few yards, without the horses seeming the least frightened; and at one time the passengers by the engine had the pleasure of accompanying and cheering their brother passengers by the stage coach, which passed alongside, and of observing the striking contrast exhibited by the power of the engine and of horses; the engine with her six hundred passengers and load, and the coach with four horses, and only sixteen passengers.[2]

The journey successfully accomplished, a twenty-one-gun salute was fired from the company's wharf from which point the official guests of the

THE

STOCKTON & DARLINGTON

RAILWAY COMPANY

Hereby give Notice,

THAT the FORMAL OPENING of their RAILWAY will take place on the 27th instant, as announced in the public Papers.—The Proprietors will assemble at the Permanent Steam Engine, situated below BRUSSELTON TOWER*, *about nine Miles West of* DARLINGTON, *at 8 o'clock, and, after examining their extensive inclined Planes there, will start from the Foot of the* BRUSSELTON *descending Plane, at 9 o'clock, in the following Order :——*

    1. THE COMPANY'S LOCOMOTIVE ENGINE.
    2. The ENGINE'S TENDER, with Water and Coals.
    3. SIX WAGGONS, laden with Coals, Merchandize, &c.
    4. The COMMITTEE, and other PROPRIETORS, in the COACH belonging to the COMPANY.
    5. SIX WAGGONS, with Seats reserved for STRANGERS.
    6. FOURTEEN WAGGONS, for the Conveyance of Workmen and others.

    ☞ *The WHOLE of the above to proceed to STOCKTON.*

    7. SIX WAGGONS, laden with Coals, to leave the Procession at the DARLINGTON BRANCH.
    8. SIX WAGGONS, drawn by Horses, for Workmen and others.
    9. Ditto   Ditto.
    10. Ditto   Ditto.
    11. Ditto   Ditto.

The COMPANY'S WORKMEN to leave the Procession at DARLINGTON, and DINE at that Place at ONE o'clock; excepting those to whom Tickets are specially given for YARM, and for whom Conveyances will be provided, on their Arrival at STOCKTON.

TICKETS will be given to the Workmen who are to dine at DARLINGTON, specifying the Houses of Entertainment.

The PROPRIETORS, and such of the NOBILITY and GENTRY as may honour them with their Company, will DINE precisely at THREE o'clock, at the TOWN-HALL, STOCKTON.— Such of the Party as may incline to return to DARLINGTON that Evening, will find Conveyances in waiting for their Accommodation, to start from the COMPANY'S WHARF there precisely at SEVEN o'clock.

The COMPANY take this Opportunity of enjoining on all their WORK-PEOPLE that Attention to *Sobriety* and *Decorum* which they have hitherto had the Pleasure of observing.

The COMMITTEE give this PUBLIC NOTICE, that all Persons who shall ride upon, or by the sides of, the RAILWAY, on Horseback, will incur the Penalties imposed by the Acts of Parliament passed relative to this RAILWAY.

* Any Individuals desirous of seeing the Train of Waggons descending the inclined Plane from ETHERLEY, and in Progress to BRUSSELTON, may have an Opportunity of so doing, by being on the RAILWAY at ST. HELEN's AUCKLAND not later than Half-past Seven o'clock.

RAILWAY-OFFICE, *Sept. 19th*, 1825.

ATKINSON's Office, High-Row, Darlington.

9   The formal notice of opening of the Stockton and Darlington Railway, September 1825.

proprietors, numbering 102 and preceded by the Yarm band, marched to Stockton town hall to be entertained at a banquet punctuated by congratulatory speeches and the astonishing number of twenty-three toasts. The latter encompassed the predictable royal and civic dignitaries, as well as the proprietors of the Liverpool and Manchester and Hull and Leeds Railways. A guest speaker representing the former expressed the feelings of the gathering with the generous sentiment that 'facility of communication by means of railways had been fully established by the experiment of that day'.[3]

In the sober light of day the proprietors were confronted with the immediate task of managing a business 'in which they had not the advantage of a single example' in terms of operational practice.[4] As Edward Pease commented to Thomas Richardson, 'I can see nothing but our way must one day be a good concern yet thou art a bold man to venture so deep in an untried speculation – tis like these American mines – all promise'.[5] The reference to the El Dorado of South America was entirely apposite in view of Robert Stephenson's profitless sojourn in Venezuela.[6] It also serves as a reminder of the worry that was uppermost in the minds of the proprietors in 1825, namely the need to generate traffic revenues sufficient to service the company's debts. So serious was the situation in this respect that in the week prior to the official opening of the railway the management committee of directors had proposed that in order to facilitate the repayment of the Gurneys' debt every shareholder should be 'bound formally for £100 towards the money borrowed or to be borrowed for the use of the Railway'.[7] As late as May 1826, after eight months of operation, Jonathan Backhouse was still referring to the company's 'pecuniary embarrassments' arising from cumulative borrowings amounting to £74,800. Such large-scale borrowing had facilitated the issue of a relatively low number of shares, thereby maintaining the 'concord of the Company'. There was, however, an immediate requirement for the repayment of £30,000 to creditors.[8] It was in these circumstances that the management committee applied to the Exchequer Loan Board for financial assistance. As a statutory body with power to grant loans in aid of public works projects the Board submitted the company to a detailed interrogation in which it was revealed that the sum of £50,000 was required – £30,000 to meet outstanding debt obligations and the remainder 'to complete the works – viz Black Boy branch, Croft branch, and sundry land purchases, Engines, etc.'.[9] There is no record of the company's request being met and it is reasonable to presume that the application was rejected on the grounds that the Board was unwilling, or unable, to extend loans for the purpose of redeeming existing debts, even though the latter may have been incurred as a result of fixed expenditures on land, plant, and equipment.

The Exchequer Loan Board interrogation highlighted the company's further dilemma. In order to bring the line to fruition within the authorised capital sum and to limit borrowing, work on essential infrastructure projects, ranging from shipping staithes and depots, to engine sheds and repair shops, had been held in abeyance. In addition, the construction of important branch lines to Croft, the Black Boy Colliery, and to Hagger Leases had been suspended.[10] All of these shortfalls impaired the company's operations and hence its ability to generate revenues. Jonathan Backhouse may have taken comfort in the fact that 'every mile of railway in its first year was maintained at *double* the cost of succeeding years' and that costs had been inflated by non-recurring 'sundry expenses', but there could be no denying that by May 1826 the company was in the grip of a liquidity crisis. To make matters worse, some colliery lessees were continuing to lead their own coals by road with the result that the company was hardly in a position to raise its tolls and charges.[11] This difficulty was in all probability the result of irrational prejudice against the company, but it was certainly exacerbated by problems encountered with the company's rolling stock which served to retard the growth of traffic on the line.

The Stockton and Darlington Company's response to rolling stock difficulties is an important issue which raises some key aspects of entrepreneurship, in particular the relationship between technological choice and cost effectiveness. Insofar as the issue has been discussed in established accounts of the company's history, it has tended to be dominated by partisanship and the extreme interpretation of events, especially on the subject of locomotive haulage. It is possible, however, with the aid of a range of sources to provide an objective and accurate account of the company's early problems in the management of traffic and the manner in which they were surmounted.

Within a month of the opening of the line the company began to receive complaints from colliery owners about a shortage of waggons, the result in part of 'unfair' allocations between adjacent pits.[12] At the same time, Thomas Storey, resident engineer to the railway, informed the management committee that the 150 waggons owned by the company were below the statutory capacity for the export of coal (53 cwt) and that in constructional terms they were 'as bad a set of waggons as were ever turned out on a Railway' due to inferior wood and 'flimsy sides'.[13] In their existing state they could hardly be expected to last for more than two years.[14] Confirmation of the poor design of these early waggons is provided by the comments of an independent observer who wrote to the management committee in November 1825 drawing attention to 'the grinding or friction experienced at every turn on the road by the wheels of the several waggons on which they move, and consequently [the need for] more power from the

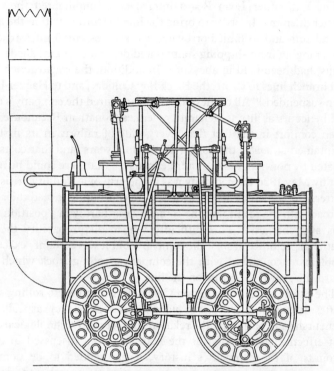

10   *Locomotion No. 1*, the Stockton and Darlington Railway Company's first locomotive, 1825.

engine to draw them along ... than in the straight line'. The problem arose due to the use of fixed axles which produced excessive wear and tear as the wheels tended 'to run off the curve in a tangent'.[15] One reason for George Stephenson's modifications to Overton's original route in 1821 (see above, p. 40) was the need to straighten the line to accommodate fixed axles.[16] Stephenson was well aware that such a design would lead to high maintenance costs both for wheels and rails and it seems an astonishing oversight on his part that he had failed to apply his practical skills and attention to detail to resolving the problem by 1825. It is hardly surprising, therefore, that the early operational records of the company contain several large orders for replacement waggon wheels and rails.[17] In September 1826 the company embarked on experiments with a new design of waggon employing 'anti-friction rollers', but it was not until 1829, after Robert Stephenson and Co. had introduced a new spring-mounted waggon utilising the 'anti-friction' principle, that the company possessed an efficient and well-constructed waggon fleet.[18]

So too with locomotive haulage, the Stockton and Darlington Company encountered severe difficulties almost from the outset of operations. To some contemporary observers locomotive haulage was the most spectacular aspect of the company's activities. As the Reverend James Adamson commented in the *Caledonian Mercury* in 1826,

it is the locomotive engines which show, in the most striking light, the extent of power which the Rail-Way system places at our command. Each of these, of which there are two constantly at work, and one, if not two additional in preparation, draws after it 20 waggons, and frequently 24, and forming in all a mass of 77 tons in the one case, and 92 in the other; and this enormous load is now regularly conveyed by each of these engines from Brusselton Plane to Stockton, a distance of 20 miles, in four hours; the engine returns again in five hours with the empty waggons; and, including an hour spent in stoppages, completes the journey in ten hours; so that, if necessary, it could easily make two trips in one day and one night, and thus deliver ... between 500 and 600 tons per week, which is equal to the work of 12 or 14 horses in the same circumstances.[19]

This eulogistic account, however, fails signally to convey any impression of the company's difficulties during this early phase of locomotive haulage. Troubles began following the delivery of a second locomotive from Robert Stephenson and Co. in November 1825. So badly constructed was this engine that the railway company's smiths had to be 'employed a whole week before it could be got to work'.[20] Disillusion with Stephenson's products was reflected not only via an approach to Fenton, Murray and Jackson of Leeds (see above, p. 47), but also in the resolution adopted in November 1825

that Robert Stephenson and Co. be requested that in any engine they may furnish us with, not to send any engines with new and experimental apparatus, but such fitting up as hath, been tried and approved already, and that as the disadvantage arising from not having duplicate wheels for the engines are very great, Robert Stephenson and Co. are requested to send some spare wheels fit on the axles which it is desired may be always of the same pattern not only for the Engines but for the Waggons.[21]

A further resolution, adopted one week later, provides a graphic illustration of the management committee's frustration:

Innumerable accidents and inconveniences having arisen from some defects in the Locomotive Engines and this Committee considering the great expenses they have incurred in alterations and repairs ... – direct the Clerk to make out an account of the expenditure and transmit the same to [Robert Stephenson and Co.], and request they will *protemporare* place a Smith or person sufficiently acquainted with Locomotive engines at Brusselton or elsewhere in order to superintend the alterations and repairs which attach to the said Engines on account of [them] not being perfect and complete when set at work.[22]

By May 1826 the company possessed four locomotives, all built to a common pattern. Boiler pressures were 25 lb per square inch with two vertical cylinders placed within a single straight-flue boiler. None of these engines was equipped with bearing springs or malleable iron tyres and in these respects were inferior to those employed at Killingworth Colliery in the mid-1820s. In operation they all suffered from a crippling weakness, namely, the failure to generate an effective head of steam due to their limited heating surface amounting to only sixty square feet. Inclines proved difficult to negotiate even when conditions were favourable, and 'in awkward slippery weather or on some long, greasy incline, the speed would flag rapidly; the engineman first lavishing oil on the rods and bearings, and then prising the wheels round with a crowbar'.[23] Such tactics were not always successful and it was not an unusual sight for drivers and their firemen to be seen patiently waiting by the trackside whilst a stationary locomotive built up steam.[24] The effects on traffic of disrupted journeys as a result of poor locomotive performance were compounded by stoppages arising from derailments. These were invariably the result of the failure of crudely constructed point switchings. Moreover, the locomotive drivers themselves were hardly 'the most manageable class of beings' having a tendency to careless and wreckless driving and the abuse of their engines as when the company's second locomotive ran out of control along the Stockton wharves in 1827 as a result of the fireman rendering the safety valve inoperable.[25] These difficulties were exacerbated by the manner in which the line as a whole was worked with its combination of stationary engines, locomotives, and horse haulage for the conveyance of merchandise and passengers. As Robert Stephenson commented in 1830,

scarcely a single journey is performed by [the] engines without being interrupted by the horses or other trains of carriages passing in a contrary direction there being only a single line of road with passing places. At each end of the distance traversed by the engines great delay is occasioned from the irregular supply of carriages which from the nature of the trade and other local circumstances it is impossible to avoid.[26]

Moreover, there are numerous apocryphal stories of the disruption to traffic caused by the abrasive relations between locomotive drivers and horse leaders. These were the result of arguments over the right of passage in relation to the many sidings on the line. The company had adopted a strict rule in this respect in that passenger vehicles were expected to make way for locomotives and horse-hauled waggons, but this did not prevent the occasional fist fight from breaking out, lubricated by the consumption of ale from the several inns along the way. As for the inclined planes, their breakdown had the potential to disturb the entire traffic on the line. There was one stationary double engine at the top of each ridge at Brusselton and Etherley which worked the two inclined planes via a single vertical drum. Early operational problems arose from the irregular coiling of the ropes leading to breakage and the consequent destruction of waggons. The engines together had cost the company well over £5,000 and on financial grounds alone there could be no substantial remodelling of this aspect of the company's operations. Instead, the company's superintendent of 'the permanent and locomotive engines', Timothy Hackworth, succeeded in devising a new haulage arrangement whereby 'the momentum of the waggons descending one incline assisted the engine in hauling the ascending waggons up the other'.[27] Further improvements were applied to the ropes themselves, together with ingenious devices for throwing waggons off the plane if they threatened to run over the bank-head or crash back into waggons at the foot of the incline. Eventually, in 1831 the Brusselton engine was replaced by a more powerful eighty horsepower unit designed by Hackworth and built by R. and W. Hawthorn of Newcastle upon Tyne. This had the effect of greatly accelerating the flow of traffic with six sets of waggons passing over the incline every hour at the remarkable speed of 15 mph.[28]

It is on the subject of the possible abandonment of locomotive haulage that a considerable controversy had arisen in the early history of the Stockton and Darlington Company. It originated in the published opinion of John Wesley Hackworth that, but for the fact of 'two of the most influential members of the Company (Messrs. Edward Pease and Thomas Richardson) being partners with Stephenson in the Forth Street Engine Works, Newcastle, from whence four of the first locomotives were supplied – they would have been abandoned long before an experimental period of eighteen months had been allowed'.[29] Hackworth, a direct descendant of the company's first locomotive superintendent, possessed a missionary zeal to secure for his relative an important place in the history of locomotive engineering, an aspiration which was well reflected in his claim that the Stockton and Darlington Company's management committee 'as a last experiment' took up Timothy Hackworth's request 'to be allowed to make an engine in his own way'.[30] This version of events in 1826–7, portraying Timothy Hackworth as the saviour of the company's fortunes, was summarily dismissed by W. W. Tomlinson in his historical account of the company and also by J. G. H. Warren, the official historian of Robert Stephenson and Co.[31] For Tomlinson the fact that there was not 'the slightest foundation' for Wesley Hackworth's view rested on the existence in the company's records of a report to the management committee stating that experiments had shown that the cost of carrying 4,263 tons of coal by horses was £163 8s 0d compared to only £70 6s 6d by locomotive haulage.[32] In Tomlinson's view this finding was corroborated by the comment in the annual report to shareholders for 1827 that 'there appears to be a saving of nearly 30 per cent in favour of haulage by Locomotive Engines when compared with its being done by Horses'.[33] According to Tomlinson, these statements were hardly consistent with the claim that the abandonment of locomotive

11   Timothy Hackworth (1786–1850), first locomotive superintendent of the Stockton and Darlington Railway.

haulage was being actively considered within the management committee in 1827.

That there was evidence in support of the pessimistic view of the future of locomotive haulage was amply confirmed by Robert Young in his detailed study of Timothy Hackworth's role in early locomotive development. Citing correspondence contained in biographies of the Stephensons by Samuel Smiles and J. C. Jeaffreson, Young was able to show that in 1826–7 both Edward Pease and Thomas Richardson were seriously worried as to the safety of their investment in the Forth Street Engine Works. Both partners were especially concerned that Robert Stephenson should return from South America. As Pease commented in a letter addressed to Stephenson in April 1826, 'I can assure thee that thy business at Newcastle, as well as thy father's engineering, have suffered very much from thy absence, and unless thou soon return the former will be given up, as Mr Longridge is not able to give it that attention it requires, and what is done is not done with credit to the house'.[34] Smiles went as far as to claim that Pease actively wished to terminate his association with Robert Stephenson and Co. but that since George Stephenson was unable to buy him out, 'the establishment had to be carried on in the hope that the locomotive might yet be established in public estimation as a practical and economical working power'.[35] Other more circumstantial evidence for 'the failure of the locomotive' is provided by the withdrawal of the Stephenson-built engines from part of the line at Hetton Colliery, an apparently serious blow to the credibility of locomotive traction in view of the fact that steam haulage had come to be regarded as permanent at Hetton after its introduction in 1822.[36] Further damage to the Stephensons' reputation arose from the contemporary decision of the management committee of the Newcastle and Carlisle Railway to employ horse haulage only on their line. The directors of this concern were 'local men with full knowledge of local doings' and their decision to dispense with steam power can be taken as *prima facie* evidence of public awareness of the Stockton and Darlington Company's crisis of confidence in the locomotive,[37] fully reflected in the management committee's decision in March 1827 to employ additional horses.[38] Finally, there is the telling point raised by Robert Young that the company's claims for the cost effectiveness of locomotives cannot be entertained seriously in view of the gross disparity between the savings reported internally and the far less impressive results presented to shareholders (see above, p. 61). As Young points out, there is no indication how the latter had been obtained and the very vagueness of the relevant statement, without supporting figures, does indeed suggest that the management committee had as yet no clear idea of the comparative costs of locomotive and horse haulage.[39] If the internally reported figures were correct, then the company was guaranteed financial security and that was manifestly not the case in 1826–7.

There is thus a modicum of evidence to lend support to Young's claim that it was Timothy Hackworth who was responsible for the ultimate success of the locomotive, and hence a substantial fall in operating costs on the Stockton and Darlington Railway. Certainly, Hackworth was a talented engineer endowed with immense practical abilities. According to William Patter, his former employer at Walbottle Colliery, he was 'ingenious, honest [and] industrious'[40] and it was this endorsement, together with the strongest possible recommendation from George Stephenson, which had secured his appointment to the Stockton and Darlington Railway. He had

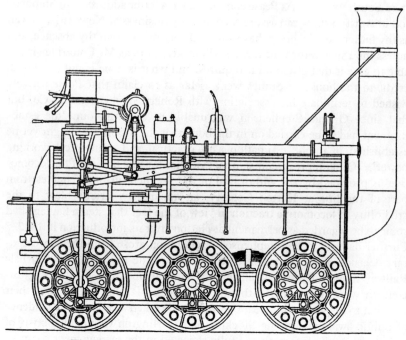

12   The *Royal George* locomotive, designed by Timothy Hackworth for the Stockton and Darlington Railway, 1827.

been employed for a time at the Stephenson's Forth Street works and had supervised the construction of the railway company's first locomotive.[41] It was Hackworth who had the onerous task of repairing and maintaining the company's early locomotives, rectifying design faults in the search for greater reliability and improved steaming performance. Early in 1827 he was engaged in the design of no less than three new locomotive types and it was in this context that the management committee authorised him to construct a locomotive that would 'exceed the efficiency of horses'. The resulting product, the *Royal George*, has an honoured place in the evolution of locomotive design as the most powerful engine of its day. This distinction it owed to a return-flue boiler operating at 52 lb per square inch with 141 square feet of heating surface. It employed a direct drive from the cylinders to the wheels and it was the first locomotive to have three axles with the wheels coupled via outside coupling rods. These properties, together with its weight (12 tons 7½ cwt compared to 8 tons 5 cwt for the early Stephenson-designed engines), gave it the considerable advantage of greater tractive adhesion. The more even distribution of weight on the track, moreover, helped to limit damage to the permanent way.[42]

As an ardent defender of the Stephensons Tomlinson damned the *Royal George* with faint praise, claiming that contrary to general supposition it was not the first locomotive to exceed the efficiency of horse haulage. Neither did it establish the credibility of steam traction or the future of the railway system generally. It was no more than 'a good serviceable engine', and in its much vaunted use of a blast pipe with its orifice placed centrally in the chimney – a critical development in early locomotive technology – it merely capitalised on the achievements of other locomotive designers, from Richard Trevithick to George Stephenson himself.[43] Further support for Tomlinson's view is provided by Warren in his observation that although the *Royal George* had a nominal capacity 'about 50 per cent greater' than the Stockton and Darlington Company's other locomotives, working results for 1828 indicate that it hauled loads only 15-30 per cent in excess of the Stephenson-designed engines.[44] In these respects, table 2, setting out the details of locomotive drivers, their earnings, and work done in 1828, is revealing. Gowland was the driver of the *Royal George* and although his earnings and performance were superior to those of the other enginemen it is clear that Stephenson, Morrow and Law, driving older and less powerful locomotives, achieved creditable results. On this basis, there-fore, it would appear that the unique contribution of Hackworth's locomo-tive should not be overemphasised. Tomlinson's strictures, moreover, carry considerable weight from the perspective of railway development as a whole. The really decisive event in the inauguration of the 'Railway Age' was the opening of the Liverpool and Manchester Railway in September 1830. From the outset of operations exclusive reliance was placed on locomotive haulage and the success of the line in this respect was founded upon the technological breakthrough represented by Robert Stephenson's *Rocket* powered by a multitubular boiler and the unequivocal victor in the 1829 Rainhill Trials.[45] As representatives of a distinctive school of engi-neering, Hackworth's locomotives, with their vertical or steeply inclined cylinders, and single return-flue boilers, were doomed to ultimate obsole-scence, if only because of their low operating speeds.[46] In a major sense, however, these points offered in denigration of Hackworth's achievements miss their mark. In operational terms the outstanding need for the Stockton and Darlington Railway in the years after 1825 was for a reliable and cost-effective form of haulage. This was provided by the *Royal George* and its successors. As Young comments,

Costing £425, the *Royal George* in the year 1828 conveyed 22,422 tons of coal over 20 miles at the rate of a farthing per ton per mile, or including all repairs and maintenance, and interest on sunk capital at 10 per cent, £466; an economy in working rarely exceeded. The cost of the same work performed by horses was £998, showing a difference of £532 in favour of the engine, a saving of 53.3 per cent, on

Table 2. *Enginemen's earnings and comparative haulage performance, 1828*

Enginemen	No. of days employed	Net earnings (£ s d)	Total no. of miles run	Tonnage of coals led	Tons carried 1 mile	Average no. of miles per day	Average quantity of coals per day		Tons carried 1 mile per day
							tons	cwt	
William Gowland	269	344.19. 7	10,679	20,231	340,099	39.70	75	4	1,264
James Stephenson	260	254.18. 0	9,941	14,336	252,403	38.24	55	5	971
Robert Morrow	271	276. 9. 2	10,820	15,356½	274,364	39.94	56	13	1,012
Michael Law	244	269.15.10	9,923	13,911	266,938	40.67	57	0	1,094
John Cree	125	121.11. 5	4,906	6,456	120,710	39.25	51	12	966
Edward Corner	79	75. 2. 4	2,973	4,230	74,346	37.63	53	11	964

Source: Tomlinson, *The North Eastern Railway*, pp. 150, 151.

what was up to this period the cheapest working cost, and throughout its journey of 20 miles it was able to maintain a speed of nine miles per hour in all weathers.[47]

The *Royal George* was the prototype for a sequence of heavy mineral engines, built to Hackworth's designs either under his own supervision at New Shildon or by outside contractors. In addition to Robert Stephenson and Co. the latter included the Darlington engineering partnership of William and Alfred Kitching as well as R. and W. Hawthorn of Newcastle upon Tyne. They served the Stockton and Darlington Company well for two decades. Most of them were reliable in service and their six coupled wheels 'gave the engine perfect command over heavy loads in all states of weather'.[48] On a network dominated by the transhipment of heavy minerals slow haulage speeds were no disadvantage, especially during the early phases of the company's operations when the single line of track was traversed by horses and even slower locomotives, averaging only 4–5 mph. A further defence of Hackworth's reputation rests on the fact that up to the end of the 1820s most of the locomotives supplied by Robert Stephenson and Co. were either poorly constructed or unreliable in service. In itself this should occasion no surprise. These early Stephenson locomotives were necessarily constructed on the basis of experience gained from short colliery lines and in this respect 'it was to be expected that defects would be found in complicated locomotives working under new and extremely defective traffic conditions'.[49] But it was Hackworth, largely devoid of skilled assistance, who transformed them into effective operational vehicles. E. L. Ahrons, the doyen of locomotive historians, provides an apposite and unbiased judgement:

[Hackworth] was the man, a part of whose duties consisted in investigating reports and causes of failures, and he, and not Robert Stephenson and Co., had the first opportunity of finding the remedies. It was the keen observation which he brought to bear upon the working of the details of the locomotives and engines under his charge which made Hackworth the excellent practical locomotive superintendent which he undoubtedly was.[50]

The effectiveness of Hackworth's engineering talents were reflected in the number of miles run and tonnages hauled by Stephenson-built locomotives in 1828 (see table 2 above, p. 66). This was, indeed, the critical year for locomotive operations and, as the figures in tables 3 and 4 reveal, steam haulage achieved a significant breakthrough.

Horse haulage was to persist on the Stockton and Darlington network well into the 1850s by virtue of 'a simple and ingenious contrivance which economised their [horses'] powers to the extent of one-third'.[51] This was the dandy cart designed by George Stephenson himself and popularised by a Liverpool barrister, Thomas Shaw Brandreth. It was nothing more than a

Table 3. *Tonnages conveyed and operating costs, May 1828*

	Tonnage	Cost
Horses	9,029	£354 19s 4½d
Locomotives	7,416	£132 18s 8d

Source: Timothy Hackworth's memorandum book, cited in Young, *Timothy Hackworth,* p. 168.

Table 4. *Tonnages conveyed by locomotives and horses, 1828*

	Locomotives	Horses
Jan.–June	35,201	31,855
July–Dec.	39,349	23,349

Source: Tomlinson, *The North Eastern Railways,* p. 149.

four-wheeled truck attached to the rear of a train and equipped with a hay box. On reaching a descending section of the line the horse could be unhitched and placed in the cart, enabling it to restore its energies before the next incline was reached. The dandy cart certainly proved effective but it could not prevent the ascendancy of the locomotive. At the very time of its introduction in July 1828 Hackworth was instructed by the management committee that 'the engines are in future to take all coals possible' with horses receiving the residue. This was followed in September by the order that 'the coal owners, east of Brusselton plane, are to send their coal by locomotive engines as formerly, and if they are unwilling, they must apply to the Company'.[52] A further act of coercion for recalcitrant colliery owners came in July 1829 with the decision of the management committee that waggon facilities should be witheld from traffic senders who refused to cooperate with the company's policy on locomotive haulage.[53]

It took the Stockton and Darlington Company the greater part of four years to resolve complex motive power and rolling stock problems. In this respect, the history of the company in the years 1825–9 does indeed vindicate Henry Booth's contemporary judgement that south Durham was at that time 'the great theatre of practical operations on railways'.[54] It is hardly surprising, therefore, that the company's activities attracted the close attention of other aspiring railway proprietors, notably the promoters of the Liverpool and Manchester Railway.[55] The fact that the latter were sufficiently uncertain of the practicability of locomotive haulage to arrange the

ABSTRACT

Of the Cash Account for the Year ending 30th of June, 1827.

Dr. Jonathan Backhouse, Treasurer, in Account with the Stockton & Darlington Railway Co.				Cr.				
	£.	s.	d.		£.	s.	d.	£. s. d.
To Cash received in Sundry Loans .	30,753	11	6	*By Balance due to the Treasurer*		10,459	3 9	
Do. do. on account of Tonnage &c. .	16,876	8	7	*Cash paid on account of dividends* .		726	1 10	
				Stephenson & Co. for permanent Engines		4,000	0 0	
				H. Birkbeck, repayment of his Loan .		1,000	0 0	
				Interest, Discount, and Commission .		3,371	5 4	
				Cash paid on account of Land for the				
				Main Line, Croft Branch, Black Boy				
				Branch, and Hagger Leases Branch		4,598	4 2	
				Newmarch and Co. for Kenton Engine,				
				purchased for Black Boy Branch .		528	4 6	
				Cash on account of Law Expences		300	0 0	
				Allowance to Owners of Black Boy Col-				
				liery, to the 1st June last, ⅌ order				
				of General Meeting . . .		1,037	9 4	
				Do. to W. L. Wharton, ⅌ do. . . .		151	13 0	
				Additional outlay (viz) Depots, Erec-				
				tions, &c. on the Main Line and				
				Branches, Locomotive Engines, &c.		8,698	12 0	
				Cash paid for sundry Materials and				
				Labour, for Waggons, &c. for in-				
				crease of Carrying establishment .		3,674	17 5	
				Sundry contingent Expences (viz) Smith				
				and Wright's Work, Labour, Dam-				
				ages, Freight, Carriage, Agents' and				
				Clerks' Salaries, Rates, Stationary,				
				Travelling Expences, Postages, &c.	4,612 18 4			
				The Monthly Pay Bills (viz) Labour				
				and Consumable Articles, at the fixed				
				and Locomotive Engines, and for ad-				
				ditional Horses employed in leading				
				Coals and Lime	2,807 7 9			
				Do. as under :—				
Balance due to the Treasurer . .	2,691	1	6	*Repairing the Way & Materials* 1818 16 2				
				Sundry Contingent Labour 1060 2 4				
				Cleaning Cuts and repairing				
				embankments . 514 15 6				
				Repairing Waggons, Engines, &c 527 1 7				
				Leading, &c. . . 434 8 7—4355 4 2—11,775 10 3				
	£.50,321	1	7			£.50,321	1	7
Amount of Two Instalments of 20 ⅌ Cent.								
New Share Account . . .	13,000	0	0	*Balance*		2,691	1	6

13 First printed statement of the Stockton and Darlington Railway
Company's accounts, as presented to the body of shareholders in 1827.

Rainhill Trials should not be allowed to detract from the Stockton and
Darlington Company's achievements where, as indicated already, the
nature of the traffic placed little premium on rapidity of movement.

The question remains, however, as to the means by which the company
sustained its financial position during such an extended period of its
operations, and when other net drains on its reserves were being experienced. Reference has been made to the limitations on traffic expansion as a
result of the failure to complete projected branch lines (see above, p. 57). In
1826 the company felt bound to compensate the owners of the Black Boy
Colliery to the extent of 1s 6d per ton for all coal delivered to the railway
terminus by road. By June 1827 the cumulative rebate exceeded £1,000 by
which time the company had also extended compensation to William Lloyd
Wharton, the lessee of Coundon Colliery, who was similarly penalised in
having to use road transport to gain access to a branch line.[56] At a time when
liquidity problems were pressing such expenditures were a major irritant to

the company. Yet the means to end them entailed further substantial expenditure of capital on branch lines and other facilities.

The Stockton and Darlington Company's financial difficulties were resolved in successive stages after 1825, initially on an *ad hoc* basis to sustain liquidity, and subsequently by departing from the declared aim of restricting the number of shares. In October 1825 Thomas Richardson's offer to 'guarantee the Bond of the Company to the extent of £10,000' was gratefully accepted by the management committee,[57] and in the following year Edward Pease 'laid the proprietors under new obligations by advancing the money to pay the wages of the workmen'.[58] He advanced £1,000 on 27 January 1826 and a further £895 on 18 March.[59] Quaker largesse was also reflected in the agreement of the Gurney banking partnership to the further postponement of their loan repayment. According to an agreement negotiated in January 1827 the outstanding sum of £40,000 was to be paid off in four equal instalments in the period July 1827 to January 1829. It was also agreed that a further £20,000 borrowed from Overend, Gurney and Co. should be repaid in two instalments of £10,000 in January and July 1828.[60] By these means the company's immediate financial requirements were eased. As for capital needs, these were substantially met by the decision taken in January 1827 to issue 325 new shares, the original total of 675 being judged 'inadequate to the purposes contemplated by the proprietors'.[61] By 27 March 1827 the whole of the share issue had been taken up within the existing proprietorship,[62] thus perpetuating that 'concord of the company' which had been lauded by Jonathan Backhouse in 1826 (see above, p. 56).

With new funds at its disposal the company was able to resume the construction of branch lines. The first to be completed was the Coundon branch serving the Black Boy, Coundon, Eldon, Adelaide, and Deanery Collieries. It was opened on 10 July 1827, from which time the compensatory payments to aggrieved colliery proprietors were terminated. In the following month work began on the Croft branch and after its opening on 27 October 1829 'large quantities of goods and minerals' began to be delivered into the North Riding of Yorkshire.[63] In July 1828 work recommenced on the Hagger Leases branch and when it was completed in November 1830, collieries at Butterknowle, Copley Bent, Norwood and Cockfield gained access to the Stockton and Darlington network. All of these projects had been sanctioned by the company's parliamentary Acts before 1825 and with their completion the Stockton and Darlington Company could look forward to increased traffic and revenues. There was, however, a further project for extending the network which began to be considered by the management committee early in 1826 with a view to improving the company's financial position. Reference was made at the end of the previous chapter to the interest shown by Thomas Richardson and Jonathan Backhouse prior to the opening of the line in the possibility of a coastal trade in coal from the River Tees in competition with the Tyne and Wear (see above, p. 50). The direct result of their collaboration was the formation of the Tees Coal Company in association with Thomas Harris and Joseph Taylor.[64] After an uncertain beginning, with the company sustaining losses of £2,000 in the financial year 1825–6, it soon became clear that a substantial coastal market for Tees coal awaited exploitation, despite the statutory burden of a significant differential in the rate of carriage for land-sale and sea-sale coal imposed by the Stockton and Darlington Company's original Act of Incorporation in 1821 (see above, pp. 38–9). In 1825–6 the railway carried 7,296 tons for shipment from Stockton, in 1826–7, 18,589 tons, with a surge forward to 54,290 tons in 1827–8. Even a severe diminution in this rate of expansion would lead to port congestion if Stockton remained the sole shipping point. As early as February 1826 the Stockton and Darlington Company's resident engineer, Thomas Storey, wrote to Edward Pease bemoaning the lack of suitable coal staithes at Stockton. Lack of investment in dockside facilities was holding up traffic so that the company was 'like a ship without sails'.[65] But Storey was concerned to emphasise a further constraint on the development of a coastal trade. Even if the company were to invest in Stockton as a coal shipping port the trade would fail to reach its full potential as a result of shoal water in the lower reaches of the river at Jenny Mill's Island. Grounding was a common occurrence, whilst ships of more than 100 tons burden were obliged to depart from Stockton staithes with limited cargoes. Full loading was only possible after replenishment by keels involving much cost and inconvenience.[66] There was a clear argument, therefore, for a new deep-water port further down the river estuary. In this context Storey drew attention to Haverton Hill on the north bank of the Tees as a possible site for enlarged coal shipments.[67]

The issue of port development was to prove highly contentious for the Stockton and Darlington Company since it was to provoke rivalries in the coal trade which the proprietors had long discounted following the demise of Christopher Tennant's project of 1819 and the parliamentary rejection in 1825 of the Tennant-inspired Tees and Weardale Railway scheme. One influential source of opposition to the Stockton and Darlington project prior to incorporation was the Misses Hale, joint lessees of the Coxhoe and Quarrington Collieries (see above, p. 36). With their mining interests well to the north of Darlington the Hale sisters' complaints that they would be unfairly disadvantaged were only propitiated by the Stockton and Darlington Company's offer to purchase their lease at a fair valuation. Arbitrators were appointed but no agreement was forthcoming. It was this circumstance which provided the rationale for the Tees and Weardale project. Launched in 1823, the scheme envisaged the construction of a line from the Tees to the

Hale sisters' colleries and extending from there into the Wear valley to the margin of extensive limestone deposits. In November 1825 it was rumoured that the Stockton and Darlington Company itself was considering an extension into Weardale.[68] All of these events served to keep alive the Stockton and Darlington Company's bête noire of 1819 – a direct 'northern' route from the Tees into the Auckland coalfield. That this was to come about can be ascribed to the management committee's refusal to cooperate with the Tees and Weardale interest in developing deep-water coaling facilities. In June 1826, Henry Blanshard, a Stockton and Darlington shareholder and close associate of Christopher Tennant, wrote to Thomas Richardson proposing collaboration in the projection of a northern line with a common port of shipment for both interests, possibly at Haverton Hill.[69] The initial response appeared favourable due to Jonathan Backhouse's public statement that the proposal was worthy of consideration. A file of letters in the Stockton and Darlington Company's records, addressed by Christopher Tennant to its secretary, Richard Otley, provides additional evidence of the northern party's desire for cooperation.[70] Within a few months of the Stockton and Darlington Railway opening Tennant had become a significant traffic sender on the company's network, requiring up to forty waggons a day to service his lime kilns at Thickley. The initial letters concern his requirements in this respect, whilst the later correspondence calls for 'a joint port of shipment at Haverton Hill'. As Tennant commented, 'a part of the annual increase of [coal] consumption in London of 150,000 tons would make the Darlington Railway flourish'. In other words, the continued buoyancy of the London market, combined with the competitive edge of rail-borne coal from the Tees, would ensure ample profits for both interests. Tennant even envisaged joint action to raise the necessary funding and also to secure the passage of legislation through Parliament, preferably when Charles Lambton, representing the hostile Tyne and Wear interests, 'was out of the Kingdom'.

The olive branch was thus well and truly extended but, according to Tennant, it was peremptorily rejected without hint of the grounds for opposition.[71] No records have come to light explaining the Stockton and Darlington Company's intransigence. Reasoned conjecture, however, would suggest the following scenario. Discounting personal prejudice against Tennant, the management committee could well have taken the view that as an existing enterprise there was no reason why the Stockton and Darlington Company should share any portion of the coastal trade in coal with another interest. Objective business strategy dictated that the company should retain exclusive access to localised monopoly profits for as long as possible, all the more so since its current financial position was uncertain, if not precarious. In any event, if a rival scheme was to be projected on the basis of adequate funding there was no guarantee that it would win acceptance in Parliament, and even if it did, the pre-existing monopoly supplier of rail facilities on Teesside would be in a position to give a good account of itself in any competitive struggle for traffic.

In October 1826 the Stockton and Darlington Company gave parliamentary notice of its intention to construct a branch line from the Stockton terminus to Haverton Hill. Within a month second thoughts had set in on account of the 'highly inexpedient parliamentary situation',[72] and it was not until January 1827 that surveys were authorised for a route survey pending agreement by the body of shareholders to the submission of a parliamentary bill in the session of 1828.[73] In the meantime, the following report setting out the case for a deep-water port was circulated to shareholders:

without additional facilities the export of coal can never become of that consequence or prove of that advantage to the Railway which otherwise might be reasonably anticipated. Your Committee is of the judgement that the quantity of coal exported from the Tees might be increased three or four fold on such terms as would materially increase your revenue, terms of which the coalmining and those interests in the shipment of coal would be glad to accept.[74]

As events were to prove this was a gross underestimate of the potential coal traffic to be shipped via the Tees.

When the shareholders met in July 1827 they had before them the above report and a further statement pointing out that 'with respect to the shipping trade the quantity of coals exported has surpassed your Committee's most sanguine expectations, having in the last three months alone considerably exceeded the total amount contemplated in the prospectuses which were issued at the commencement of the undertaking'.[75] They were also provided with the results of two surveys for a deep-water extension, the first connecting Stockton to Haverton Hill as originally envisaged, and the second leading to the small hamlet of Middlesbrough on the south bank of the river. The routes had been surveyed by Thomas Storey and Richard Otley, and it was their proposed extension to Middlesbrough which found favour in view of its shorter length and saving in construction costs amounting to £1,000.

The general body of shareholders ratified the Middlesbrough extension in October 1827 and a parliamentary bill was introduced early in 1828. It met little opposition in the House of Commons but was subject to opposition in the House of Lords as determined as that manifested in 1819 and 1821 against the Stockton and Darlington Company's own bills of incorporation. Once again the Tyne and Wear colliery interests were united in opposing a measure which it was claimed would endow south Durham coal with an unfair competitive advantage in the London market due to the absence of wayleave payments. But even the combined influence of such powerful coal magnates as Lord Londonderry and the Earl of Durham was insufficient to prevent the passage of the bill, and the Act for the Middlesbrough extension received the Royal Assent in May 1828. As Tomlinson pointed out, the bill's opponents were unable to dispute the fact that there was a rising demand for Tees coal on account of its price competitiveness and that this expanding trade, fully in accord with the public interest, was being hampered for lack of deep-water facilities.[76] It is also the case that as in 1819 and 1821 the Stockton and Darlington interests were able to call upon influential forces of their own, in particular Richard Hanbury Gurney of Norwich, 'who being well-known as a hunting man in Leicestershire and his own county, induced a considerable number of Norfolk noblemen and others to come down and support the railway'.[77] The Gurney's financial stake in the Stockton and Darlington Company was sufficient to guarantee their active cooperation, but so too were the kinship links which had played such a vital role in mobilising capital funding after 1818. These links had only recently been enhanced by the marriage in March 1826 of Edward Pease's second son Joseph, to Emma, the co-heiress of Joseph Gurney and younger sister of Jonathan Backhouse.[78]

After some delay, the product of disputed land prices with the agents of the Bishop of Durham, and lengthy negotiations with the Tees Navigation Company to determine the most appropriate means of bridging the Tees, the Middlesbrough extension was declared open for traffic in December 1830. The most notable features of the works were the suspension bridge designed and erected by Captain Samuel Brown RN at a cost of £2,300, and the steam-powered coal shipping staithes capable of loading six colliers at a time. The latter, designed by Timothy Hackworth, were an outstanding success whereas the bridge was a costly failure from the outset, being incapable of bearing the weight of fully loaded coal trains. In operation, batches of waggons had to traverse the bridge four at a time and nine yards apart. Predictably, as traffic grew, the bridge became a highly inconvenient bottleneck. It was replaced in 1844 by an iron girder bridge designed by Robert Stephenson.

The decision to create a deep-water coaling facility down stream from Stockton on the south bank of the Tees had momentous consequences for the Stockton and Darlington Company. In the first instance, by producing a division within the management committee it helped to consolidate the position of the Quaker-dominated Darlington interest, led by the Peases and Backhouses. Up until 1828 outward appearances suggested that the Quaker influence was counterbalanced in some measure by the presence of individual directors occupying influential positions who were sympathetic to the commercial needs of Stockton, either as residents of that town, or of Yarm. This certainly applied to Thomas Meynell, the chairman of the management committee and also to Leonard Raisbeck, the company's joint solicitor. In January 1928, when the proprietors were considering the draft bill for the Middlesbrough extension, they were informed by George Stephenson that in his opinion an extension of the railway was unnecessary in view of the Tees Navigation Company's intention to spend more than £20,000 on a new cut in the river at Newport. In consequence of this, some shareholders favoured postponement of the Middlesbrough extension in order to assess the traffic implications of improved navigation facilities. At a meeting to discuss the draft extension bill on 5 January 1828 a motion in favour of postponement was moved but defeated. It was followed by a successful resolution proposed by Edward Pease and seconded by Jonathan Backhouse, that the company should proceed with a railway extension whilst maintaining friendly relations with the Navigation Company. As chairman, Thomas Meynell signed the minutes of the meeting, but appended a dissenting note. This was soon followed by his resignation as chairman of the management committee which he justified in the following terms:

I dissent because, first, I consider the extension of the railway beyond Stockton to be a measure solely calculated to promote the export of coal, and beyond the limits of the original proposal on the faith of which the subscribers agreed to take their shares; secondly, that another project, calculated to facilitate the coal trade of the port of Stockton, being decided upon [the proposed Newport cut], if the sanction of Parliament can be obtained, I deem the investing of £35,000 to be a precipitate expenditure of the funds of the Railway Company.[79]

This gesture of opposition followed close on the resignation of Leonard Raisbeck, the most prominent resident of Stockton to have supported the Stockton and Darlington project since its inception. Raisbeck's view that the extension of the railway would 'materially prejudice the interests of the town of Stockton'[80] attracted a vituperative reply from Joseph Pease which referred to Raisbeck's 'violation of former engagements' and 'breach of gentlemanly conduct and professional etiquette'.[81] Such language was hardly calculated to mollify the feelings of the Yarm and Stockton interests. In this respect it is significant that Meynell's resignation led immediately to the departure of Benjamin Flounders of Yarm from the management committee. Like Raisbeck, Flounders was another long-standing supporter of the railway.

By the late 1820s Edward Pease's involvement in the day to day affairs of the Stockton and Darlington Company was far less prominent than in the constructional phase. Indeed, in 1827 he is reported to have terminated his active business career 'with a resolution never to enter a railway meeting again'.[82] Although he continued to attend management committee meetings intermittently to 1834, and adjudicated on breaches of discipline by locomo-

14   Benjamin Flounders of Yarm, a leading Quaker supporter of the Stockton and Darlington Railway in the 1820s. Flounders resigned from the company's management committee in 1828 in opposition to the Middlesbrough extension.

tive drivers and firemen, this period witnessed the emergence of a new generation of entrepreneurial Peases who were to exercise far more control over the company's affairs, not just in routine management, but also in strategic direction. Prominent among them was Joseph, Edward's second son, destined to become an elder and eventually a minister within the Society of Friends, and achieving a place in history as the country's first Quaker Member of Parliament sitting for the South Durham constituency in the reformed Parliament of 1832.[83]

Joseph Pease's first independent business adventure was as a colliery entrepreneur. From October to December 1827 he was engaged in leasing various coal properties in Co. Durham, mainly in the Auckland coal field at the St Helens and Adelaide Collieries. It is significant that these colliery interests were being acquired at the time when the Middlesbrough extension was under construction and, despite Joseph's wish to avoid 'sanguine expectations', it is clear that even before the project had received parliamentary approval he was anticipating a substantial expansion in the Tees-based coal shipping trade. His ambitions were confirmed in 1828 when he 'took [a] boat and entering the Tees Mouth sailed up to Middlesbrough to take a view of the proposed line of the contemplated extension of the Railway'. After viewing the farmhouse that constituted the core of the hamlet he recorded in his diary that he was 'much pleased with the place altogether' for 'Imagination here had ample scope in fancying a coming day when the bare fields ... will be covered with a busy multitude and numerous vessels crowding to these banks denote the busy seaport'. The vista of Middlesbrough from the river at that time was dominated by extensive salt flats, but Joseph waxed lyrical in his expectations. As his diary entry for the day concluded, 'Who that has considered the nature of British enterprise, commerce and industry will pretend to take his stand on this spot and pointing the fingers of scorn at these visions exclaim that it will never be? If such an one appears he and I are at issue'.[84] Joseph's intention, therefore, was to achieve far more than the construction of a railway extension terminating in coal staithes. It was to plan and build a new town – a model urban community free of squalor and disease, and with its prosperity underpinned by expanding shipments of coal. In the former he was to be disappointed. The original estate plan, with thoroughfares drawn up in a symmetrical grid-iron pattern, was already being eroded within twenty years of its conception due to the needs of industry and building speculation. Much of the housing, moreover, was of poor standard on account of its low elevation and consequent dampness.[85] An appropriate verdict on Middlesbrough's first half-century of urban and industrial development was provided by Joseph's own grandson, Alfred Edward, who commented of Middlesbrough's jubilee celebrations that 'my grandfather and his

15   Joseph Pease (1799–1872) as a young man in 1832. Pease succeeded
Jonathan Backhouse as treasurer to the Stockton and Darlington Railway
Company in 1833. Co-founder of the port of Middlesbrough, he dominated
the affairs of the company from the 1830s to the 1850s.

contemporaries managed to lay the foundations of a large hideous town, a den of misery, dirt and debauchery planted by the once green fields on the banks of the Tees'.[86] The obverse of this condemnation was that economically and commercially Middlesbrough, by the standards of the nineteenth century, was an outstanding success. Little did the young Joseph Pease realise that by the time of his death in 1872 Middlesbrough would be a booming industrial town with extensive metallurgical industries and a thriving shipping trade based not upon coal but upon the export of iron manufactures.

At first sight it might be thought that the Stockton and Darlington Company itself would be directly involved in the financing and development of Middlesbrough's urban facilities. This was not, however, the case. The purchase of the necessary land was undertaken by a small group of Quaker bankers and financiers from London and Norwich – Thomas Richardson, Joseph Gurney, Henry Birkbeck, Simon Martin and Francis Gibson. In several accounts of the development of Middlesbrough Joseph Pease is commonly identified as the principal founder of the town,[87] but whilst he too is named as one of the original 'Middlesbrough Owners', his contribution of £7,000 to the purchase price of £35,000 for the 520 acre estate was loaned by his father-in-law, Joseph Gurney, at an interest rate of 4 per cent. In retrospect, the lack of formal involvement on the part of the railway company is understandable. Extra capital borrowing was unacceptable in the light of the existing debt structure and further share issues were to be reserved for the construction of a network of branch lines. The Middlesbrough extension itself was a case in point, as was the Hagger Leases branch stretching for 4¾ miles from St Helens Auckland further into the coalfield. Indeed, the Act for the Middlesbrough extension compelled the Stockton and Darlington Company to complete the latter, a concession granted to the Reverend William Luke Prattman who had threatened opposition to the company's eastwards extension on account of the continued isolation of his Butterknowle and Copley Bent collieries from a rail terminus.

The purchase of the Middlesbrough Estate provides further striking evidence of the strength of Quaker financial networks. The existence of such a personalised capital market certainly lends support to the notion that as businessmen Quakers were unusually advantaged. In other words, the critical contribution of Quakerism to economic and industrial development is to be found in its distinctive institutional aspects rather than in its religious precepts. It is also important to note that from its inception in the late 1660s the London Yearly Meeting of the Society of Friends sent out advices periodically to local meetings containing guidance on the conduct of daily life, including business pursuits. The *Rules of Discipline and Advice*, published in 1834, contained eleven pages of guidance on business conduct, hardly surprising in view of the fact that bankruptcy provided *prima facie* grounds for disownment. Further research in this area is necessary to test the proposition that the overrepresentation of Quakers among the ranks of successful businessmen in the early phases of British industrialisation was the product of effective financial networks and close internal surveillance of business conduct rather than any inherent entrepreneurial qualities arising from a particular religious ethic.[88]

There is one respect, however, in which religious factors probably did have a positive role to play in motivating Quaker business conduct. Capital was forthcoming from London and Norwich to Teesside precisely because Quaker lenders and investors had the necessary confidence in the Backhouses and Peases, this in turn being derived from the allegiance of these family groupings to the Quaker code of conduct as set forth in the Yearly Meeting advices. It is reasonable to presume that the Gurneys, for example, had little independent means of evaluating the commercial prospects of the Stockton and Darlington Railway, still less Middlesbrough's potential for port development. But they did know that their northern 'cousins' were devout members of the Society of Friends, with unimpeachable records of honesty and scrupulosity in business dealings. Edward Pease himself was well known as a deeply conservative evangelical Quaker observing a personal lifestyle in conformity with eighteenth-century advices and worrying incessantly about the corrupting influence of great riches.[89] Moreover, it is salutary to remember that the principal reason for Jonathan Backhouse's formal resignation as treasurer to the Stockton and Darlington Company in 1833 was his wish to embark upon full-time ministry for the Society of Friends.[90] Backhouse's replacement by Joseph Pease served as final and decisive confirmation of Quaker ascendancy in the affairs of the company. Not that Joseph was especially concerned to perpetuate his father's austere lifestyle. He may have attained the position of recorded minister in the Society of Friends but, as his political ambitions revealed, he was a 'wordly' Quaker. His diaries are replete with scriptural injunctions, but they convey no impression of the anguish which characterised his father's reaction to the acummulation of wealth. Thus, in contrast to Edward Pease, Joseph was guilt free. Why should it have been otherwise at a time when the Yearly Meeting was coming to be dominated by men of business and commercial standing? Indeed, the time was not far off when mainstream Quakerism would sanction and encourage the pursuit of wealth.[91] Joseph's quoted remarks on the birth of Middlesbrough reveal him in his true colours – 'a man of business, consciously in the vanguard of human progress, the prophet of a new and enlightened civilisation, urban and capitalist, which would challenge the economic and political supremacy of land-owning Toryism'.[92]

If open acknowledgement of the Quaker ascendancy was one result of the decision to extend the railway to Middlesbrough, a second and equally important consequence was the revival in fortunes of the 'northern' railway party. His proposed scheme of collaboration rejected by the Stockton and Darlington Company (see above, p. 72), Christopher Tennant seized the opportunity opened up by the availability of Haverton Hill as a port of shipment to project a line from the north bank of the Tees, via Coxhoe to the edge of the Auckland coalfield at Simpasture. That the resulting Clarence Railway would be a potentially powerful competitor to the Stockton and Darlington Company was neatly understated by Tennant's own calculations of comparative distances:

Distance from Simpasture, near School Aycliffe to Stockton by the Stockton and Darlington Railway	17½ miles
Distance from Simpasture by the Clarence Railway (Being a saving of 6 miles, or rather more than one-third of the distance)	11½ miles
Distance from Simpasture to Middlesbrough, the place of shipment of the Stockton and Darlington Railway Company	21½ miles
Distance from Simpasture to Haverton Hill, the place of shipment of the Clarence Railway Company (Being a saving of 7½ miles, upwards of one-third of the distance).[93]	14 miles

There could be no doubting the attractions of the Clarence scheme, especially since the Stockton and Darlington Company's own traffic development pointed to a rising market for coal shipments from the Tees. In view of the directness of the route from Haverton Hill to the coalfield there appeared to be every prospect that the Clarence Railway would fulfil Tennant's long-standing ambition to become a major force in the coal shipping trade. It was a considerable coup when he received the support of Henry Blanshard. As noted already, Blanshard was shareholder in the Stockton and Darlington Company itself, and as a prosperous London merchant he was able to play a vital role in mobilising the necessary financial support to facilitate the issue of a parliamentary bill of incorporation for the Clarence Railway in 1828.[94]

As the parliamentary deliberations on the Stockton and Darlington Company's Middlesbrough extension had revealed, the advocates of a Tees-based coal shipping trade could still count on the determined opposition of the Tyne and Wear exporters. The projectors of the Clarence Railway were confronted by the same hostile forces. Their task, however, was to be doubly difficult due to the emergence of an unholy alliance between the Stockton and Darlington Company and the Marquis of Londonderry. The former, determined to protect its local monopoly profits, opposed the Clarence projectors in both Houses of Parliament. The management

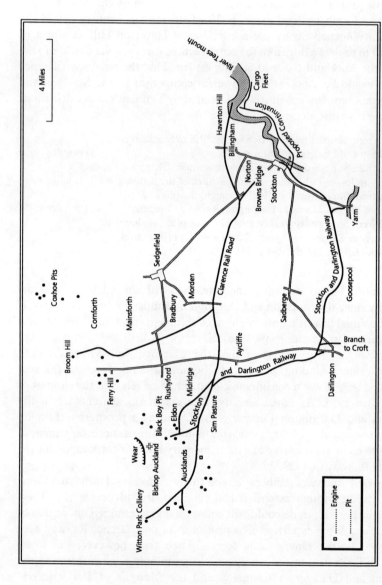

4 Map of the Stockton and Darlington and Clarence Railways published by Christopher Tennant in January 1828.

Table 5. *Comparison of toll charges on the Clarence and Stockton and Darlington Railways, 1829*

	Clarence Railway	Stockton and Darlington Railway	
	Main line toll per ton per mile	Main line toll per ton per mile	Middlesbrough branch toll per ton per mile
Coal, culm, coke, cinders for exportation	¾d	½d	1½d
Coal, culm, coke, cinders for home consumption	1½d	4d	4d
Lime	¾d	4d	4d
Manure, road metal	½d	4d	2d
Stone, marl, sand, clay, lead, bar-iron, timber, deals, and staves and all other goods	½d	4d	4d
Wares and merchandise	3d	6d	4d

Source: Clarence Railway Company, *Act of Incorporation*, 1829.

committee alloted the sum of £1,705 10s – 'equivalent to a dividend of 1¾ per cent of their share capital of £100,000'[95] – to a fighting fund to defend its interests. The results of the expenditure, as reported to the body of share-holders in 1829, were 'the removal of many objectionable clauses' in the parliamentary legislation with 'others ... so modified and amended as to remove the apprehensions of your Committee, and to induce them to believe that many years will probably elapse ere it will become needful (if ever) to refer to anything connected with that extraordinary scheme'.[96]

Lord Londonderry was by this time a veteran opponent of any project calculated to increase coal shipments from the Tees. By the late 1820s, however, his vested interest had been enhanced greatly by the decision to develop a new port at Seaham Harbour for the shipment of coal from his own collieries. The House of Lords was thus obliged to listen to a further appeal to self-interest, buttressed by claims that the Clarence works would never be completed for lack of funds and that the scheme, as presented, would be 'a nuisance and inconvenience to the landowners', leaving in its wake 'heaps and mounds of rubbish'.[97] The Marquis was no more success-ful on this than on any other occasion, and the Clarence Railway Bill received its final reading on 1 June 1829. Under the Act of Incorporation the company was empowered to raise the sum of £100,000 in shares and the unusually large sum of £160,000 by borrowing on bonds or by mortgage to facilitate the construction of a network of branch lines penetrating as far north as the City of Durham and north-west to Byers Green.

16   Christopher Tennant, the leading projector of the ill-fated Clarence
Railway.

Table 6. *Colliers cleared from the Tees, 1826–32*

Year	Number of Vessels
1826	97
1827	280
1828	530
1829	450
1830	1,026
1831	1,665
1832	2,415

Source: PRO RAIL 667/1858, Stockton and Darlington Railway accountant's records.

The Stockton and Darlington Company's traffic monopoly on Teesside was thus breached. As table 5 reveals, the Clarence Company enjoyed the competitive advantage conferred by the direct northern route, but this was offset to some extent by a higher statutory toll payable on coal for export. It also undercut its rival in all other charges, although this was of no great advantage in view of the line's primary purpose as a route for coal shipments. There can be no doubting the jubilation in Stockton at the coming to fruition of the scheme for a northern route, or that it represented a personal triumph for the indefatigable Christopher Tennant. There was, however, a serious and potentially crippling weakness in the Clarence project. It is true that the new railway would receive coals from collieries in the area of Coxhoe and to the north-west, but its rationale in financial terms was dependent on its ability to encroach upon the Stockton and Darlington Company's Auckland traffic. But the Clarence project in its final form did not provide the company with independent access to the Auckland coalfield. That was to be via running powers on the Stockton and Darlington line from the Simpasture terminus. In a very real sense, therefore Tennant's ambitions rested on the goodwill of the Stockton and Darlington Company. Yet there was nothing which had occurred in either the distant or more recent past to suggest that this would be forthcoming.

The first coals for export on the Clarence Railway reached Stockton in October 1833, Haverton Hill in January 1834 and the final terminus at Port Clarence, with its newly constructed coal staithes, towards the end of the year. In the meantime, the Stockton and Darlington Company continued to enjoy the fruits of its traffic monopoly. As appendix 1 reveals, coal was from the outset of operations the overwhelmingly preponderant form of traffic. Compared to the rate of expansion of landsales, the growth of coal exports was dramatic. In the period from 1826 to 1833 shipments faltered in only one year, 1828–9, reflecting a short period of free competition – the so-called

Table 7. *Collieries served by the Stockton and Darlington Railway, 1826–7 and 1834 (owners/lessees indicated where known)*

Collieries served 1826–7	Collieries served 1834
Old Etherley (William Stobart and R. W. Pierse)	Old Etherley
New Etherley (Dixon and Co.)	New Etherley
Eldon (Burton and Co.)	Eldon
Coundon (John Manners)	Coundon
Black Boy (Jonathan Backhouse and Joshua Ianson)	Black Boy
Witton Park (William Chaytor)	Witton Park
	Butterknowle (Rev. William L. Prattman)
	Cockfield (Jonathan Backhouse)
	Norwood
	St Helens (Joseph Pease)
	Shildon
	Shildon Lodge
	Deanery
	Adelaide (Joseph Pease)

Sources: PRO RAIL 667/4, Stockton and Darlington Railway management committee minutes; ibid. 667/1458, Stockton and Darlington Railway accountant's records.

'fighting trade' – in the coastal trade, pending the renegotiation of the Tyne and Wear Vend. In the following twelve-month period the upward growth of traffic was resumed to the extent that exports began to exceed landsales by a considerable margin. From 1831–2 the growth in coal exports was carried forward by Middlesbrough following the completion of the railway extension and shipping staithes. Thereafter, exports from Stockton stagnated and ultimately began to decline in the 1840s. Further indications of the growth of coal traffic were the rise in the number of colliers cleared from the Tees and collieries served by the railway (see tables 6 and 7). In the former case there was a twenty-five fold increase between 1826 and 1832. The number of collieries using the railway's facilities more than doubled between 1826 and 1834. This was the result of two critical factors, first the completion of the network of branch lines within the Auckland coalfield and secondly the fact that the innovation of the railway effectively lowered the cost of entry for new firms into the colliery business. The end product of these developments was to endow the Auckland collieries with a competitive edge in the coastal trade to the detriment of the Tyne and Wear exporting interests. The breakdown of the Vend in 1829 was precipitated by overselling by collieries in the ownership of the Earl of Durham, but it was also a reflection of the onset of a new phase of instability within the cartel which

Table 8. *Share prices of the Stockton and Darlington Railway Company, 1823–32*

Date	£	Date	£
11 Dec. 1823	80	12 Nov. 1828	170
24 Jan. 1824	90	27 Apr. 1830	177 10s
1 Jan. 1824	100	7 Apr. 1831	210
17 May 1824	112	18 Oct. 1831	250
12 Aug. 1824	115	25 Jan. 1832	275
30 Oct. 1824	121	19 Apr. 1832	298
23 Jan. 1826	150	10 July 1832	315
12 June 1828	160	9 Jan. 1832	310
16 June 1828	165	23 Nov. 1832	200

Source: PRO RAIL 667/264/1, Stockton and Darlington Railway financial statistics.

would lead to its demise after 1840. Significantly, of the twenty-one new colliery winnings in the north-east of England in the period 1829–36, ten had their main export outlet via the Tees.[98] A further explanation for burgeoning coal exports was the miners' strike in the Tyne and Wear collieries in 1831. According to Francis Mewburn the crippling effect on production 'had the effect of advancing the Tees coal full 20 years in London and the outports'.[99] Indeed, with only a single line of railway the Stockton and Darlington Company was hard pressed to meet the demand for export coal.

The Stockton and Darlington Company's traffic revenues increased fourfold between 1826–7 and 1832–3, from £14,455 in the former accounting period (July–June), to £57,819 in the latter. Inevitably, buoyant traffic and revenues – far in excess of any predictions made before the opening of the railway – were reflected in share prices and dividends. From a low of £80 in 1823, the peak value of each £100 share was reached in July 1832 at £315 (see table 8). There was a substantial fall before the end of the year, but the value had climbed back to £280 by February 1834. The dividend record was also satisfactory (see table 9). From 1831 the shareholders began to receive dividends in excess of Edward Pease's minimum requirement of 1818 (see above, p. 32). Throughout this period the whole of the dividend due to shareholders was paid over. For the Pease family the 1831 dividend of 6 per cent produced the results indicated in table 10. In January 1832 Edward Pease's shares were valued at £33,825, rising to a peak of £38,755 in July of that year. This was the reward for his tireless efforts as railway promotor, projector, and manager. In the following year he finally retired from the active affairs of the company. From then until his death at the age of ninety-one in 1858 he was to see his fortunes ebb and flow at the dictates of

Table 9. *Dividend record of the Stockton and Darlington Railway Company, 1826–33*

Year	Dividend (%)
1826	2½
1827	5
1828	5
1829	5
1830	5
1831	6
1832	8
1833	8

Source: PRO RAIL 667/158, Stockton and Darlington Railway: reports of management committee to shareholders.

Table 10. *Dividends ordered to be paid to the Pease Family, 1 January 1832*

	No. of shares	Amount of ordinary shares (£)	Dividend of 6% (£)
Edward	123	12,300	738
John	6	600	36
Joseph Jr	26	2,600	156
Edward Jr	7	700	42
Henry	5	500	30
Rachael	10	1,000	60
Elizabeth	15	1,500	90
Thomas B.	2	200	12
John and another	10	1,000	60

Source: PRO RAIL 667/1329, Stockton and Darlington Railway Company's accountant's records.

commercial conditions. His greatest anxieties, however, were to be caused by the speculative activities of his sons, Joseph in particular. For Edward Pease, the strategic task had been simple enough – to construct a landsale mineral railway – in effect an extended coal waggonway, albeit with steam haulage. Joseph, however, was obliged to confront the onset of railway and port competition, the effects of severe commercial depression, and the need to sustain the prosperity not only of the Stockton and Darlington Company, but also its growing number of traffic senders. As subsequent chapters will reveal, competitive and commercial pressures were at times intense, and the personal strain on management committee members in general and Joseph Pease in particular, considerable.

Table 11. *Stockton and Darlington Railway coach traffic, November 1832*

Proprietors	Travelling between	Length of stage (miles)	Journeys per week	Passengers per week	Average no. of passengers per journey
Messrs Pickersgill	Darlington and Stockton	12	12	126	10½
Messrs Scott and Co.	Darlington and Stockton	12	12	124	10½
Messrs Ludless and Buckton	Darlington and Stockton	12	12	218	18
Messrs Adamson	Darlington and Shildon	8	12	24	6
Messrs Wastell	Darlington, Yarm, and Stockton	Darlington and Yarm	2	42	21
		Darlington and Stockton	2	42	21
Messrs Harris	Stockton and Middlesbrough	3¼	36	324	9

Source: PRO RAIL 667/3, Stockton and Darlington management committee minutes, 2 November 1832.

RAPID, SAFE, AND CHEAP TRAVELLING
By the Elegant NEW RAILWAY COACH,

THE UNION,

Which will COMMENCE RUNNING *on the* STOCKTON *and* DARLINGTON RAILWAY, *on* MONDAY
the 16*th day of October*, 1826,
And will call at Yarm, and pass within a mile of Middleton Spa, on its way from Stockton to Darlington, and *vice versa.*
FARES.   Inside 1½d.—Outside, 1d. per Mile.   Parcels in proportion.
No gratuities expected by the Guard or Coachman.
N.B. The Proprietors will not be accountable for any Parcel of more than £5. value, unless entered and paid for accordingly.
The UNION will run from the Black Lion Hotel and New Inn, Stockton, to the New Inn, Yarm, and to the Black Swan
Inn, near the Croft Branch, Darlington; at each of which Inns passengers and parcels are booked, and the times of starting may
be ascertained, as also at the Union Inn, Yarm, and Talbot Inn, Darlington.
On the 19th and 20th of October, the Fair Days at Yarm, the Union will leave Darlington at six in the morning for Yarm,
and will leave Yarm for Darlington again at six in the evening; in the intermediate time, each day, it will ply constantly between Stockton and Yarm, leaving each place every half hour.

(From the *Durham County Advertiser*, 14th October, 1826.)

17   The horse-drawn 'Union' coach which ran on the Stockton and
Darlington Railway after October 1826.

The year 1833 marks the end of the first operational phase of the Stockton
and Darlington Railway. At the time of the opening in 1825 the working of
the line bore striking resemblance to established canal practice insofar as it
practically allowed public rights of way. Thus, colliery owners were permitted, on payment of a toll, to lead their own coals, a practice which was soon
extended to the carriers of general merchandise. To contemporary eyes, the
most overt example of the company's commitment to canal procedures was
its policy on passenger traffic. The company's second parliamentary Act
provided for the conveyance of passengers by 'coaches and other carriages'
with locomotive haulage as an option. As Tomlinson observed, the proprietors 'were no doubt looking a long way ahead, for, at that time, there was
little prospect of revenue from this branch of traffic, when one coach
running between Stockton and Darlington three times a week afforded
facilities, more than ample, for communication between the two towns'.[100]
For a few months after the official opening the company operated its own
passenger coach, but during the course of 1826 the practice was adopted of
renting out coaches to private contractors and even permitting them to use
their own vehicles. By the beginning of 1827 up to seven horse-drawn

coaches were operating between Stockton and Darlington. Taking the accounting year July 1826 – June 1827 their cumulative mileage was in excess of 45,000 with more than 30,000 passengers conveyed. Table 11, taken from the management committee report of November 1832, provides details of the 'coach traffic'. By the standards of the Liverpool and Manchester Railway, let alone the later trunk line companies, the numbers are miniscule. Revenues, moreover, were extremely modest, rising to £576 in 1827–8, a figure which was not exceeded again until 1832–3.[101] Yet in 1833 the management committee decided to buy out the coach proprietors and terminate all horse leading preparatory to operating a scheduled locomotive passenger service under the auspices of the company. There were two principal reasons for this action. In the first instance it was a further instalment in the company's attempts to resolve mounting operational difficulties. As indicated already, in order to work the traffic on a single line of track the management committee had devised a complicated order of precedence. Locomotives enjoyed the first right of way, horse-drawn waggons the second, and coach traffic the third. In principle, loaded waggons enjoyed preference over empty vehicles. Inevitably, such rules were made to be broken, and in the years after 1826 the management committee delegated to Edward Pease responsibility for adjudicating on a multitude of disciplinary offences.[102] Courtesy and consideration were at a premium among the horse drivers – the operating conditions ensured that, all the more so given the difficulties in reversing unwieldy waggons into the passing loops. Disputed rights of way involving frayed tempers, verbal abuse and fist fights were frequent, causing Timothy Hackworth to exclaim to the management committee, 'Gentlemen, I only wish you to know that it would make you cry to see how they knock each other's brains out!'[103] One obvious way of alleviating the problem was to double the line. This had been envisaged as long ago as 1819, but a prophetic warning that a single line would cause 'vexation, confusion and inconvenience' had been discounted on the grounds of cost.[104] In 1831 Hackworth revived the issue in circumstances that ensured a positive reaction from the management committee: operational difficulties were one consideration, but so too was the continuing expansion of traffic following the opening of the Middlesbrough extension. Thus, in 1831–2 a second line of track was laid down from Brusselton to Stockton and this was complemented by the installation of a new and more powerful high-pressure steam engine to work the Brusselton inclined plane.[105] The effect of this was to facilitate the flow of traffic, but in such a way as to underline the absurdity of continuing to combine horse haulage with locomotive operations. Tomlinson, utilising a contemporary source, provides an illuminating description of the operation of the line in the early 1830s:

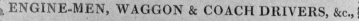

CAUTIONS

TO

ENGINE-MEN, WAGGON & COACH DRIVERS, &c.,

ON THE

Stockton and Darlington Railway.

I. THE STOCKTON & DARLINGTON RAILWAY COMPANY, direct that all Engine-Men, Waggon and Coach-Drivers, employed on the Railway, go at a moderate speed down the Runs.

II. That in crossing all Turnpike and other Roads, the speed of Locomotive Engines, Waggons, and other Carriages, to be very slow, especially when any Coaches, Carts, or other Carriages are seen travelling on such Roads, and on coming near the same, the Engine-Men are directed to ring their Bells.

III. The Coaches hereafter named, cross the Railway near Darlington daily. Engine-Men and Drivers are directed to keep a good look out for the same, and in all cases not to cross Turnpike or other Roads, whilst any Coaches are near the Crossings on the said Roads.—

The MAIL Coach going North, crosses the Railway near the Merchandize Warehouses, at Darlington, about half-past 11 o'Clock, every Night.

The MAIL Coach going South, and the COURIER and WELLINGTON Coaches cross the Railway, about half-past 1 o'Clock every Morning.

In the course of every Forenoon, there are Three or Four daily Coaches cross the Railway, going South, and about the same number every Afternoon, going North, from Darlington.

IV. Engine-Men to avoid, as much as possible, letting off Steam near public Roads, and should any Horse or Horses take fright at the Engine or Waggons when passing, immediate assistance to be rendered by the Engine-Men and their assistants.

V. All Engine-Men, Coach and Waggon Drivers, to carry good and sufficient Lights, affixed in conspicuous parts of their Train, in conformity with the Company's Bye-Laws.

VI. Engine-Men and Waggon-Drivers not to allow Persons to ride on the Engines or Waggons, as directed by the Company's Bye-Laws.

Signed, By Order,

RICHARD OTLEY.

Railway Office Darlington, Nov. 7, 1831.

Coates & Farmer, Printers, Darlington.

18   Notice of traffic regulations of the Stockton and Darlington Railway Company, 1831.

STOCKTON & DARLINGTON RAILWAY COACHES.

The SUMMER ARRANGEMENTS will cease on the 30th Instant, and the Trains run the same as last season until further notice: viz.—

Winter Arrangements, commencing October 1st, 1840.

ST. HELEN'S AUCKLAND TO DARLINGTON.

First Trip	-	at half-past Eight o'Clock.
Second Trip	-	at One "
Third Trip	-	at Five "

DARLINGTON TO ST. HELEN'S AUCKLAND.

First Trip	-	at half-past Eight o'Clock.
Second Trip	-	at One "
Third Trip	-	at Five "

DARLINGTON TO STOCKTON.

Merchandize Train	-	at half-past Six o'Clock.
First Class Train	-	at half-past Nine "
Merchandize Train	-	at Eleven "
First Class Train	-	at Two "
Merchandize Train	-	at Four "
First Class Train	-	at Six "

STOCKTON TO DARLINGTON.

First Class Train	-	at 10 min. bef. Eight o'Clock.
Merchandize Train	at 10 min. bef. Nine "
First Class Train	-	at 20 min. past Twelve "
Merchandize Train	at 20 min. past Two "
First Class Train	-	at 20 min. past Four "
Merchandize Train	at 20 min. past Six "

STOCKTON TO MIDDLESBRO'.

First	Trip	-	at Eight o'Clock.
Second	do	-	at Nine "
*Third	do	-	at Ten "
Fourth	do	-	at Eleven "
Fifth	do	-	at half-past Twelve "
Sixth	do	-	at half-past One "
*Seventh	do	-	at half-past Two "
Eighth	do	-	at half-past Three "
Ninth	do	-	at half-past Four "
Tenth	do	-	at half-past Five "
*Eleventh	do	-	at a quarter bef. Seven "

MIDDLESBRO' TO STOCKTON

*First	Trip	-	at half-past Seven o'Clock.
Second	do	-	at half-past Eight "
Third	do	-	at half-past Nine "
Fourth	do	-	at half-past Ten "
*Fifth	do	-	at Twelve "
Sixth	do	-	at One "
Seventh	do	-	at Two "
Eighth	do	-	at Three "
*Ninth	do	-	at Four "
Tenth	do	-	at Five "
Eleventh	do	-	at Six "

* Are in connexion with the first class Trains to and from Darlington.

Tickets must be taken at least Five Minutes before the Trains start.

NO SMOKING ALLOWED IN ANY OF THE COMPANY'S COACHES.

MARKET COACHES.

A Coach and Cattle Carriage will leave St. Helen's Auckland, on Mondays, at half-past Six o'Clock; and Shildon, at Seven in the Morning.

HORSES, CATTLE, AND CARRIAGES, CAREFULLY CONVEYED BETWEEN STOCKTON AND DARLINGTON, BY THE MERCHANDIZE TRAINS:

Horse, 2s.—Gig, 2s. or Horse and Gig, 3s.—Four-wheeled Carriage, 5s., or with Two Horses, 8s.—Horned Cattle, 1s. 6d. each.—Sheep, 4d. each, or 5s. per Score.—Dogs, 1s. each:

If by the FIRST-CLASS Train; Horse 3s.—Gig, 3s.—Horse and Gig, 4s.—Four-wheeled Carriage, 5s., or with Two Horses, 9s.

Railway Office. Darlington, September 25th, 1840.

COATES AND FARMER, PRINTERS, HIGH ROW, DARLINGTON.

19   Passenger timetable for the Stockton and Darlington Railway, 1840.

Two of the [horse leaders] who left Shildon on the 1st March 1832, drunk, after driving recklessly along for some miles and committing several breaches of the bye-laws, met the *William IV* engine ascending the line. They refused to go into the siding and not only laid a rail and chair before the engine with the object of throwing it off the line, but got onto the footplate and collared the enginemen. Several others on the 23rd April 1832 made the *Rocket* engine follow them from Redhall to Darlington, a distance of over two miles, before they would allow the engine to pass. The horse-leaders were constantly leaving the switches wrong, travelling by night without lights, driving furiously across the roads and lanes (which were unprotected by gates at this time), going down the *runs* at headlong speed, numerous horses being killed and lamed and locomotive engines damaged by the breaches of the bye-laws. Not infrequently they left their horses and waggons standing on the line for a considerable time ... while they were drinking in a public house adjoining the line. On one of these occasions, the *Globe* engine ran into the waggons which were standing without a light at Aycliffe Lane; ... Two of the leaders on the 30th June 1832 stood their horses and waggons at the top of Darlington Run and went into the lane to fight.[106]

By 1832 horse haulage could no longer be justified on the company's main line. By that time the company possessed nineteen locomotives, twelve of them having been constructed in the period 1831–2. Hackworth's engineering ability was beyond dispute and he could be relied upon to maintain an effective engine fleet. He had even designed a locomotive specifically for passenger traffic as early as 1830. The resulting *Globe*, constructed by Robert Stephenson and Co., is reported to have attained speeds of up to 50 mph when circumstances permitted. The final decision to terminate horse haulage on the main line was taken in August 1833. The relevant minutes of the management committee suggest that the precipitating factor was the discovery of 'fraudulent behaviour' on the part of some of the haulage contractors, in particular the underrecording of journeys in order to evade toll charges.[107] In October the leading coach operators were bought out by the company for the sum of £316 17s 8d,[108] and thereafter the adoption of steam haulage proceeded apace. The leading of coal waggons by horses had been eliminated by the end of the year and arrangements were well in hand for steam-hauled passenger and goods services between Shildon and Middlesbrough. The transition was finally accomplished in April 1834 with the inauguration of a passenger and goods service on the Middlesbrough extension.[109] By that date the main line services of the Stockton and Darlington Railway approximated to the operational standards current on the Liverpool and Manchester Railway, the latter company having opted for complete mechanical traction under its own auspices from the commencement of operations in 1830. Beyond the main line, horse-drawn services continued in operation and a limited number of private contractors were permitted to run coaches on specific days. The last horses on the network were removed from the Hagger Leases branch in September 1856.[110]

The abandonment of the 'public way' concept was the direct consequence of operational and traffic considerations and it marked the end of an innovative phase in the Stockton and Darlington Company's development. In other important respects, however, the managerial structure of the company continued to reflect its pioneering origins. The elimination of a majority of the private haulage contractors may have provided a sharper edge to the boundaries of the firm, but elsewhere in the company's operations the business of subcontracting remained entrenched. The following chapter, therefore, will examine the continuing rationale of subcontracting, as well as the company's competitive strategy and commercial performance until the onset of commercial crisis in the later 1840s.

5   Growth and competition, 1834–1847

In the history of British economic development the decades of the 1830s and 1840s, punctuated by the great speculative manias of 1839–40 and 1845–7, marked the full flowering of what Sir John Clapham termed 'The Early Railway Age'.[1] If the Stockton and Darlington Railway had been the curtain raiser to the new era, the first decisive act was performed by the Liverpool and Manchester Company whose line opened for business in 1830.[2] With all the advantages of hindsight the portent of this event, following close on the Rainhill Locomotive Trials of 1829, should have been clear to all but the most obscurantist observer. Completely reliant on steam locomotive power under the control of a board of directors the new undertaking provided a far more convincing demonstration of the economic and commercial potential of railways than the Stockton and Darlington Company. For one thing, it linked two large metropolitan centres, and although the promoters had focused their initial attention on the transport requirements of the Lancashire cotton trade, the railway began to draw up to one half of its revenue from passenger traffic from the outset of operations. The Stockton and Darlington Company may have provided a theatre of practical railway operations in the later 1820s, but because of its overwhelming concentration on the bulk shipment of heavy minerals at low speeds it failed to alert railway promoters and investors to the wider possibilities of the new transport medium. It was in the wake of the Liverpool and Manchester Railway, therefore, that the 1830s witnessed the promotion and construction of the first trunk lines for the conveyance of passengers and merchandise, linking London with Birmingham, Southampton and Bristol. The process continued apace into the following decade. Already, by 1844, 104 railway companies operating 2,000 miles of track were in existence and by that time it was possible to travel by railway from Birmingham to Exeter, from London to Dover and Brighton, and from Crewe to Manchester, Birkenhead and Fleetwood. North of the border, the cities of Edinburgh and Glasgow had both been linked to Greenock and Ayr by 1842, and in Wales the Taff Vale Railway connected Merthyr Tydfil and Cardiff. Although these early lines were 'a veritable house-that-Jack-built', they were to provide the sinews of a nationwide trunk rail network, interconnected by a plethora of branch lines, which was to come to fruition in the two decades after 1850.[3] Two other notable features of these years were the rising expectations of investors and the emergence of a trend towards company amalgamations. In the former case speculative pressures reached a climax of 'bubble' proportions in 1837 and again in 1845–6. Taking the period as a whole, economic growth was rapid by the standards of the nineteenth century. In the 1830s raw material prices were falling, money was cheap, and the agricultural sector was staging a revival from the depressed conditions of the post-1815 era. These factors in themselves were sufficient to stimulate business confidence and they help to explain why so many investors were prepared to sink their capital in the most dubious of railway projects. In the following decade a combination of monetary stability and a bull share market produced an unprecedented wave of company promotions after 1844. In 1845, ninety-four new lines received parliamentary sanction with an authorised capital in excess of £59 million. At its height in 1847, railway investment accounted for 6.7 per cent of national income, equivalent to 'about two-thirds of the value of all domestic exports, and ... over twice as great as the maximum level of the Bank of England's bullion reserve in the decade'.[4] Speculation was rife, especially in the form of transferable subscription, or 'scrip' certificates entitling the holder to an allotment of shares after incorporation.[5] Even though the share market peaked in August 1845 railway investment continued to be attractive, and by the end of the following year a further 219 Acts of Incorporation had reached the statute book. In the event, both manias were broken by extraneous events – in 1837 by a drain of gold to the United States and instability in the domestic financial system, and in 1847 by a renewed outflow of gold to fund grain imports in the aftermath of the agricultural crisis of 1846.

In a number of industrialising countries in the nineteenth century railway networks bore the impress of centralised planning, the product in part of governmental interest in a form of transport with important strategic implications. In Britain, however, railway development was, from the outset, infused with the spirit of competitive private enterprise. The inevitable result in a small island with localised transport requirements was the proliferation of small undertakings. Indeed, by the end of 1844, of the 104 railway companies then in existence, only 11, accounting for more than half of the total route mileage laid down, possessed lines in excess of fifty miles in total length. As the system developed, the management of through traffic necessitated cooperation between companies and this was facilitated at a relatively early stage by the establishment of the London-based Railway Clearing House in 1842. Initially restricted to nine companies, by the end of the decade, in advance of its legal authorisation in 1850, it embraced most of the larger undertakings then in existence save for some notable exceptions in the south of England. It is a point well taken that although the organisation 'aimed at removing one of the penalties of dispersed control of railway operations, [it] probably tended in practice to demonstrate some of the advantages which amalgamation would bring, and it is arguable that its very existence hastened the process for which it had been designed as an alternative'.[6] In this context, the movement towards combination which gathered momentum after 1844 becomes readily understandable as a rational response to the practical difficulties of railway operations. There is, of course, a human dimension to the company promotions and amalgamations of these years focusing on the person of the York draper and furnisher, George Hudson. It was Hudson who, by force of personality and entrepreneurial flair, gave birth to 'the new era of big business' in the railway industry. Castigated at the time of his fall from grace in 1849 as a fraudulent and ill-bred bounder, The *Times* commented after his death in 1871 that he was 'a man who united largeness of view with wonderful speculative courage – the kind of man who leads the world'.[7] Despite his speculative excesses and outright disregard for financial proprieties Hudson's contribution to the founding of a tolerably rational railway system was invaluable. In the first instance, as a pioneer of amalgamations, he succeeded in producing an element of coordinated control over the emergent railway network of eastern England, from London to the Scottish border. This fact in itself encouraged more economical working of the system and helped to improve managerial standards. Also, to his eternal credit, he only promoted lines that had a genuine commercial rationale, unlike many of the projects laid before the investing public in the 1840s. Responsible for the first great amalgamation of English railway undertakings – that of the Birmingham and Derby Junction, Midland Counties, and North Midland Railways in 1844 – to form the new Midland Railway, he laid the groundwork for the subsequent creation of the Great Eastern and North Eastern Railways, the latter possessing the most complete territorial monopoly of any railway undertaking after its formation in 1854.[8] Other significant amalgamation schemes of the 1840s included the formation of the Lancashire and Yorkshire Railway after the merger of six separate undertakings in 1845, and the Manchester, Sheffield and Lincolnshire Railway, the product of a four-company merger in 1846.

In many ways the most impressive amalgamation scheme of these years was the formation in 1846 of the London and North Western Railway (LNWR) following the merger of the trunk line London and Birmingham and Grand Junction Railways (the latter having already absorbed the Liverpool and Manchester undertaking in 1845). Five years later, the new concern was capitalised at more than £29 million, employed a workforce in

excess of 12,000, and operated more than 800 miles of track. By contemporary and later standards the LNWR was a giant enterprise, bearing in mind
that as late as 1905 only three British businesses were capitalised in excess of
£10 million. A concern as large as this was dependent for its success upon an
effective managerial structure and in this respect the LNWR was one of a
number of leading railway companies which recruited military men with
administrative experience to senior managerial positions. Indeed, the company's first and most influential general manager was Captain Mark Huish,
the former chief executive of the Grand Junction Railway and one-time
serving officer in the East India Company's Bengal Native Infantry. In a
detailed study of the managerial structure of the LNWR Dr Gourvish has
provided a graphic reminder of the organisational problems imposed by the
sheer size of the amalgamated undertaking.[9] On an extensive rail network
carrying a variety of goods, as well as large numbers of passengers, the
traffic management requirements were intricate to a degree. Methods had to
be devised to keep track of rolling stock, to avoid jams and the accumulation
of idle stock along the network. Such a large commercial operation,
moreover, entailed more than rudimentary accounting procedures. With
revenues collected on a daily basis from numerous ticket offices, as well as
freight and passenger conductors, the system gave rise to large cash flows,
the efficient handling of which was an art in itself. This aspect of the
company's operations was matched in complexity by the interregional
movement of traffic with all the difficulties that this entailed for the fixing of
agreed rates for goods travelling across more than one railway system.
Complicating matters even further was a company financial structure characterised by high fixed costs and mounting capital expenditures as the
volume of traffic expanded. In the light of all these factors an undertaking of
the size of the LNWR required precise information about maintenance and
operating costs, and this entailed some degree of sophistication in the
collection of statistics, the recording of data, and the transmission of information to company managers.

The managerial strategy adopted by the LNWR to cope with extensive
commercial operations was to opt for a geographically divided structure but
with strongly centralised overall control. Three divisions were created,
Northern, North Eastern, and Southern, each possessing its own secretary,
superintendent, locomotive superintendent and goods manager. All of these
senior company officers were responsible to Captain Huish as general
manager. Huish in turn possessed his own managerial staff directly responsible to the London-based board of directors. As Gourvish reveals, Huish
made effective use of this structure to implement new administrative and
managerial procedures, the results in part of his experiences with the Grand
Junction Railway, one of a number of pioneering trunk line companies

20 Captain Mark Huish (1808–67), general manager of the London and North Western Railway. Huish was an outstanding pioneer of railway management techniques.

which had laboured since their inception under a regime of high-cost operations, the result in part of excessive promotional and construction costs, deficiencies in the management of the permanent way and traffic, and ill-devised pricing policies. The managerial innovations associated with Huish included accounting procedures which made appropriate allowances for depreciation and plant valuation (especially important given the heavy fixed capital costs inherent in railway operations), and extensive collection of operating statistics thereby facilitating the continuous revision of long-run costs and an element of forward planning. The board of directors, meeting monthly, was presented with detailed information on costs, augmented where necessary by working papers from Huish and his under-managers, a number of which in Huish's case represented path-breaking contributions to the theory and practice of railway management. Thus, the hallmarks of Huish's managerial regime were threefold, first the recruitment of professional salaried managers, differentiated by specialist function, secondly the collection and interpretation of operating statistics, and thirdly the internalisation of market functions in order to reduce transaction costs. The strategy of internalisation was exemplified by the early policy of the LNWR in expanding to the point of self-sufficiency its own locomotive and rolling stock building capacity. The motives for this were the desire to monitor construction techniques and costs closely, to create a locomotive fleet attuned to the company's specific requirements, and thirdly to ensure security of supply at those times in the business cycle when private locomotive building establishments enjoyed full order books.[10] As the coordinator of activities at the centre, and responsible for the company's strategic direction, Huish 'approximates to the modern chief executive to an extent remarkable for a founder member of a new profession, a man merely on the threshold of a nascent science'.[11] In Gourvish's considered judgement, therefore, it was the early railway companies, and the LNWR in particular, which 'made the first concerted attempt to solve the overriding problems of large-scale business, and developed important and possibly novel forms of business management'.[12]

The purpose of this lengthy introduction has been to provide some indication of the major trends in railway development from the mid-1830s until the late 1840s as a reference point in analysing the strategies pursued by the Stockton and Darlington Company in the second phase of its development. As the chapter will indicate, the company continued to operate predominantly as a heavy mineral railway serving localised traffic needs after 1833. However, despite this comparatively limited focus the company could not escape from the wider forces of railway development. In relation to the themes discussed above it was, for example, directly involved, albeit as a comparatively minor player, in the development of a trunk rail network between London and Edinburgh. Moreover, the expansion of the Hudson empire in the 1840s raised the issue in an acute form of the continued independence of a localised mineral railway with a limited commitment to the carriage of passengers and light freight. Above all, the period after 1833 witnessed the rise of competition in heavy mineral transport on the north bank of the Tees estuary, a development which threatened the very roots of the Stockton and Darlington Company's prosperity. As the chapter will reveal, the company's response to the loss of its traffic monopoly was a mixture of defence and aggression which gave rise to considerable personal animosities between the leading participants in the competitive struggle for traffic revenues.

Before examining the development of the Stockton and Darlington Company from the mid-1830s to the commercial crisis of 1847 it is necessary to consider a feature of its operations which stands in marked contrast to the procedures adopted by the main trunk line companies during the 1840s. If the LNWR stood at the most advanced end of the spectrum of business structures in the early Victorian economy, the Stockton and Darlington Company's managerial practices remained ossified at an immature level of development. It has already been noted that in opting for a public right of way for non-mineral traffic the management committee was conforming to the established practice of canal companies. In contracting out the building of the line the company was also following well-established precedents in the construction of the canal network. In the latter case, the company's experience cast a long shadow forward: most of the rail network in existence by 1870 had been laid down by independent contractors. Men of the calibre of Joseph Locke, Thomas Brassey, Sir Morton Peto and E. L. Betts were outstanding in this respect, not only for their prodigious labours, but also for their role in helping to consolidate the emergent profession of civil engineers.[13] It is, however, in the operational management of the undertaking that the Stockton and Darlington Company remained distinctive. Whilst the trunk line railway companies began to recruit professional salaried managers from the later 1830s, the management committee remained committed to the practice of subcontracting in major aspects of the company's business. Thus, the buy-out of the independent carriers in 1833, however much it was conducive to the efficient handling of traffic, did not herald a managerial revolution in the company's affairs.

The practice of subcontracting was a 'pre-capitalist method of industrial organisation' with its roots in the domestic system of manufactures in the eighteenth century.[14] That it survived into the nineteenth century and beyond is well known, suggesting that it could in certain circumstances be a rational form of business organisation. In the case of the Stockton and Darlington management committee, however, it would appear that subcontracting became 'if not a method of management, at least a method of evading management'.[15]

The rationale of subcontracting lay in the reduction of direct supervisory functions and also in the sharing of risks, capital, and technical knowledge with the subcontractor. Where the latter was in receipt of a fixed price per unit the originating business was relieved of a complicating element in its cost structure. Most importantly, in the early phases of industrialisation, when work incentives for managers and workers alike could be uncertain, 'the great advantage of this system ... was that it supplied a "self-acting stimulus"', which dispensed with the necessity of incessant supervision of the managing foreman by the employer'.[16] The disadvantages of subcontracting lay in the maximising of short-run returns, as when subcontracting in mines and quarries led to physical damage which pre-empted effective programmes of mineral exploitation. That it was hardly conducive to efficient management and working was conceded by the Stockton and Darlington Company itself – but only in regard to the independent merchandise and passenger contractors. The company in fact clung to the system in one form or another for the greater part of its independent existence. Before examining the reasons for a strategy which in contrast to the LNWR rendered the true boundaries of the firm uncertain it is worthwhile highlighting the extent of subcontracting by the Stockton and Darlington Company.

The most celebrated subcontractor to the company was Timothy Hackworth. His original appointment was dated as 13 May 1825 when he was given responsibility for 'the superintendence of the permanent and locomotive engines' at an annual salary of £150, 'the Company to find a house, and pay for his house, rent and fire'.[17] In this capacity Hackworth served as an employee of the company until 1833 when, as his biographer records, 'some other arrangement became desirable'.[18] It seems that this 'other arrangement' was precipitated by Hackworth's desire 'to extend his sphere of work by engaging in a general engineering business which should include the building of locomotives for other railways'. A further consideration, which could well have made the management committee more receptive to his proposal, was that by this time the company had achieved reliable locomotive haulage, the result in large measure of Hackworth's own efforts. With these considerations in mind,

An agreement was therefore concluded by which [Hackworth] took over from the Railway Company the whole contract for working it, including the locomotives, the workshops, the tools and machinery. A valuation was made on which the Company received 5 per cent interest annually. Hackworth was to provide and maintain in good condition all the necessary locomotive power, to find all workmen and material, including fuel and lubrication for rolling stock, while the Railway Company

21   William Gowland, first driver of the *Royal George* and of Hackworth's *Sanspareil* at the Rainhill Trials, 1829.

undertook to take back all stock on conclusion of the contract on a second valuation. The consideration to be paid was four-tenths of a penny per ton of goods per mile exclusive of carriages laden and empty.[19]

Hackworth's contract lasted until May 1840 from which time he devoted himself entirely to his own engineering business at the Soho Works, Shildon, building locomotives and stationary steam engines for the

Stockton and Darlington and neighbouring railways, as well as winding engines for colliery companies, and hydraulic presses and grinding mills for local engineering concerns.[20] During the subcontract period itself he achieved some fame as the builder and supplier of the first locomotive to the Imperial Russian Government and also as the builder of heavy mineral engines for the Albion Coal Mining Company of Nova Scotia. At those times when his own business took precedence Hackworth had no hesitation in subcontracting work to others. In this respect he made particular use of the brothers William and Alfred Kitching of Darlington, who not only built locomotives for the Stockton and Darlington Railway to his designs at their Hope Town Foundry, but also engaged in repair and maintenance work for Hackworth.[21] As for Hackworth's treatment of his locomotive drivers there is the following graphic description provided by James Gowland, the brother of William Gowland who was the driver both of the *Royal George* and *Sanspareil*, Hackworth's own entry at the Rainhill Trials in 1829:

We had a farthing per ton per mile . . . For that figure we found everything except the engine, coal and oil and firemen . . . An engine could then make perhaps 10s. per day after all was paid. We were paid better than anyone else and we always had plenty of money. Some men took a contract with an engine. They paid the enginemen, say, 5s. and the fireman 3s. 6d. per day, and then there was a grand living for doing nothing. I have seen an engineman drinking for a whole week, never going near his work at all. I have gone and run the engines for him at 5s. or 6s. per day . . . When we were on by the ton, we were allowed to go into any market and purchase our stores, so that we could always buy at the cheapest rate . . . I was 27 times to Middlesbrough for Harry Joyce in one week. Harry had been having a drinking bout, and he never came near the place. He paid me 5s. per trip, and I made a good week's wages, but then I was working night and day.[22]

Such lengthy drinking bouts are suggestive of generous remuneration. What evidence there is, however, demonstrates that Hackworth was able to earn a reasonable return on his contract – despite having to pay the Stockton and Darlington Company '5 per cent on the capital value of the engines along with rents of buildings' amounting to nearly £1,000 per annum.[23] Surviving ledgers for the period from May 1834 to March 1837 indicate a balance accruing to him of £3,000 over the cost of locomotive haulage, inclusive of drivers' wages, recurring repairs and materials used.[24] It is significant, perhaps, that in 1836 the management committee reduced Hackworth's contract rate of 'four tenths of a penny per ton of goods per mile' to 0.34 of a penny per ton per mile.[25] This arrangement lasted until 1 March 1837 when the management committee took over the direct management of all haulage operations on the line.[26]

On the termination of Hackworth's contract in 1840 the Stockton and Darlington Company's 'New Shildon Works' were taken over by Oswald

Table 12. *Contracts entered into by the Railway Company, 1834–5,
1 February 1836, 1 February 1837*

Nature of contract	Name of contractor	Particulars of contract
Contract entered into by the Railway Company, 1834–5		
Repairing railway	Joseph Stephenson Matthew Bains	24¼ miles: £2,470 including labour, blocks, ballast, small materials; 13¼ miles: £1,800, including labour, blocks, ballast, small materials.
Permanent engines	Hackworth and Downing	Black Boy plane: 5s 2d per 100 Tons. Brusselton: 6s 4d per 100 tons. working and repairing of engines and sheaves, but exclusive of ropes.
Locomotive engines	Hackworth, Kitching, and Lister	$\frac{4}{12}$ of a penny per ton mile. Hackworth 12 engines, Kitching 3 engines, Lister 3 engines.
Hauling coaches	Timothy Hackworth William Lister	On Middlesbrough branch: 7d per mile for engine power.
Weighing coals and pumping water	Percival Tully Hackworth and Downing	At Darlington station, £130 per annum. On Black Boy branch £4 16s 0d per month, pumping water only.
Contract entered into by the Railway Company, 1 February 1836		
Repairing railway	Joseph Stephenson	2nd and 3rd divisions: £2,500 – £10 additional if done satisfactorily – from 1 Feb. 1836 to 31 Jan. 1837.
	Matthew Bains	1st division: £1,800 per annum.
Permanent engines	Hackworth and Downing	Brusselton: 7s 4d per 100 tons; Black Boy: 5s 10d (they find ropes) – from 1 Feb. 1836 to 31 Jan. 1839.
Locomotive engines	Timothy Hackworth	$\frac{4}{12}$ of a penny per ton mile on coals and merchandise descending, and $\frac{5}{12}$ ascending. Merchandise engine guaranteed 180 tons per day – from 1 Feb. 1836 to 31 Jan. 1837.
	William Lister	$\frac{4}{12}$ of a penny per ton per mile on coals: coaches at 7d per mile until 31 Jan. 1837.
	William and Alfred Kitching	Coals: $\frac{4}{12}$ of a penny per ton per mile, from 1 Feb. 1836 to 31 Jan. 1837.
Shipping staithes	Nesham and Welsh	To repair, uphold, and maintain lifting engines, coal staithes, and other works: £300 per anum, £50 bonus on signing contract. To ship coals: $\frac{1}{8}$ of a penny per keel of 8 chaldrons. Penalty to break contract £50 with 3 months' notice.

Table 12. (*cont.*)

Nature of contract	Name of contractor	Particulars of contract
	William Cranston	15s 6d per 100 waggons and 5s per day attending staithes until 31 Jan. 1837.
Weighing coals	Percival Tully	Weighing coals, £100 per annum until 31 Jan. 1837 renewed until 31 Jan. 1838.
Depots	Thomas Daids, Darlington	$1\frac{1}{4}$d per ton on coal, lime, and cinders from 1 Feb. 1836 to 1 Jan. 1837.
	Martin Richmond, Yarm	$1\frac{1}{2}$d per ton until 31 June 1837.
	William Alderson, Stockton	$1\frac{1}{8}$d per ton from 1 Feb. 1836 to 31 Jan. 1837.
	Robert Saxton, Croft	$1\frac{1}{2}$d per ton until 31 Jan. 1837.
Ballast staithes	Thomas Wilkinson	Rent £50 per annum. Ballast for every 100 yards beyond 250 yards: $\frac{1}{4}$d per ton. Not to charge ships more than 6d per ton for taking out ballast. Until 1 Feb. 1837.
Bishop Auckland Car	John Proud	3 times a day, 3s 6d per day, to charge 3d for each passenger, 12 months from 15 Aug. 1836.
Clocks	John Harrison	To wind, regulate and keep in repair, 5 clocks, 8 guineas per annum for 1 year from 9 Sept. 1836.
Leading coals	William Walton	To Darlington and Haughton Lane: $1\frac{1}{2}$d per waggon. Bank Top and Croft: $1\frac{1}{2}$d per ton: until 31 Jan. 1837.
Additional contracts, 1st February 1837		
Repair of railway	Matthew Bains	1st to 8th mile posts: £1,700: relaying blocks as last year, until 31 Jan. 1838.
Repair of railway	John Bell	From 8th mile post to the end: £2,400 until 31 Jan. 1838.
Coaching	William Walton	Coach to Croft until 17 April 1838. Co. to pay him 6s per week and no dues. 3s 6d to Fighting Cocks and 4s to Croft.
Porterage	Joseph Clapham	Porterage at Stockton: £40 per month until 1 Feb. 1838: subject to review in 6 months [increased to £42].
Porterage	George Longstaff	Porterage at Darlington for 15 months to 31 Jan. 1839: £38 per month.

Source: PRO RAIL 667, miscellaneous papers, 1822–79.

Gilkes and William Bouch, the latter the younger brother of Thomas Bouch, designer of the ill-fated Tay Bridge. As far as it is possible to judge, Gilkes and Bouch were also appointed as subcontractors to the company, with Bouch remaining in that capacity until the Stockton and Darlington Company merged with the North Eastern Railway (NER) in 1863. By that time the company was in the process of building new locomotive construction and repair facilities at the North Road Works in Darlington, and following the merger Bouch was appointed superintendent of the works at an annual salary of £450, a post which he retained until 1875.[27]

The remarkable extent of subcontracting on the Stockton and Darlington Railway is revealed in a surviving notebook of the company's records, possibly the property of a management committee member. Table 12 sets out details of contracts entered into by the company in the period 1834–7. Contracts ranged from the comparatively trivial, such as the winding and maintenance of clocks to the upkeep of the permanent way and haulage by locomotives and permanent engines. The continuing importance attached by the Stockton and Darlington Company to subcontracting can be gauged by the management committee's response to a report tendered by John Dixon in 1843. Dixon had acted as assistant to George Stephenson during the constructional phases of the Stockton and Darlington and Liverpool and Manchester projects and had been employed as a surveying engineer by the London and Birmingham and Grand Junction Railways in the later 1830s.[28] He thus possessed considerable experience of railway operations. In 1842 he had been appointed civil engineer to the Stockton and Darlington Company at a time when the management committee was confronted by a significant deterioration in the permanent way. Dixon's report called for a substantial ongoing programme of investment in new rails: previous subcontracting arrangements had provided insufficient allowance for this at a time of rising mineral traffic. In this respect Dixon estimated that the gross weight of traffic on the Stockton and Darlington network was five times that on the trunk line London and Birmingham Railway.[29] His recommendation, therefore, was that the company should offer 'a fair remuneration for a person who might be willing to enter into a contract to maintain [the] Railway in good and sufficient repair for a term of ten years'. Such a contract might operate in the first three years on the following basis.[30]

If 3 miles of New Single Way should be laid down per year for the next three years the estimates will stand as follows:

Maintenance of Way and other Works	£ 8,760 per year
Laying down new Rails	£ 3,088 per year
Total	£11,848 per year

Dixon's recommendation was adopted, the report to shareholders for

1843–4 stating that after 'long and mature deliberation' the management committee had let the maintenance and repair of the permanent way to John Harris for a period of ten years.[31] This was to extend from Crook to Middlesbrough, whilst Dixon was appointed 'Inspecting Engineer' on the company's behalf, as well as 'Mutual Arbiter' between the management committee and Harris.

The question remains as to why the Stockton and Darlington Company persisted with a management form which was antediluvian by the standards of other contemporary railway undertakings. One obvious reason is that it was cost effective. Clearly, the management committee thought so, and it was this aspect of subcontracting which it chose to stress to shareholders. As the annual report for 1835–6 commented,

The system of contracting for repairs, labour, use of machinery, haulage, etc. has been satisfactorily pursued and reductions to a considerable amount have been annually made with the Contractors: in one case only has any advance in price been given, with the view of securing additional dispatch in the teeming of the Waggons at Middlesbro', an augmentation of the remuneration before paid to the Contractors was agreed to.[32]

It is one thing, however, to reduce the cost of a contract and quite another to secure a satisfactory standard of service. As indicated already, a potential weakness of subcontracting was that the elimination of 'direct supervisory functions' rendered the originating company open to the maximising of short-run returns on the part of the contractor. Even the conscientious Hackworth could be called to account for less than satisfactory perform- ance, as when the management committee, in drawing attention to the 'disgraceful state' of the *Earl Grey* coaching engine, ordered him to avoid the 'recurrence of similar annoyance' since it was 'prejudicial to the Char- acter and Interests of the Company'.[33] Happily, such events were a rare occurrence and the reason is not far to seek. It was the very smallness and compactness of the Stockton and Darlington Company's network which facilitated close internal surveillance of contractors' standards. Sub- contracting could never have worked satisfactorily on the LNWR: its route mileage was sixteen times as great as that of the Stockton and Darlington Company and its daily managerial arrangements far more complex in view of the concentration on a varied passenger and merchandise traffic. The nature of LNWR operations, therefore, called for the internalisation of functions which in the Stockton and Darlington Company's case could be left to independent agents. It appears, however, that there were limits to the extent to which direct management could be evaded. The appointment of John Dixon as inspecting engineer of the permanent way in 1842 is *prima facie* evidence of the management committee's concern to maintain effective monitoring of contractor's performance. It is significant also that Dixon was

simultaneously appointed inspecting engineer of the locomotive establishment, his brief being to oversee the Gilkes and Bouch contract.

The fact remains that in the years up to 1860 the managerial revolution
resulting from problems of increased scale was confined largely to the
expanding trunk line companies. There remained in existence an entire
sub-stratem of smaller undertakings whose managerial procedures continued to be determined by 'the precedents of stage-coach and canal'.[34]
Until the very end of its independent existence the Stockton and Darlington
Company employed few individuals who could be described as salaried
professional managers.[35] Beyond the offices of company engineer, surveyor,
and secretary, the professional managerial hierarchy was virtually non-
existent, at least until Dixon's recruitment. How could it have been otherwise when the boundaries of the firm were so indistinct? The few salaried
officers employed were, of course, assisted in their task by individual
members of the management committee the more active of whom performed direct managerial functions. The brothers Joseph, John and Henry
Pease are cases in point. There is ample evidence in the surviving records of
the company to illustrate the ubiquitous presence and influence of these
individuals as decision makers. They were, in effect, 'managerial' directors,
responsible for a range of executive functions and also for determining the
company's strategic direction.

In the later 1830s and 1840s the Stockton and Darlington Company was
an expanding enterprise but one subject to sustained competitive pressures,
the consequence of the loss of its monopoly position. In analysing this phase
of the company's development three interrelated themes can be identified.
The first concerns the growth of port competition on the north branch of the
Tees estuary and the determination of the Clarence Railway not only to
break the Stockton and Darlington Company's hold on mineral traffic from
the Auckland coalfield, but also to develop the west Durham coalfield
further to the north. The Stockton and Darlington Company's response to
these developments provides the second theme. In this respect the company's strategy of containing the Clarence Railway by physical and parliamentary obstruction looms large, as do the management committee's
attempts to enhance traffic revenues by improving shipping facilities and
exploiting the mineral wealth of Weardale. Finally, the period witnessed the
development of the east coast route between London and Edinburgh,
traversing the Stockton and Darlington Company's Tees-based network.
Strategic and tactical considerations dictated that the company should
participate in this movement. In doing so, the management committee
discovered, to its cost, that experience gained in the operation of a mineral
railway provided few points of guidance for the business of trunk line
projection.

In the 1830s there was one individual who, more than any other, proved to be a thorn in the flesh of the Stockton and Darlington Company. Christopher Tennant's role in founding the Clarence Railway and associated coal shipping facilities on the north bank of the Tees has already been noted. But Tennant was not content to limit his activities as a railway and port projector. Following the opening of the Clarence Railway he took up residence at Hartlepool at the extreme northern end of the Tees estuary. Ever mindful of the need for improved shipping facilities he rapidly concluded that Hartlepool possessed considerable natural advantages as a coaling port.[36] It would also open up the possibility of exploiting the productive potential of those collieries lying to the north-west towards the City of Durham. In 1831, therefore, he projected the Hartlepool Dock and Railway Company with a capital of £209,000 and loan-raising powers of £70,000. With only limited opposition from landowners and a muted protest from the corporation of Newcastle upon Tyne at the absence of wayleaves on coal shipped at Hartlepool, an Act of Incorporation was passed in June 1832. In the ensuing years the project advanced slowly due to considerable difficulties in constructing the dock and harbour facilities, but by the end of 1835, 14½ miles of railway were open, together with two coal drops and shipping space extending to 17½ acres.[37]

The Stockton and Darlington Company did not oppose the Hartlepool project, possibly because it appeared to have little relevance to the Auckland coal traffic. This did not apply, however, to other schemes on the north bank of the Tees. In 1835–6 Tennant launched a major bid to encroach on the Stockton and Darlington Company's mineral traffic, first by projecting the Durham South-West Junction Railway to link the Auckland and Coundon coalfields with the Chilton branch of the Clarence Railway, and secondly by forming a link with the limestone deposits of Weardale via the projected South Durham Railway, running from Frosterley and Wolsingham to the Clarence Railway via the latter's Byers Green branch. The Stockton and Darlington Company's response to these new projects was openly hostile, the management committee denouncing the Durham South-West Junction Railway as 'a *sinister* attempt to obtain the sanction of the legislature to a branch railway calculated to injure their line by depriving it of traffic'.[38] It would therefore present the project with its 'determined and unyielding opposition'.[39]

In the event, the Durham South-West Junction scheme failed to receive parliamentary sanction. The initial opposition focused on the Tyne and Wear exporting interests led once more by Lord Londonderry who advanced the time-worn argument that the new railway would be unfairly advantaged in the coastal trade in view of the absence of wayleave payments. Having listened to this kind of special pleading on previous occasions

Members of Parliament sitting for London and adjacent county constitu-
encies reacted by asking for the establishment of a select committee to
investigate the working of the coal trade. This was clearly to Tennant's
advantage, although it could only have been a source of considerable
irritation that his arch-rival, Joseph Pease, was elected to serve on the
resulting committee. It was Pease, in fact, who laid the groundwork for
destroying the South-West Junction scheme by focusing attention on the
parlous financial state of the Clarence Railway as the principal sponsor. It is
instructive to note that the Stockton and Darlington Company was in some
measure responsible for this situation.

Under its Act of Incorporation the Clarence Railway had been given
running powers over a section of the Stockton and Darlington network.
Within a month of the new line opening for business the Stockton and
Darlington Company began to engage in obstructive tactics, 'prohibiting
the Clarence horse-leaders from travelling on the [Stockton and Darlington]
railway one hour after sunset or one hour before sunrise, though their own
horse-leaders might do so'.[40] Further interference was forthcoming in the
separate weighing of Clarence coal waggons at the Thickley Weigh House
when Stockton and Darlington traffic was merely counted as it went past. At
the end of October 1833 the Clarence Railway began the export of coal and it
was at this point that the Stockton and Darlington management committee
took decisive action. The company's 'master move' was neatly summarised
by Tomlinson:

Upon all coals delivered at Simpasture, as at other intermediate points on their line,
they [the Stockton and Darlington Company] charged landsale dues. Now let us see
how this plan worked. In December 1833, some coals from Butterknowle Colliery
were sent down the Clarence Railway for exportation. They travelled 10 miles on the
Stockton and Darlington Railway and were charged at the rate of 2¼d per ton per
mile, which included – somewhat unfairly, it must be added – a farthing for depot
rent and agency. The cost of transport to Stockton was therefore increased by at least
3½d per ton if the coals went to the Clarence, instead of the Stockton and Darlington
staiths. In other words, the owner of the colliery had to pay 3s 2½d instead of 2s 11d,
when the Stockton and Darlington Company charged the full dues; but, as the dues
at this time upon coals for exportation were subject to a considerable reduction – a
drawback of 50 per cent had been allowed between July and November – the contrast
between the two charges was very much more striking. This was a lesson not to send
any more coals down the Clarence Railway.[41]

In these circumstances it is not surprising that in the first year of operation
the gross receipts of the Clarence Railway amounted only to £2,206 6s 2d, a
sum barely enough to meet maintenance charges on the line. Lacking access
to the personalised credit network which had done so much to sustain the
Stockton and Darlington Company in the 1820s, the Clarence directors had
been obliged to borrow £100,000 from the Exchequer Loan Board at an

interest rate of 5 per cent in order to complete the construction of their line. It was the inability to meet interest charges that forced the company to place its administration in the hands of the London-based Board in July 1834, a move which was hardly conducive to efficient management. In October 1834 the company was further embarrassed by the muted public response to a share issue to raise extra capital. The 1,000 shares had to be issued at a 65 per cent discount, 'thus saddling the concern with £100 of liability for every £35 received'.[42]

The unfortunate financial history of the Clarence Railway thus provided its detractors with ample material to undermine the credibility of the South-West Junction project. As the Stockton and Darlington management committee announced to shareholders in 1836, the project was 'an attempt to bolster up a ruminous speculation at their expense'.[43] In the House of Lords, Lord Londonderry, intent upon bringing 'this iniquitous job forward to public exposure', cast doubt on the ability of the Clarence Railway to repay its debt to the Exchequer Loan Board.[44] With Parliament fully informed of the Clarence Railway's financial predicament the rejection of the South-West Junction project was inevitable.

The fate of the proposed South Durham Railway was more complex. As Tomlinson pointed out, its rationale was well founded, insofar as it 'would open out an extensive coalfield, connect Weardale with Hartlepool and Stockton, and put new life into the Hartlepool and Clarence Railway Companies'.[45] It was, moreover, well supported within Co. Durham itself, and included George Hudson among its subscribers. The relevant bill was passed in the House of Commons with a large majority but succumbed in the Lords to an unholy alliance between Lord Londonderry and the Dean and Chapter of Durham Cathedral. The project, re-christened as the West Durham Railway, was later revived in truncated form as a wayleave line pending an application for incorporation. A parliamentary Act was eventually obtained in July 1839, but the ensuing history of the line was bedevilled by its dependent relationship on the Clarence Railway.

In the meantime, a further project designed to complete the rail link from Hartlepool to the Auckland coalfield had been inaugurated. This was the Stockton and Hartlepool Railway, linking the Clarence Company's Stockton terminus with Hartlepool itself. Construction began in May 1837 without parliamentary authority and from the outset the new undertaking sought to cooperate with the Hartlepool Dock and Railway Company in the shipment of coal. Constant friction between the two companies, however, resulted in the Stockton and Hartlepool directors promoting their own dock scheme. A parliamentary Act of Incorporation was obtained in May 1844 and the resulting Hartlepool West Harbour and Dock Company opened its facilities at New Stranton in June 1847. In practical terms the Stockton and

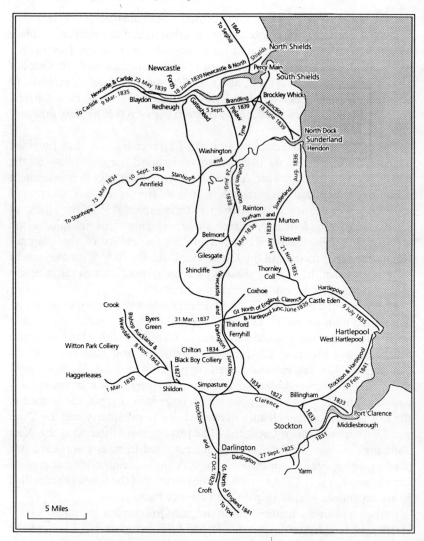

5   The Stockton and Darlington Railway and its regional linkages in the early 1840s.

Hartlepool Railway was the eastern extension of the Clarence Railway, whilst the dock was dependent on both lines. In these circumstances a unification of interests was advantageous and in August 1844 the Stockton and Hartlepool Railway took a lease on the Clarence Railway for a period of twenty-one years. By this time, Christopher Tennant was long dead, having succumbed to illness in Leeds in September 1839 whilst negotiating contracts for the delivery of fresh fish from Hartlepool.[46] He had been out-manoeuvred at virtually every turn by the Stockton and Darlington interests after 1818, and although he had succeeded in projecting the Clarence Railway the company's dismal financial history provided the sharpest contrast with the experience of his principal competitors on the south bank of the Tees estuary.

It was the leasing arrangement of 1844 which proved to be the financial salvation of the Clarence Railway. In 1842 the company's gross receipts had amounted to only £26,736 compared with an equivalent figure of £98,394 (1842–3) for the Stockton and Darlington Company.[47] By 1845, however, the Clarence Railway's receipts had climbed to £42,449 on a rising trajectory, and in that year the company declared its first dividend – of 1½% – on its original share capital. The guiding hand behind these developments was the Hartlepool solicitor, Ralph Ward Jackson. He was to prove to be a far more implacable opponent of the Stockton and Darlington Company than Tennant. As chapter 7 will reveal, Ward Jackson was to carry the fight for traffic revenues directly into the North Riding of Yorkshire – a brilliant move designed to outflank the Stockton and Darlington Company and the product of a master strategist.

Physical obstruction and parliamentary machinations had certainly damaged the Clarence Railway, but the development of Hartlepool called for a more considered response from the Stockton and Darlington interests. In the face of a competitive threat traffic revenues could be safeguarded not only by obstructive tactics, but also by investing in improved facilities. For the Stockton and Darlington Company the Middlesbrough extension and the doubling of the permanent way in 1832 are cases in point. In addition, new sources of traffic could be developed by projecting and extending lines to hitherto unexploited coal and mineral deposits. Both strategies were implemented by the company from the later 1830s onwards.

The effect of an expanding coal trade on Middlesbrough was profound. At the census of 1831 the population had amounted to 154. A decade later it had reached 5,463. In 1838 this new community of railway employees, coal heavers and seamen was sufficiently noteworthy to receive its first royal visitor, the Duke of Sussex, whose congratulations on 'the rising prosperity of your little town' were acknowledged by William Fallows, the Stockton and Darlington Company's agent, with the observation that whilst Middlesbrough had yet to acquire the paraphernalia of civic institutions 'yet we have far greater pleasure in seeing those institutions rising up in the midst of us, by our own industry and exertions, growing with our growth and strengthening with our strength'.[48] In 1839 the company's management committee noted that in view of the increasing trend of coal shipments, new drops and staithes were required.[49] At the same time the committee endorsed an

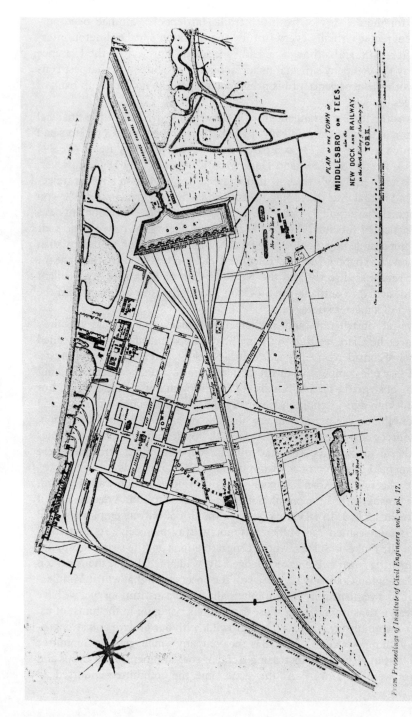

PLAN of the TOWN of
MIDDLESBRO' on TEES,
also the
NEW DOCK and RAILWAY,
in the North Riding of the County of
YORK.

From Proceedings of Institute of Civil Engineers vol. v. pl. 17.

6   Plan of Middlesbrough and the new docking facilities, opened in 1842.

earlier decision to collaborate with Thomas Richardson, Joseph Pease and Henry Birkbeck, acting in the name of the Middlesbrough Owners, in constructing a new dock at Middlesbrough 'to keep pace with the improvement of adjacent ports'.[50] This was a clear reference to the growth of Hartlepool and the competitive threat posed by the projected Stockton and Hartlepool Railway. Construction of the dock, to the plan of William Cubitt, commenced in 1840 and was completed in May 1842. It was an impressive installation capable of accommodating 150 colliers and 1,200 loaded waggons. A short branch railway was constructed from the Stockton and Darlington terminus, ending in ten double-line sidings extending over fifteen acres. The dock also encompassed ten new coal drops with a total loading capacity of 105 tons per hour.[51] The total cost of construction amounted to £140,000. This was shared between the railway company and the Middlesbrough Owners. Under an agreement of 1841 drawn up by Francis Mewburn the Stockton and Darlington Company agreed to take a 999 year lease of the dock at an annual rental equivalent to 6 per cent of the total construction cost.[52] Outright purchase of the dock and associated facilities by the railway company at some future date was not, however, ruled out.

With the new dock in place Middlesbrough's shipping capacity was substantially increased. A persistent problem with shoal water in the old shipping berths was also effectively resolved. However, in order to appreciate the full extent of the Stockton and Darlington Company's traffic expansion strategy it is important to note that the enhancement of Tees shipping facilities was a complement to developments at the western end of the Stockton and Darlington network.

In 1837 the management committee projected a new line from the southern tip of the Black Boy branch to Frosterley in Weardale. The chosen route entailed the construction of a tunnel, 1,300 yards long, underneath the magnesian limestone ridge carrying the Black Boy line. By these means the mineral wealth of Weardale and coal deposits currently being exploited by the Pease family in the vicinity of Crook could be transported into the Tees valley and thence to Middlesbrough. In the event, the strenuous opposition of local landowners resulted in a severely truncated version of the project being submitted to Parliament. The resulting Bishop Auckland and Weardale Railway Bill received the Royal Assent in July 1837. Whilst it fell far short of Frosterley it did reach into the west Durham coalfield, and in so doing held out the prospect of diverting traffic from the Clarence Railway. Capitalised at £96,000 the new line was the first in a sequence of subsidiary undertakings to be floated by the Stockton and Darlington Company with a guarantee of interest payable on the capital. The habitual procedure was for the parent company either to lease or to purchase outright the new line at some future date. The close links between the two companies were reflected in the funding arrangements. At the general meeting of Stockton and Darlington Company shareholders in August 1837 the management committee proposed that the cost of the tunnel, amounting to £30,000, should be met by the creation of 1,000 half-shares to be offered to the present proprietors, 'that is to say one half-share for each original share held by a Proprietor. That the said shares be deemed £100 shares and the half-shares £50, but that £100 be the price of the said half-shares being a premium of £50 upon each of said half-shares'. In endorsing the proposal the meeting received the assurance that the new shares were to be paid for in instalments of £2 10s per half-share at intervals to be determined by the company, 'but that in no case more than £5 to be called for in any 3 consecutive months'.[53] The fact that the two companies established the Shildon Tunnel Company to oversee the project should not be interpreted as a shared burden since the Bishop Auckland and Weardale Railway share list was dominated by Stockton and Darlington Company proprietors, notably those with an interest in the Middlesbrough Estate.[54] At the end of August 1838 the management committee agreed that the Stockton and Darlington Company should take 1,000 shares of £50 each in the new line 'and that the same be entered in the following names as Trustees':[55]

Shares	Name of proprietor
100	John Pease and Henry Birkbeck
100	Leonard Raisbeck and George Stacey
100	Henry Stobart and David Bevan
100	Henry Pease and Thomas Newman
100	Thomas Meynell and Thomas Fowler
100	Joseph Pease Jr. and John Birkbeck
100	Francis Gibson and Jonathan Backhouse
100	Thomas Richardson and John Flintoff
100	William Kitching and John Alleard
100	Edward Pease Jr. and John Kitching

The above list includes a number of proprietors of the Stockton and Darlington Company itself. It is also a testament to the continuing Quaker financial interest in the company and further underlines the extent to which it was differentially advantaged compared with the capital-constrained Clarence Railway.

The Bishop Auckland and Weardale Railway opened for traffic in November 1843. Less than a year later, in August 1844, the Stockton and Darlington Company's management committee decided on 'the extension of railway enterprise in Weardale'.[56] By this time the opposition of landowners had clearly dissipated, for the plan entailed the construction of a 10½ mile extension from Witton Junction to the limestone deposits of Frosterley, with a branch to Bishopley. The resulting line, jointly projected with the Bishop Auckland and Weardale Company, received parliamentary authorisation in July 1845 as the Wear Valley Railway. Capitalised at £82,000 with borrowing powers of £27,000, the new line was destined to be leased by the Stockton and Darlington Company on completion at a rental equal to 5 per cent on the capital invested.[57] The eight directors appointed by the Act (see appendix 4) were drawn from the upper echelons of shareholders in the Stockton and Darlington and Bishop Auckland and Weardale enterprises. The entrepreneurial leaders were Joseph Pease, John Castell Hopkins and Thomas Meynell. These three had earlier pressed for an extension of the proposed Wear valley line to penetrate beyond Alston via a 2¼ mile tunnel under Cross Fell, in order to link up with Newcastle and Carlisle Railway at Brampton. That they failed to carry the Stockton and Darlington Company management committee can be ascribed to the large expenditure involved and likely engineering difficulties, combined with the high operating costs of a line which would have ranked as the most arduous and exposed in the country.[58]

Joseph Pease and his associates were, however, successful in persuading the management committee to adopt an alternative extension scheme which was much more soundly based, practically if not financially. The project entailed cooperation with the Derwent Iron Company, founded as recently as 1841, but possessing fourteen blast furnaces and thirty-five coal and limestone mines in 1846. By then it was the largest iron-making concern in England and second only to the Dowlais Company of south Wales in the entire country.[59] The extraordinary growth of the firm had been made possible by the receipt of large advances from the Northumberland and Durham District Bank. In 1842 it had purchased a section of the ailing Stanhope and Tyne Railway, operating it as the Derwent Railway from Consett to Stanhope. This gave access to major limestone deposits in the Wear valley, but it also opened up the prospect of a valuable link with Middlesbrough, via the Stockton and Darlington network. All that was required was a ten-mile link between Waskerley and Crook. The resulting Weardale Extension Railway was built as a wayleave line, but under an agreement of 1844 financial support was obtained from the Stockton and Darlington interest in return for the surrender of the wayleaves to Joseph Pease, Thomas Meynell, and John Castell Hopkins.

The Weardale Extension Railway opened for traffic in May 1845. In the meantime the Stockton and Darlington Company had expressed the desire to take over the Derwent Railway, but negotiations with the company were frustrated by the absence of parliamentary powers. However, under an agreement of November 1844, Pease, Meynell, and Hopkins, together with Henry Pease and Henry Stobart, acquired the Derwent Railway lease and wayleaves, a move which paved the way for an amalgamation with the Weardale extension line. This was accomplished in March 1845 when the lines were united as the Wear and Derwent Junction Railway.

In organisational terms this burst of activity in Weardale pointed to an eventual rationalisation of company structures. In November 1845 the Stockton and Darlington Company's management committee agreed that the Wear Valley Railway should acquire the Bishop Auckland and Weardale Railway, the Wear and Derwent Railway, the Weardale Extension Railway and the Shildon Tunnel Company, as a prelude to the leasing of the entire network to the Stockton and Darlington Company itself. Such a scheme would result in 'Unity of Interest, Unity of Management Economy [and] such Parliamentary powers as will enable the Directors for the time being the better and more effectively to discharge their duties'. Moreover, 'A larger capital on a sound basis will be received [and] such improvements and alterations as may hereafter be found necessary will be facilitated.'[60] Thus, in September 1847 the Stockton and Darlington Company accepted the offer of the lease of the Wear Valley Railway and its associated undertakings for a period of 999 years. The annual rent, to be paid biennially, was £47,037, and the Stockton and Darlington Company agreed to commit the sum of £60,000 to the 'improvement' of the Wear Valley system over a period of seven years. At the same time the management committee agreed to take on the lease of the Middlesbrough and Redcar Railway at an annual rent of £2,880, 'and at the additional yearly rent of a sum equivalent to pay the interest on the present and future borrowed capital of that Company'.[61] The Middlesbrough and Redcar Railway was a 7¾ mile eastwards extension to the Stockton and Darlington Company's Middlesbrough Dock terminus. Projected in 1845 by the management committee, it opened up the prospect of recreational travel along the coast of north-east Yorkshire. Indeed, the company soon inaugurated holiday excursions for its own employees and their families, transporting 1,016 passengers in 1848 and 2,200 in 1850.[62]

As indicated already, the rationale of the infrastructure investments at Middlesbrough and the penetration of Weardale was to maintain the competitiveness of the Stockton and Darlington network in the face of the growth of coal shipments at Hartlepool, and if possible to generate new sources of traffic. In terms of traffic volumes the investments of the 1840s can be judged a success. As appendix 1 indicates, after a dip in landsale coal traffic in the early 1840s, the remainder of the decade, from 1844, was marked by strong recovery. Coastal shipments also fell off in the early 1840s but had recovered to the second highest recorded level by 1844–5. Lime and stone shipments exhibited a similar pattern, with especially rapid growth after 1845. It is important to note, however, that the later 1840s marked a transitional phase in the Stockton and Darlington Company's traffic

Table 13. *Coal shipments from Hartlepool, 1845–50*

Year	Coastwise (tons)	To foreign ports (tons)	Total (tons)
1845	726,183	158,225	884,408
1846	601,481	186,437	787,918
1847	703,113	186,478	889 591
1848	922,568	243,060	1,165,628
1849	1,037,390	253,704	1,291,094
1850	1,232,500	329,900	1,562,400
Total	5,223,235	1,357,804	6,581,039

Source: Jeans, *Jubilee Memorial*, p. 179.

pattern. As chapter 7 will demonstrate, the growth of the iron industry on Teesside was to lead to a marked fall in coastal and foreign coal shipments in the face of buoyant landsale deliveries after 1850.

In the period 1821–30 total coal shipments from the Tees amounted to only 110,211 tons, reflecting in part the limitations of Stockton as a coaling port. In the 1830s, however, the impact of the growth of Middlesbrough was spectacular with shipments rising to 8,239, 984 tons in the years 1831–40. The equivalent figure for the period 1841–50 was 11,019,714 tons, representing a substantial falling off in the rate of growth of the coal trade conducted from the south bank of the Tees.[63] On the north bank shipments from Hartlepool amounted to 441,707 tons in 1840.[64] However, as table 13 demonstrates, in the later 1840s the volume of coal shipments rose substantially following the opening of the new dock facilities at West Hartlepool.

There can be little doubt that traffic movements on the Stockton and Darlington network would have been even greater from the mid-1840s but for the physical limitations of the route connecting Stanhope with the Derwent Iron Company at Consett. A major obstacle was provided by the infamous Hownes Gill ravine. Waggons were raised and lowered on the sides of the ravine, one at a time, with the assistance of a winding engine. Further bottlenecks were provided by the Crawley and 'Nanny Mayor's' inclines, the former entailing rope haulage to the summit, 1,500 feet above sea level, by the Weatherhill winding engine.[65] However, even on the basis of existing traffic volumes, one major consequence of the expansion of the rail network in west and south Durham was to render untenable the Regulation of the Vend.

In the years 1836–43, sixty-one new collieries were opened up in the

Table 14. *Growth of the Teesside coal shipping trade, 1822–50*

Year	Number of collieries shipping coal via the Tees	Coal shipments (millions of tons)[a]	Tonnage of shipping registered at the port of Stockton-on-Tees
1822	9[b]	nil	5,731
1829	10	0.04	7,295
1836	20	0.85	17,318
1841	—	—	54,516
1843	47	1.55	51,193[c]
1847	—	—	42,597
1850	60	2.13	50,507

[a] Includes coastal and foreign shipments, but excludes shipments through Seaham Harbour.
[b] Landsale collieries only.
[c] Registered tonnage for 1842.
Source: Kenwood, 'Transport capital formation', table 2, p. 58.

north-east coalfield, twenty-seven of them connected with the Tees shipping trade. From 1844 to 1850, twenty-nine new winnings were developed with the Tees and the Tyne in rough parity as shipping outlets.[66] A further, related index of expansion was the growth in tonnage of ships registered at Stockton which rose to a peak of 54,516 tons in 1841. Thereafter, as table 14 reveals, the tonnage declined to a low point of 42,597 tons in 1847 before recovering to 50,507 tons in 1850. By 1840 there were at least a dozen shipping companies located on the south and north banks of the Tees. Most, like the Tees Coal Trade Shipping Company, and the Stockton and Port Clarence Steam Packet Company, were joint stock enterprises. The most significant concentration of such companies was located at Hartlepool where five firms with a combined capital of £179,144 were founded in the period between 1835 and 1843. These five alone operated 61 vessels, although the total number of vessels belonging to the town probably numbered 90 in 1839, rising to 116 by 1850.[67]

Even before 1840 the Vend had begun to show signs of serious instability as a result of overselling by member firms and the failure to submit accurate statistical returns to the controlling 'United Committee' of colliery owners. By 1843, according to the secretary of the committee, 'the maintaining of prices and obtaining adequate vends' was becoming 'utterly impracticable' because of the proliferation of new collieries and improvements in competing dock and harbour facilities.[68] The Vend disintegrated for the last time in 1844 in the midst of a pit strike during which Lord Londonderry had sold in excess of his quota in an attempt to minimise losses. Thereafter, there were intermittent attempts to revive the regulation, but these stood no chance of success, especially when, after 1850, rail-borne coal from the east Midlands began to reach the London market in increasing quantity.[69]

RATES,
TOLLS & DUTIES,
ON THE
STOCKTON AND DARLINGTON
RAILWAY
AND
BRANCHES.

MILEAGE RATES.

		d	
No. 1.	For all Coals, Culm, and Cinders, for Home Consumption	$2\frac{1}{4}$	per Ton per Mile
2.	For all Coals, Culm, and Cinders, shipped at Stockton or Middlesbrough, for the purpose of Exportation: and all Stone and Gravel, for public or private Roads	$\frac{1}{2}$	per Ton per Mile
		1	per Ton per Mile
3.	For all Lime, Building Stone, Bricks, Tiles, Clay, Marl, and Manure		
4.	For all Grain, Flour, Meal, Hay, Straw, Slate, Lead in Pigs or Sheets, Bar and Pig Iron, Bark, Timber, Staves, and Deals	$1\frac{1}{2}$	per Ton per Mile
5.	For all Goods, Commodities, and Merchandize, not above specified	$2\frac{1}{2}$	per Ton per Mile
6.	For each Carriage conveying Passengers	3	per Mile.
7.	For each Ditto ditto on Sundays	6	per Mile.

WHARF TOLLS, &C.

8.	For all Coals, Culm, or Cinders, put into any Vessel by the Company, including Porterage, and Labour of Men employed	2	per Ton.
9.	For all Articles, Matters, and Things (save as above specified) loaded or unloaded on the Property of the Company	1	per Ton.

BRIDGE TOLLS.

10.	For all Coals, Culm, Cinders, Stone, and Lime, conveyed over the Chain Bridge	1	per Ton

INCLINED PLANE DUTIES.

11.	For all Articles, Matters, and Things, over and above the before-mentioned Rates	6	per Ton.
12.	For all Articles, Matters, and Things, when one Plane only is descended	2	per Ton

N. B. For Information as to the CHARGE FOR HAULAGE, by the Company's Locomotive Engines, enquire of

Mr. S. BARNARD, Secretary.

RAILWAY OFFICE, DARLINGTON

EDWARD TOWNS, Collector at Darlington.
THOMAS LONGSTAFF, Ditto at Croft.
ARCHIBALD KNOX, Ditto at Yarm.
EDWARD ROBINSON, Ditto at Stockton.
JOHN GLASS, Ditto at Thickley.

(Signed.)
THOMAS MEYNELL, JUN., CHAIRMAN.

Railway Office, Darlington, March 22nd. 1839.

Coates and Farmer, Printers, High Row, Darlington.

22   Table of tolls and duties on the Stockton and Darlington Railway, 1839.

Before concluding the chapter with an examination of the Stockton and Darlington Company's financial and dividend record in the later 1830s and 1840s, there remains to be considered the company's involvement in the trunk line development of the east coast route from London to the Scottish border. According to Tomlinson, the Great North of England project, announced to the investing public in October 1835, was the product of 'the deeply-planning brain of Joseph Pease'.[70] The primary object of the line was to connect Leeds and York with Newcastle upon Tyne thereby forming 'a continuation of all the proposed lines from the metropolis towards Scotland'.[71] The project was especially attractive to the Stockton and Darlington interests on two grounds. First, it would secure for the company a valuable strategic position in the developing trunk rail network of eastern England. It would also increase the company's mineral traffic by means of 'a cheap and expeditious transit of coals into the heart of the North Riding and to the City of York itself; as well as . . . a communication between the Port of Stockton and every part of the Kingdom'.[72] Following the announcement of the project every Stockton and Darlington shareholder received a copy of the Great North of England Company's prospectus together with a statement from the management committee 'that it is exceedingly desirable that those who are interested in the Stockton and Darlington Railway should also become shareholders in the said undertaking . . . and thus [bring] in aid of the direction of the new Concern . . . that experience which may eventually promote the interests of both Companies'.[73]

The Great North of England Railway received parliamentary sanction under two Acts. The first received the Royal Assent in July 1836 and authorised the construction of the northern section linking Darlington with Newcastle. A second Act, covering the southern portion of the line from Darlington to York, was obtained in the following year. Under the Act of 1836 the company was capitalised at £1 million with authorised loans of £150,000 for the construction of the northern section. The subscription contract for the line accounted for shares to the value of £948,500 of which £338,800 was drawn from the local counties of Yorkshire, Durham, and Northumberland.[74] Of the £72,500 invested by the board of directors the sum of at least £62,600 was accounted for by individuals directly associated with the Stockton and Darlington Company. Other large subscriptions came from Liverpool (£209,300) and London (£224,600). Some of the laragest individual subscriptions were forthcoming from the wider Quaker community, reflecting the drawing power of a project associated with the Peases and their local Quaker associates. Thus, seven members of the Darby family of Coalbrookdale were prepared to invest £17,000, Francis, Richard and Joseph Fry of Bristol, £5,500 and Henry Birkbeck of Norwich (soon to be Joseph Pease's collaborator in the construction of the Middlesbrough

Dock), £5,000. Under the second Act the company was empowered to raise its borrowing requirement by £180,000, although the original capitalisation of £1 million was deemed to be sufficient for the construction of the entire line. In the intervening period the public was treated to a verbal confrontation between Joseph Pease and Christopher Tennant, the latter incensed that 'Darlington and the Darlington Railway were to get the lion's share of the benefit from the Great North of England Railway'.[75] Tennant accused Pease of attempting 'to get possession of the county' and that the public interest would be better served by a route to the north utilising part of the Clarence Railway network.[76] Although Pease was able to rebut the charge that Tennant's preferred route could lead to savings in construction of £300,000, the imputation of financial laxity was to linger on for some time to come.

The first signs that all was not well with the Great North of England project appeared in August 1837 when the projectors announced that construction would not begin first on the Co. Durham section, as originally intended, but from Darlington southwards. The reasons preferred for the change were that the southern section could be constructed more rapidly and cheaply, and would enable the company to form links with other undertakings whose lines extended as far as Leeds, Hull, Manchester, Liverpool, and London. Superficially, this was a logical move, but its effect was to bring allegations from shareholders in Co. Durham that the all-powerful Stockton and Darlington interests were deliberately delaying the construction of the northern section in order to protect their Yorkshire markets for Auckland coal. This led to a growing lack of confidence in the Great North of England board which was reflected in mounting arrears for share payments. Legal proceedings were threatened against the laggards and board members even advanced loans to the company amounting to £50,000 out of their own pockets. A financial crisis, however, was in the making. By August 1839, when only £40 per share had been paid, there were more than 3,000 scrip certificates in existence on which the company had received only the minimum deposit of £2. Defaulting subscribers were eventually prosecuted successfully by the company, but in January 1841, when the southern section opened for mineral traffic, a renewed crisis of confidence was precipitated by the resignation of Thomas Storey, a former Stockton and Darlington employee and the company's engineer. Storey's departure was the result of the long delay in the opening of the line compounded by the fact that construction of the southern section had absorbed the whole of the company's resources. Coincidentally, suspicions were aroused that Thomas Meynell, Henry Stobart and Henry Pease – Stockton and Darlington directors who were also members of the Great North of England board – were attempting to undermine George Hudson in his efforts to form the Newcastle and Darlington Junction Railway in order to complete the route to the north.

It is unnecessary to describe in detail the final stages in the Great North of England saga. It is sufficient to note that by January 1843 a total of 1,611 scrip certificates and 794 registered shares had been declared forfeit, a sufficiently dismal record to ensure that before the spring of 1844 the price of Great North of England shares on the London Stock Exchange failed to reach par. No wonder then that the editor of the *Railway Times* was moved to comment that 'the Great North of England Railway ... appears to have been, in the outset, one of the worst-managed undertakings in the Kingdom, and that is saying a great deal'.[77] In the spring of 1845, following sustained pressure from aggrieved shareholders, disappointed at the company's dividend record (it had averaged only 3 per cent in the first three years of the company's operation after 1841), the directors were relieved to negotiate a leasing arrangement with George Hudson's Newcastle and Darlington Junction Railway. The entire line from York to Newcastle was then renamed the York and Newcastle Railway. Under the terms of the lease Hudson was to pay a dividend of 10 per cent on £100 and £40 shares. The lease also provided for the eventual purchase of the line with each £100 share being valued at £250. Following Hudson's demise in 1849 the terms were revised. Instead of a cash payment, Great North of England share-holders received debentures in the York, Newcastle and Berwick Railway to the value of £2,657,237. Thereafter, as David Brooke concludes, 'the Great North of England at last became a very profitable investment for its long-suffering shareholders'.[78]

In accounting for the chronic financial difficulties of the Great North of England Railway Brooke has pointed to their early onset, within months of the launching of the project. Scrip was changing hands soon after its issue, and as late as 1841 there were still 1,500 scrip certificates which had attracted only the minimum deposit of £2. This suggests either a heavy speculative element in the subscription list or the early onset of doubts as to the expected return on the investment. Neither explanation is mutually exclusive. It seems reasonable to conclude, however, that the decision of the directors to abandon the northern section of the line was a decisive factor in eroding confidence, as was Storey's much-publicised resignation as engineer to the project. In the context of railway financing in the north-east of England as a whole the experience of the Great North of England Railway sheds further light on the effectiveness of Quaker financial networks. It is true that the project attracted Quaker interest – it could hardly fail to do so in the light of its origins. But Quaker shareholdings could not be the preponderant element in a trunk line project. Capitalised at £1 million, the Great North of England Railway was dependent for its financing on a far

Table 15. *Stockton and Darlington Railway financial statistics 1834–5 to 1846–7*

Year	Gross income ($£$ s d)			Net profit ($£$ s d)			Dividend (per $£$100 share) ($£$ s d)
1834–5	62,207	10	1	9,413	5	7	6
1835–6	68,795	6	4	12,500	14	4.	11
1836–7	72,609	4	10	17,509	8	3	11
1837–8	85,651	17	8	23,003	4	4	14
1838–9	96,288	1	3	25,614	19	10	14
1839–40	120,286	12	7	26,936	13	5	15
1840–1	118,925	0	11	33,859	15	7	15
1841–2	115,321	1	0	32,986	0	10	12 10 0
1842–3	98,394	6	2	27,258	3	5	12 10 0
1843–4	87,000	1	10	20,451	14	1	12 10 0
1844–5	108,341	7	2	34,107	8	6	14 0 0
1845–6	98,657	9	5	27,464	14	4	12 10 0
1846–7	114,275	13	9	27,976	8	8	12 10 0

Source: Stockton and Darlington Railway Company annual reports.

wider range of capital sources than the Stockton and Darlington Railway. Therein lay a critical weakness.

If this venture into the business of trunk line development during the country's first 'railway mania' was hardly an example of shining entrepreneurship then it remains to be said that in its local context the Stockton and Darlington Company proved to be an outstanding commercial success in the later 1830s and 1840s. Table 15 sets out the relevant statistics for the financial years 1834–5 to 1846–7. Net profits rose strongly from 1834 to 1837–8. The rate of growth thereafter slackened off until a renewed upsurge came in 1840–1. For the remainder of the 1840s until the financial year 1846–7 net profits averaged $£$28,734, a disappointing record, perhaps, in the light of the rising trajectory after 1834. Traffic competition in the coal trade was, of course, mounting throughout this period, especially so during the first half of the 1840s. It is thus reasonable to conclude that the Stockton and Darlington Company's strategy of infrastructural investment on Teesside, combined with route extensions in Weardale, helped to sustain revenues and profitability. Tomlinson, certainly, entertained no doubts that the company's dividend record was 'the reward of a prudent policy and good management'.[79] Between 1839 and 1841 the annual dividend to shareholders was 15 per cent, the highest by far of any railway in the country. At a time when other undertakings were dependent upon revenue from the carriage of passengers in the face of the last vestiges of competition for freight traffic from canals and turnpikes, the Stockton and Darlington line

Table 16. *Share prices of the Stockton and Darlington Railway Company,*
1834–46

Date	£	Date	£
18 Feb. 1834	280	22 Jan. 1841	260
28 Oct. 1835	235	28 July 1841	260
23 Aug. 1836	200	27 Dec. 1841	260
21 Oct. 1836	205	12 Jan. 1842	257
28 Oct. 1836	202	19 May 1842	255
23 Feb. 1838	240	26 Oct. 1843	230
24 Apr. 1838	250	15 Jan. 1844	242
7 Dec. 1838	260	7 May 1844	242 10s
23 Feb. 1839	260	6 Dec. 1844	250
16 July 1839	250	2 Jan. 1845	245
12 Oct. 1839	265	4 June 1845	292
13 Dec. 1839	260	10 July 1845	299 19s
4 Jan. 1840	265	16 Jan. 1846	285
19 Apr. 1840	265	29 Jan. 1846	280
16 July 1840	275	17 Mar. 1846	283
4 Nov. 1840	267	9 July 1846	280

Source: PRO RAIL 667/264/1, Stockton and Darlington Railway financial statistics.

throughout this period was still fulfilling the function demanded of it by the
original promoters – a mineral railway with only a secondary interest in
passenger and freight transport.

The company's dividend record was reflected in the value of its shares, as
table 16 indicates. From a low of £200 in August 1836 the value of each
£100 share climbed to £275 in July 1840. There was then a decline, but a
renewed surge began in 1844 with a maximum value of nearly £300 being
reached in July 1845. As for the pattern of share ownership, the company's
share registers display a large measure of stability throughout the period
with a tendency for holdings to rise on the part of Quaker families in
Norfolk and the Home Counties as a result of purchase, intermarriage, and
bequests within the Society of Friends. Thus, shareholders' lists for the
early 1840s show substantial holdings on the part of the Gurneys, Martins
and Birkbecks of Norwich, the Gibsons of Saffron Walden, the Hulls of
Uxbridge, the Barclays and Bevans of London, the Newmans of London
and the west Midlands, the Fowlers of London and Wiltshire, and the Foxes
of Devon and Cornwall.[80] Within these maintained holdings there was one
outstanding case of ownership concentration. At the time of the opening of
the railway in 1825 Thomas Richardson was already a major investor in the
company. Between 1823 and 1830 he more than doubled his holding from 55

to 141 shares. This substantial block remained in Richardson's hands until 1844 when, having retired from London to the North Riding of Yorkshire, he transferred 10 of these shares to himself and Joseph Pease jointly and sold the remaining 131 to Joseph and his brothers, John and Henry. Similarly, in July 1842 Joseph Gurney transferred 18 shares to Joseph Barclay (banker of Lombard Street) and John and Henry Pease collectively. He also disposed of a further 8 shares to his fellow Quaker banker, Henry Birkbeck of Heswith, Norfolk. Again, in July 1842, Edward Pease transferred 49 shares to his sons in their joint names.[81] Thus by 1844 the three Pease brothers were the largest shareholders in the company, possessing 239 shares, almost 25 per cent of the total. It is thus a notable feature of the shareholders' list for that year that it points to a movement of holdings back to the north-east of England with a particular focus on Darlington. At their peak value the Peases' shares were worth more than £70,000, compared with the family's original investment of £13,000.

There is one further aspect of the Stockton and Darlington Company's financial structure which calls for comment. This concerns the practice of borrowing without reference to authorised parliamentary limits. The financial records of the company for the 1830s and 1840s provide full information on the evolution of a complex structure of debt. The relevant figures are set out in table 17. The sources of these loans are unidentified except for those attracting a 5 per cent rate of interest. In this case, it is known that from October 1836 onwards a proportion of the dividend on shares was retained by the company on loan in return for the issue of 5 per cent bonds with the option to convert the latter into shares following the issue of new stock.[82] However, it was not until 1847 that loans in the 5 per cent class attained a significant proportion of the total debt which leaves the greater portion unaccounted for. In the absence of specific information on the sources of loan finance it is reasonable to presume that throughout this period the company had recourse, in unknown proportions, to the Quaker banking community and probably also to the open capital market. As to the motives for exceeding the authorised borrowing limits two possible reasons can be adduced. The first was the reluctance of the company to seek parliamentary authorisation for extra borrowing powers out of fear that clauses would be inserted in a bill which would entail extra expenditure. In 1842, for example, the *Railway Times* reported the management committee's concern that Parliament might insist that any bill to legitimise borrowing would contain a clause requiring the replacement of level crossings by bridges.[83] A more convincing explanation of the company's practice was the determination to resist the temptation to raise further funds by new share issues. This would certainly have been consistent with the long-standing aim of the leading Quaker shareholders to maintain 'the concord of the

Table 17. *Stockton and Darlington Railway Company loan structure with gross interest payable, July 1836–July 1847*

				Rates per cent					
Date	3½ (£)	4 (£ s d)	4¼ (£ s d)	4½ (£ s d)	5 (£ s d)	5½ (£)	6 (£ s d)	Total (£ s d)	Interest (£ s d)
1 July 1836		73,435	29,612 11 0	223,753 18 6	6,000			337,801 9 6[a]	7,244 7 10
1 July 1837		57,250	28,582 11 0	206,615 18 6	35,000			327,448 9 6	7,130 8 3
1 July 1838		41,600	18,913	209,465 18 6	32,800			302,778 18 6	6,825 8 8
1 July 1839		40,000	20,653	222,465	—			283,118	6,255 3 4
1 July 1840		33,100	33,550	228,878	13,800			309,328	6,728 19 3
1 July 1841		27,900	27,150	228,917 16 4	58,190			342,157 16 4	7,568 4 0
1 July 1842		24,600	14,050	230,225 8 10	111,305			380,180 8 10	8,227 2 10
1 July 1843		34,200	14,050	285,717 10 0	171,425			505,392 10 0	9,452 6 5
1 July 1844		140,211 12 1	13,950	370,358 13 5	60,600	4,000		589,120 5 6	10,842 8 5
1 July 1845	2,250	505,528 2 11	—	16,450	60,600			584,828 2 11	10,206 14 8
1 July 1846	2,250	482,203 11 10	4,900	100,150	60,600			650,103 11 10	10,747 17 1
1 July 1847	1,650	415,851 19 3	6,000	332,650 4 2	118,573 3 9		17,188 5 1	891,913 12 3	

[a] Includes £5,000 lent by Henry Birbeck

Source: PRO 667/264/1, Stockton and Darlington Railway financial statistics.

Table 18. *Allocation of loan finance, 1843–6 (£)*

Date	Railway[a]	Weardale Extension	Shildon Tunnel	Middlesbrough Dock	Total
1 July 1843	139,425	135,589	118,685	111,691	505,392
1 July 1844	208,608	144,620	119,305	116,586	589,120
1 July 1845	197,737	149,484	119,569	118,035	584,828
1 July 1846	257,702	151,639	121,001	119,760	650,103

[a] Stockton and Darlington line.
Source: PRO RAIL 667/264/1, Stockton and Darlington Railway financial statistics.

Company' (see above, p. 56). As to the use of the borrowed funds, table 18 sets out the cumulative deployment of loans in the period 1843–6.

In his analysis of railway investment in the formative years of railway development before 1850, M. C. Reed has identified the Stockton and Darlington Railway as a special case. This is due to the fact that 'the financial management of the concern was more appropriate to a close partnership than a joint-stock company with a share capital of over £100,000'.[84] As this chapter has revealed, Reed's judgement can be refined further. For all practical purposes after 1830 the company was managed as a successful family firm. This view is justified by the distinctive capital funding arrangements, the evolving pattern of share ownership, and the fact that the managerial direction of the firm was the prerogative of the dominant Pease family. Throughout the period to 1847 no member of the family served as chairman of the company or of any associated undertaking. This can only have been the result of deliberate policy: why pursue the shadow of titular office when the substance of power was guaranteed by Quaker wealth and finance? By the 1840s the Peases were well established as part of the superstructure of Quaker financial fortunes. In a broad context, younger members of the family had already embarked upon the process of 'conformity to the world' which was so unsettling for older generations of Quakers. The acquisition of ornate mansions and the pursuit of increasingly affluent lifestyles was accompanied by unprecedented involvement in political affairs. A nascent political dynasty was in the making, but its foundations were firmly rooted in the reality of economic power and influence.[85]

At the time of the leasing of the Wear Valley Railway in 1847 the Stockton and Darlington Company presented a robust image of commercial success and prosperity. Its dividend record was enviable, its infrastructure investments impressive, and its route configuration strategically located in relation to mineral traffic flows. The only flaw in this seemingly attractive position was the company's potential vulnerability with respect to fixed charges on its revenue arising from leasing arrangements and the payment of interest on loans. As long as revenues from mineral traffic were maintained all would be well. By the mid-1840s, however, there were signs that the rate of economic growth on Teesside was faltering. Capital formation as a whole had been falling persistently since 1840, as had the rate of population growth.[86] If and when national economic recession was reflected in regional economic trends, the Stockton and Darlington Company's vulnerability would be exposed with unfortunate consequences for its financial position.

6   Crisis, 1847–1850

In the wake of the coal trade Middlesbrough began a slow process of industrial diversification. The first enterprise of any note was the Middlesbrough Pottery, inaugurated in 1834 by Richard Otley, surveyor and first secretary of the Stockton and Darlington Company, and several associates. The site was purchased from the Middlesbrough Owners for the sum of £300 and production of 'everyday earthenware' began in 1835.[1] At the same time the construction of boat and shipyards was commenced by John Gilbert Holmes, the leading light of the town's first temperance society and subsequently described as 'the only gentleman' resident on Middlesbrough's 'turbulent industrial frontier'.[2] Further developments in the mid-1830s included the establishment of a repair shop for rolling stock by the Stockton and Darlington Company. This was an essential requirement in view of the expansion of traffic and the company's policy of exclusive reliance on locomotive haulage on the main network. The most significant venture by far, however, was the iron foundry and rolling mill opened by Henry Bolckow and his partner John Vaughan on a modest six-acre site in August 1841, employing about 150 men for the manufacture of bar-iron, anchors, chains, cables, rails and castings. It seems likely that Joseph Pease was personally involved in persuading Bolckow and Vaughan to invest in an untried industrial location: as one of the Middlesbrough Owners he was certainly able to secure land and coal supplies for the new concern at favourable rates, and also to provide the partners with letters of recommendation.[3]

By 1841 the population of Middlesbrough had grown to 5,463 from 154 in 1834. The town's labour force numbered 2,199 men, women and children. The distribution of occupations is shown in table 19. According to these figures two-thirds of the labour force were employed in the high growth sectors of the 1830s and 1840s.[4] It was the urban and industrial development of Middlesbrough, together with the growth of population on the south bank of the Tees estuary, which caused the historian and antiquary, J. W. Ord, to describe the town in 1846 as 'one of the commercial prodigies of the nineteenth century', as evidenced by its 'proud array of ships, docks,

133

Table 19. *Occupational distribution of Middlesbrough's labour force, 1841 (%)*

Building and construction	Iron, engineering, shipbuilding, pottery	Labourers	Shipping and coal trades
21	20	12	12

Source: Kenwood, 'Transport capital formation', p. 63.

warehouses, churches, foundries, wharves etc'.[5] In reality, this 'Arabian Nights' vision of human and economic progress was premature on several counts. The new town, for example, contrary to the original intentions of its Quaker founders and Joseph Pease in particular, was failing to conform to any notion of a 'model' community. As noted already, the rigid symmetry of the original estate plan was soon subject to the depradations of land and building speculation resulting in overcrowding and poor living conditions.[6] By the early 1840s, moreover, Richard Otley was in poor health and his pottery enterprise in severe financial difficulties. It was for these reasons that Joseph Pease provided fresh capital for the firm and attempted to revive the flagging management by persuading Otley to accept the young Isaac Wilson as a partner. Born in Kendal in 1822, Wilson was a Quaker who was destined to become a member of the Peases' 'cousinhood', and also to play a leading role in Middlesbrough's commercial and civic affairs. By 1842 he was already a shareholder and management committee member in the Stockton and Darlington Company with family interests in the carpet and iron industries. Coincidentally, Wilson joined forces with his fellow Quaker, Edgar Gilkes, formerly employed as an engineer at Shildon, to lease the Stockton and Darlington Company's repair workshops in Middlesbrough. The partnership was henceforth known as Gilkes, Wilson and Co., and by 1847 the Tees Engine Works was combining maintenance and repair work for the Stockton and Darlington Company with the manufacture of locomotives, stationary and marine engines, blowing engines for ironworks and mines, blast furnace equipment, and agricultural engines.[7]

The problems confronting Bolckow and Vaughan, however, were not so easily resolved. Almost from the commencement of business they were handicapped by the precipitate rise in the price of Scottish blackband pig-iron, their major raw material. Under the stimulus of national railway construction the price per ton rose from £2 in 1842 to nearly £6 in 1846, sufficient to undermine the economic rationale of the location of the Middlesbrough Ironworks.[8] In 1845, therefore, Bolckow and Vaughan took the apparently sensible decision to construct their own blast furnaces at

Witton Park in the centre of the Auckland coalfield. This would reduce the transport cost of their coal supplies, eliminate the transport cost of imported pig-iron, and also give access to such local clayband ironstone deposits as were available.[9] The new works were laid out on a large scale with three blast furnaces and extensive puddling-plant capacity, sufficient to meet the current needs of the Middlesbrough Ironworks. However, the local supply of ironstone proved to be inadequate and the partners were obliged to use other ore supplies. In 1845, therefore, Bolckow and Vaughan received their first shipment of ironstone from the Roseby brothers of Skinningrove on the Cleveland coast of north Yorkshire. This was landed at the Middlesbrough Dock for transport by rail to Witton Park. Thus, from the mid-1840s onwards, Bolckow and Vaughan were in the unfortunate position of having to ship iron ore from the north Yorkshire coast to the Tees for transhipment on the Stockton and Darlington Railway to Witton Park, whilst the resulting pig-iron had then to be transported back along the line to the Middlesbrough Ironworks for the final stages of manufacture.

As long as the level of economic activity was sustained and credit cheap Bolckow and Vaughan's vulnerability in the face of high transport costs would be masked. Indeed, the firm participated fully in the railway construction boom which developed after 1844, stimulated by low interest rates and favourable investor expectations. As noted already, a heavy speculative element in railway scrip began to develop in 1845 which helped to boost share values. The insatiable demand for investment funds for railway promotions produced a 'crowding out' effect elsewhere in the economy, one consequence of which was mounting speculation in commodity markets. In these circumstances of overextension the economy was ill-prepared to confront the catastrophic failure of the wheat and potato crop in 1846. At the same time, a reduced cotton crop in the United States provoked a downturn in the Lancashire cotton industry marked by rising unemployment and short-time working. In macroeconomic terms these supply contractions were reflected in mounting gold outflows which threatened bank liquidity. Between 23 January and 17 April 1847 the bullion reserves in the Issue Department of the Bank of England fell from £13.4 million to £9.3 million. Credit contraction followed in the wake of interest rate rises provoking a severe crisis of confidence in the railway sector. In October 1847 the Bank Act was suspended due to the Bank of England's inability to redeem its notes in gold. However, the action of the government in authorising the extension of loans (provided the rate charged was not less than 8 per cent), and the Treasury's willingness to indemnify the Bank against any breach of the 1844 Bank Charter Act entailed by this policy, had a 'magical' effect in bringing the financial crisis to an end. By January 1848 the Bank of England's reserves had climbed to £11 million with bullion reserves valued at £13 million. In consequence, 'The Bank and the country were prepared to weather the vicissitudes of the Year of Revolutions.'[10]

Contemporary interpretations of the crisis focused particular attention on the allegedly excessive capital demands of the railway sector which had provoked inflationary pressure and deprived other industries of capital resources. However, there is little evidence of general capital scarcity, whilst the railway companies themselves acted as a contracyclical element, their construction programmes between 1845 and 1850 employing 250,000 workers 'who might otherwise have been in the workhouses',[11] as well as adding 4,500 route miles to the national system. This is not to suggest that local liquidity shortages were not severe. In 1847, the failure of the Union Bank precipitated the downfall of six of the large agency houses in India, whilst the commercial distress in the Lancashire cotton industry has already been noted. On Teesside Bolckow and Vaughan were evidently similarly afflicted: in 1847 the firm laid off large numbers of workers, and in March 1848 the partners were grateful to accept the Stockton and Darlington Company's offer to stand security for a loan of £20,000 from London bankers.[12] The railway company's action is an indication of the management committee's determination to sustain Bolckow and Vaughan in existence as a significant generator of traffic and revenues.

For the Stockton and Darlington Company the crisis in the local iron trade was compounded by the growing competition of Hartlepool and West Hartlepool as coal exporting ports. As noted already, the Middlesbrough Dock had been constructed by the Stockton and Darlington interests in order to sustain coal shipments from the south bank of the Tees. Unfortunately, the usefulness of the Dock was impaired in the later 1840s by a serious decline in the navigable state of the river due to the good intentions of the Tees Navigation Company, whose laudable policy of constructing jetties to contain the channel earlier in the decade had produced the perverse effect of rendering the bed of the river uneven.[13] To make matters worse the Stockton and Darlington Company had leased the dues of the Navigation Company in 1845 for an annual rental of £8,200. At first sight this was yet a further instalment in the company's strategy of containing the Clarence Railway which had had its own shipping point at Port Clarence since 1833. The advantage of the leasing arrangement for the Stockton and Darlington interest was that the more dues which were paid at Port Clarence the less rent the company would have to pay. The flaw in this plan was exposed when the Clarence Railway was linked to the new harbour at West Hartlepool in 1847. This virtually ended coal shipments from Port Clarence and in so doing threw the burden of the rental on to the Stockton and Darlington Company. The situation could not be resolved simply by the termination of the lease since this would invoke a penalty payment of £3,000 which the company could ill afford to pay. The only acceptable solution was a transfer in the control of the river, a policy which was actively canvassed by Joseph Pease and which eventually bore fruit in the establishment of a statutory body – the Tees Conservancy Commission – under Admiralty auspices in 1852.[14]

The period from 1847 to 1850 was one of mounting crisis and uncertainty for the Stockton and Darlington Company. Whilst the unfavourable situation at Middlesbrough was a cause for concern, a further source of weakness was the onset of depression in the local coal and iron trades. The management committee's report to shareholders for the financial year 1846–7 was an optimistic document.[15] Traffic revenues in all categories exceeded those attained in the previous year, although net profits were only slightly in excess of the level for 1845–6. Exports had fallen off by nearly 80,000 tons as a result of the growing competition from the north bank of the Tees, but this was more than compensated for by a substantial rise in landsale coal traffic, from 386,594 tons to 471,746 tons. The continuing prosperity of the company was reflected in the dividend of 13 per cent payable on each of the £100 shares. The report for 1847–8, however, was markedly different in tone, referring to 'the general pressure of commercial affairs unprecedented in degree of continuance' which had served to depress the coal and iron trades.[16] As the report commented, 'The operations of three considerable collieries have been suspended', whilst local iron making firms were subject to 'languid operations'. The impact of these developments had been felt most heavily by the lines under lease by the Stockton and Darlington Company which had 'suffered not only from the ... monetary difficulties of the past year', but also from the fact that 'their resources [were] but very feebly developed'. Gross revenues had increased by more than £20,000 over the previous year, but net profits had fallen by 25 per cent due in part to an increase in 'short leading' in the haulage department which had raised working expenses. Nevertheless, despite a year of 'unparalleled commercial difficulties' at home, compounded by political disturbances in Europe, the management committee authorised a further dividend payment of 13 per cent.

The growing crisis in the company's affairs was more fully reflected in the report for 1848–9.[17] In terms of both traffic and revenues the year had been one of 'considerable disappointment'. Gross receipts had increased to £147,367, but disbursements, at £133,124, were substantially in excess of the previous year, producing a fall in net profits to £14,242. It was not until an adjourned general meeting of shareholders in September 1849 that the management committee announced a much reduced dividend of 7 per cent, pointing at the same time to the non-existent, or 'trifling dividends' paid by competing concerns, some of which had been unable to meet interest obligations on borrowed capital.

23   George Hudson, the 'Railway King'. Hudson was invited by the Stockton and Darlington Company to lease its rail network in 1849, immediately before his downfall.

A further indication of the company's discomfiture was provided by the termination of the use of the Stockton and Darlington network by the Backhouse family's Black Boy Colliery. In October 1848 the colliery agent wrote to the company secretary, Oswald Gilkes, to inform him that henceforth Black Boy coal would be shipped from Hartlepool on account of the Stockton and Darlington Company's 'excessive' toll charges. This was the culmination of a long-standing dispute between the colliery and the railway company reaching as far back as 1839 when Jonathan Backhouse had contemplated using the Clarence Railway for his coal shipments.[18] In January 1848 the management committee had considered leasing the export dues from its colliery customers for a period of up to two years.[19] Nothing seems to have come of the initiative, but another proposal of far greater consequence, involving a leasing bill for the entire Stockton and Darlington network, very nearly came to fruition. At some stage during the first half of 1849 the management committee invited George Hudson to negotiate for a lease of their lines. As the committee stated to the body of shareholders, the object was 'to secure you from contingencies and guarantee you £15 per cent per annum'.[20] By May 1849 a bill for the lease of the Stockton and Darlington Company by Hudson's York, Newcastle and Berwick Railway was under preparation. It failed to come to fruition only because of Hudson's fall from grace later in the year, a move precipitated by the revelation that he himself had profited to the extent of £9,000 after selling his Great North of England shares to his own York and North Midland Company. With Hudson's deceit proclaimed publicly the management committee prudently terminated their interest in the leasing bill.

In presenting its annual reports to shareholders in the later 1840s it is clear that the management committee was concerned to portray an image of a well-run company which was embarrassed temporarily by events beyond its control. In reality, however, the company was suffering in consequence of earlier managerial decisions concerning leasing arrangements and borrowing. It has already been noted that the extraordinarily rapid expansion of the Derwent Iron Company had been facilitated by the receipt of large advances from the Northumberland and Durham District Bank. Even without the onset of commercial crisis in 1847, the iron company would have been hard pressed to meet its annual interest commitments. As it was, it was sustained by the extension of generous credit by its bankers, a policy which kept the concern in existence but one which could not prevent a reduction in the Stockton and Darlington Company's revenues on the Wear Valley line of sufficient severity to threaten the financial stability of the entire enterprise. The combined annual rental for the Middlesbrough and Redcar and Wear Valley lines was in excess of £48,000 and to help meet this commitment the Stockton and Darlington Company used the resources obtained from the sale of the Shildon Tunnel to the Wear Valley Company as a guarantee fund applicable to the Wear Valley rental. The management committee report for 1848–9, however, noted that the fund had been so reduced that the time was rapidly approaching 'when the cost of the rental will have to be met from general revenue'.[21] In October 1847 the fund had stood at £146,303; by July 1850 it had fallen to £8,000.[22]

At the half-yearly general meeting of shareholders held in February 1850, the management committee, clearly on the defensive in relation to charges of excessive dividend payments and worries concerning the leases, responded as follows:

if an impression exists that the dividends paid were excessive, it can have been only on the part of those who judged in ignorance of facts. Any insinuation that such dividends had been paid out of capital will be best met by referring the Proprietors to the accounts. They will thereby satisfy themselves that so far from this having been the case, the revenue account has been fully debited with items indisputably belonging to the capital account.

Whilst flourishing, and increasingly so, the Stockton and Darlington Railway Company saw, during the railway-making mania, the district from which it drew its resources surveyed for at least six lines, all aimed to divert or subtract its traffic; the company being thus compelled to choose, selected and encouraged the best and least expensive undertakings. They gave 6 per cent rental when 8 and 10 per cent were not uncommon; and inevitably driven into this position, your Directors have laboured unceasingly to develop the traffic on these lines to render them profitable.[23]

In the matter of paying dividends out of capital the management committee's conscience was clear, but the nub of the issue was, indeed, the shortfall in traffic revenues on sections of the network which attracted heavy fixed charges.

In an effort to stave off a financial crisis the management committee attempted to negotiate an amalgamation with the Wear Valley Company. By the end of 1850 a draft parliamentary bill had been drawn up but it failed to secure majority support from the Wear Valley shareholders. The Wear Valley directors were, however, empowered to negotiate an alteration in the financial terms of the lease under which the company agreed to forego the full amount of the guaranteed rental until commercial conditions had improved. The crucial proviso was that if the Stockton and Darlington Company's receipts were insufficient to meet the lower rental (between 4 and 5 per cent) the lessors would be entitled to the whole of the net revenue not only of their own line, but also of the Stockton and Darlington and Middlesbrough and Redcar networks.[24]

As for the Stockton and Darlington Company's borrowing record, the published accounts for the later 1840s indicate a rising burden of interest payments – from £22,710 in the financial year 1845–6 to £36,879 in the year

Table 20. *Share capital structure of the Stockton and Darlington Railway Company before the Consolidation Act of 1849*

Number of shares	Value (£)	Total (£)
675	100	67,500
325	120	39,000
973 (½) first series	100	97,300
27 (½) first series	111	2,997
1,000 (½) second series	125	125,000

Source: PRO RAIL 667/264/1, Stockton and Darlington Railway financial statistics.

Table 21. *Authorised capital of the Stockton and Darlington Railway Company under the 1851 Act*

Ordinary shares	£400,000
Preference shares 'A'	£400,000
Preference shares 'B'	£250,000
Total	£1,050,000

Source: Stockton and Darlington Railway (Loan Conversion) Act, 19 May 1851.

1848–9. In order to secure a reduction in interest charges the management committee opted for parliamentary legislation to rationalise the company's financial structure. In 1849, the share capital of the company amounted only to £331,797 (see table 20), whereas the bonded debt had reached £710,859. Of the latter, only £52,000 had been raised under the provisions of the Acts of 1821 and 1824 and the remainder had been obtained without parliamentary authority. Under a new Act of 1849 the company was reincorporated at the same time as it was given legal title to the ownership of the Middlesbrough Dock. The Act also gave sanction to the greater portion of the bonded debt amounting to £500,000. The remaining portion was held back by the company for liquidation out of its own reserve fund. However, in view of the prospective exhaustion of the fund, the company was also obliged to secure a further parliamentary Act in May 1851. Its chief provision was the conversion of the whole of the bonded debt, both authorised and unauthorised, into share capital. As Tomlinson pointed out, by capitalising their mortgage debt the company was henceforth able to save up to £3,000 a year in interest charges.[25]

The authorised capital of the company under the Act of 1851 was divided between ordinary and preference shares as indicated in table 21. Although share registers for the 1850s point to a wider geographical spread in the pattern of ownership compared with the previous decade, Quaker share-holdings remained significant, and the Peases retained their position as the largest family holding (see below, p. 157). Their ascendancy at board level was also maintained. In August 1849 the company's managerial structure had been modified to embrace separate 'east' and 'west' sub-committees reflecting the recent extensions to the company's network. The new arrangements, with details of membership, were as follows:[26]

Sub-committee arrangements of the Management Committee after 1849

East	West
Thomas Meynell Jr.	Thomas Meynell Jr.
J. C. Hopkins	Henry Stobart
Isaac Wilson	Henry Pease
Alfred Kitching	Henry Pascoe Smith
Coach and Carrying Committee	Finance
Henry Pease	Joseph Pease
William Kitching	Alfred Kitching
J. C. Hopkins	John Pease
John Pease	
Locomotive Power (formerly Shildon Works)	Dues
Thomas Meynell Jr.	Thomas Meynell Jr.
Henry Stobart	Joseph Pease
John Pease	Alfred Kitching
Joseph Pease	J. C. Hopkins
	Isaac Wilson

The three Pease brothers were well represented, and together with their fellow Quaker, Alfred Kitching, controlled the finance committee. As chapter 7 will demonstrate, the Peases continued to dominate the company's managerial strategy throughout the 1850s, with a progressively more influential role being undertaken by Henry and John Pease, as their older brother's health began to decline.

Throughout the period of crisis in the affairs of the Stockton and Darlington company the Pease family was under considerable financial strain. As early as June 1846 Edward Pease noted in his diary that 'from the family business of the Coal Trade, Collieries, and in the Woollen Mills there is no income', and in his reflections on the year 1847 he concluded that 'in no preceding year have I passed through such a depth of conflict and trial owing to the extended trading and mining concerns of [my sons]'.[27] In that year both Joseph and his younger brother Henry received financial assistance from their brother-in-law, Francis Gibson, and the Quaker banker, Henry Birkbeck, and following the failure of the Union Bank of Newcastle in October 1847 Edward reluctantly agreed to sustain Joseph's credit as treasurer of the Stockton and Darlington Company by giving him an unlimited financial guarantee.[28] At the end of 1849 Edward noted that his family's railway shares had fallen in value by 'not less than thirty to forty thousand pounds', and following the company's revised leasing arrangements of 1850 he commented that 'S & D shares once deemed worth £360 have been sold at £30, so that property once deemed worth £60,000 [is] now worth £3,000.'[29] As for Joseph, the perpetual fear of financial insolvency began to affect his health; throughout the latter half of 1847 he was suffering from depression and insomnia, and by the early months of 1849 the first symptoms of glaucoma which were to lead to total blindness later in life had appeared.[30] There were, however, two sources of relief which eased Joseph's financial plight. In 1846 he had joined his father as a partner in Robert Stephenson and Co. and in 1849 his share of the profits amounted to £7,000 – the product of contract prices for locomotives negotiated before the onset of recession. Furthermore, the local coal trade began to show signs of revival during the course of 1849 as collieries formerly closed resumed working.[31] By that time the industry in the north-east had adjusted to the collapse of the Vend, and although there was a marked falling off in investment in new colliery winnings in Northumberland and Durham after 1844 (there were twenty-nine in the period 1844–50 compared with sixty-one between 1836 and 1843),[32] colliery owners were considerably aided by the growing demand for coke for ironworks and railways. The effect of this was to increase the demand for 'inferior' small coal so that by the end of the decade coke ovens were a common sight in the north-east, not least at the Peases' own Auckland collieries where there may have been as many as 500 coke ovens by 1850.[33]

The weakness of the Stockton and Darlington Company in the later 1840s lay in the way that it had been conceived and developed – as a mineral railway, first and foremost. This meant that at times of commercial uncertainty it did not have the staying power of the larger, if less profitable, trunk lines whose revenues were sustained by their greater concentration on passenger and light freight traffic. The company was thus dependent for its survival on the good will of its creditors, and in particular the Quaker financial connections of Joseph Pease. The latter were impressive by any standards, but the financial situation confronting the company was so serious in 1848–9 that rescue from that quarter was not possible. This was the essential background to the company's proposed leasing arrangement with George Hudson.

The experience of the Stockton and Darlington Company in the later 1840s provides a striking insight into the nature of British economic development in the mid-nineteenth century. Whilst Samuel Smiles – the arch-apostle of unbridled free enterprise and himself an employee of the South Eastern Railway – proclaimed in 1856 that 'Anybody who devotes himself to making money, body and soul, can scarcely fail to make himself rich, very little, very little brains will do',[34] the reality of the middle decades of the nineteenth century was very different. As Professor Church has pointed out, the period was, in fact, marked by 'relentless competitive pressure' as businessmen sought to deal as best they could with the squeeze on profitability following the major investment booms which were such a prominent feature of the British industrial economy after 1830.[35] As Joseph Pease stated in evidence before the Parliamentary Committee on Commercial Distress in 1848:

I know that for the last 10 or 12 years anything like the regular pursuit of business in manufacturing has, in nine cases out of ten, been entirely profitless, from the great fluctuations of capital and the value of articles; in fact the man who has made money has thriven by watching the rise and fall of his stock in trade, but the profits of industry have been perfectly minimal.[36]

It is not surprising, therefore, that by the end of 1850 Joseph was anxiously awaiting an increase in the Stockton and Darlington Company's traffic and dues from its traditional mineral traffic. As his diaries reveal, he was under no illusion that this was entirely dependent upon a revival in prosperity of the heavy industries of north-east England in general and the Tees and Wear valleys in particular.[37]

Commenting on Britain's economic history in the 1850s and 1860s the eminent Cambridge economist, Alfred Marshall, highlighted what he perceived to be the foundations of Britain's pre-eminence as a manufacturing and trading nation at that time. First and foremost was the movement towards free trade which had acted in concert with the home railway system, efficient banking and commercial facilities, and a dominant merchant marine to endow the country with 'exceptional facilities for the rapid and elastic adjustment of business'.[1] Britain's relative economic strength was also enhanced by military conflicts abroad, which not only enfeebled likely competitors, but also acted as a direct stimulus to home production in supplying the logistic needs of the warring states. All of these factors combined to increase greatly the value of overseas trade so that by the early 1870s Great Britain could justly be described as an 'export economy'. Marshall's conclusion that an exceptional period of buoyant trade enabled 'business men to make money, even when they were not throwing themselves with energy into that creative work by which industrial leadership is made and maintained'[2] was central to his thesis that Britain's relative decline as an economic power after 1870 could be ascribed in no small measure to entrepreneurial complacency and lethargy induced by the booming mid-century decades. In this respect, Marshall's view that 'rich old firms could thrive on their mere momentum'[3] dovetails well with Samuel Smiles' contemporary opinion on the ease with which profits could be made (see above, p. 144). Modern interpretations, however, lend little support to the notion of a generalised 'mid-Victorian boom'. Taking the years between 1850 and 1874 periods of recession were almost as extensive as those of expansion, whilst the three slumps of 1857, 1862, and 1865 were comparable in severity to those of 1826, 1837, and 1842.[4] Investment levels, both foreign and domestic, were not spectacular, especially when compared with those achieved in the succeeding Great Depression (1873–96) when the rate of growth of industrial production began to falter.[5] Moreover, there is little justification for the view that 'new wealth came forward in an atmosphere of exhilaration among men of business' in response to continually rising prices.[6] It is true that price inflation was noteworthy between 1853 and 1855, and again between 1870 and 1873, but in the intervening period stability of prices was the norm.[7] The idea of 'profit inflation' – the product of wages lagging behind prices – is also difficult to justify. Evidence of widening profit margins is thin with little to suggest that profits were in excess of the norms of the pre-1850 period or, indeed, of the succeeding Great Depression. In overall terms, therefore, it is difficult to disagree with the judgement that in the mid-Victorian decades, as at other times, 'For those who did not innovate and lacked the private sources required to sustain indifferent profits or losses, bankruptcy was the penalty.'[8] Failures in industry were commonplace in the 1850s and 1860s – from Coventry ribbon manufacturers succumbing to free trade, to the collapse of ship-building on the Thames after the Crimean War as a result of the move to iron-hulled vessels. Further crises occurred in the glass, boot and shoe, leather, and paper-making industries. Iron-making firms in south Wales, Shropshire, and Staffordshire were also hard pressed after 1850 as a result of new sources of competition. As Church has commented, such examples of industrial depression provide a warning against oversimplifications arising from Marshallion generalisations. They serve, in effect, to underline 'the regional basis of the mid-Victorian boom' as established producers were forced to respond to new competitive pressures arising, as often as not, from technological change.[9]

In its regional guise there can be no doubt that the mid-Victorian boom was at its most impressive in south Durham and north-east Yorkshire, with a particular focus on Teesside after 1850. The single factor which marked the onset of the decade as 'a major historical discontinuity' in the economic development of the area was the discovery in June 1850 of the Cleveland Main Seam of ironstone at Eston by the ironmaster, John Vaughan. It had been known for many years that iron ore was present in north-east Yorkshire, and during the first half of the nineteenth century geologists and naturalists had been joined by local ironmasters in a rather unsystematic search for workable deposits.[10] In 1850 Bolckow and Vaughan were themselves importing ironstone from the port of Whitby to the south of Cleveland, an area where small quantities of the raw material had been quarried from coastal outcrops or collected from beaches for at least a century before. The significance of the Eston discovery was that Vaughan had identified an outcrop of the Main Seam at a point where it was relatively pure and thick, and fortuitously located near to navigable water and the eastern terminus of the Stockton and Darlington network. Even before the end of 1850 Bolckow and Vaughan had begun to mine ironstone at Eston, and making use of a temporary tramway, soon to be replaced by a branch line to the Middles-brough and Redcar Railway, they sent 4,000 tons to their Witton Park

Table 22. *Advance of the iron trade: February 1855*

Firm	Number of blast furnaces
Consett (Derwent Iron Co.)	16
Witton Park (Bolckow and Vaughan)	4
South Durham Ironworks (Darlington)	2
Attwood, Stanhope	1
Attwood, Tow Law	4
Cochrane and Co., Middlesbrough	4
Gilkes and Co., Middlesbrough	4
Samuelson, Eston	3
Bolckow and Co., Eston	6
Hopkins and Snowdon	2
Bolckow and Co., Middlesbrough	4
Total	50

Source: Joseph Pease Diary, 19 February 1855.

furnaces. In 1851 the firm produced 118,000 tons of ironstone at Eston and in the same year the Derwent Iron Company, which had been handicapped since its inception by inadequate local ore supplies, also began to exploit the Main Seam on the Earl of Zetland's royalty at Upleatham.[11]

The commercial discovery of Cleveland ironstone acted as a major impetus to the development of the iron industry on Teesside. Bolckow and Vaughan were in the vanguard with the completion of three blast furnaces at their Middlesbrough Ironworks in 1852 with a further six coming into blast at their new Eston facility in 1853. By February 1855 fifty blast furnaces were in existence which were dependent upon supplies of Cleveland ironstone. Table 22, derived from Joseph Pease's diary, indicates the distribution of capacity at that time. Between 1851 and 1857 the production of pig-iron on Teesside increased tenfold. As Pease's table indicates, Bolckow and Vaughan were joined by Bernhard Samuelson at South Bank and Gilkes, Wilson, Leatham and Co. at Cargo Fleet in constructing ironworks along the line of the Middlesbrough and Redcar Railway. Other important pioneering firms were the Teesside Ironworks of William Hopkins and Thomas Snowdon, the Ormesby Ironworks of Alexander Brodie Cochrane, and on the north bank of the Tees, the Bell brothers' Port Clarence works headed by the talented metallurgist Isaac Lowthian Bell. Further west, at Darlington, the South Durham Ironworks completed the construction of two blast furnaces in 1855, thus inaugurating the first heavy industrial development in the old market town which had provided much of the impetus for the Stockton and Darlington Company. A number of these firms were linked to the railway company via the Pease family. Bolckow and Vaughan were an obvious case, but of the proprietors of the firm of Gilkes, Wilson, Leatham and Co., the Quaker Isaac Wilson had been induced to settle in Middlesbrough in the 1840s by Joseph Pease (see above, p. 134) and was himself father-in-law of the latter's cousin Joseph Beaumont Pease. Charles Leatham was Joseph's own son-in-law, having married Rachel, the elder of his two surviving daughters in 1851. The link with the South Durham Ironworks was even more direct: the firm was chaired by Henry Pease and contained among its directors a number of well-known Stockton and Darlington shareholders. Similarly, William Hopkins and Thomas Snowdon were closely associated with the Stockton and Darlington Railway.[12] These links are illustrative of the continuing strength of personalised entrepreneurial networks far into the nineteenth century in a general context of improving institutional arrangements for capital formation. What was emerging on Teesside after 1850 was a new geographically compact metallurgical district which owed its competitive strength to the availability of abundant raw materials, together with excellent port and transport facilities along the 'fuel artery' of the Stockton and Darlington Railway.[13]

As a distinguished visitor to Middlesbrough in 1861 W. E. Gladstone pronounced in grandiose terms that the town was 'the youngest child of England's enterprise ... it is an infant, but an infant Hercules'.[14] It was an apt description of a booming industrial town which had already outgrown the commercial limitations set by dependence on the coal shipping trade. In 1851 the population had edged up to 7,431 after the initial spurt of the 1830s. By 1861 it had reached 19,416, rising to 39,563 in 1871. During this period the town began to acquire the paraphernalia of civic institutions, as foreseen by William Fallows on the occasion of the visit of the Duke of Sussex in 1838. In 1853, when the principal civic dignitary in Darlington was the Chief Bailiff appointed by the Bishop of Durham, Middlesbrough was incorporated as a borough with Henry Bolckow as the first mayor, and following the Reform Act of 1867 it became a single-member parliamentary constituency with Bolckow again serving as the first member.

In a diary entry at the end of 1857 Joseph Pease noted, with evident astonishment, that in 1851 the Stockton and Darlington Company had booked 61,319 passengers at Middlesbrough: in 1854 the number was 89,679, and in 1857 it had reached 109,577.[15] The basis of this expansion was the iron trade in all its branches. In the year of Gladstone's visit, 334,000 tons of pig-iron were produced on the south bank of the Tees (see table 23), a figure which was probably nearer 500,000 tons for Teesside as a whole taking into account the output of furnaces on the north bank. In 1873, with the iron trade booming, the output of the whole of the Tees-based industry was over 2 million tons, accounting for one third of total British

Table 23. *The expansion of ironstone production and iron smelting on Teesside, 1861–71*

Year	Number of ironstone mines in Teesside region	Estimated output (tons)	Estimated value (£m)	Number of ironworks with smelting plants	Number of furnaces in blast	Estimated output of pig iron (tons)	Estimated value of pig iron output (£)
1861	7	1,060,000	159,000	14	49	334,000	1,000,000
1871	19	4,000,000	1,000,000	23	95	1,270,545	3,124,000

Source: Bullock, 'The origins of economic growth', tables 1 and 2, pp. 85–6.

output. In the same year, when Cleveland ironstone production was in excess of 5.5 million tons, more than ninety blast furnaces were in operation on Teesside, by which time it was the most important pig-iron-producing centre in the world. It was also in the forefront of technological advance and this had been an essential prerequisite for the industry's expansion. It is true that local ironmasters had the advantage of a river-mouth site, augmented by excellent rail communications giving easy access to the high-quality blast furnace coke of south Durham. But Cleveland ironstone, although available in prodigious quantity, was of poor quality in terms of iron content. To overcome this deficiency a series of innovations known locally as 'Cleveland practice' was introduced during the 1860s. These included larger-than-average blast furnaces, direct-acting blowing engines of high efficiency, and regenerative hot blast stoves.[16]

During these middle decades of the nineteenth century the expansion of overseas markets provided the momentum of growth for the UK iron industry. Teesside participated fully in this development. European trading links were forged, with Germany as a particularly important export market. In 1871, 269,000 tons of pig-iron were exported from Teesside, accounting for approximately a quarter of UK shipments overseas, whilst an additional 214,000 tons were sent to UK destinations. These figures represented 38 per cent of total pig-iron output on Teesside. The bulk of the output that was retained on Teesside itself was used for the manufacture of wrought-iron. Originally confined to Bolckow and Vaughan's Middlesbrough Ironworks, wrought-iron production expanded substantially after 1851. By 1861 Teesside possessed five works with an annual capacity of about 100,000 tons produced from 197 puddling furnaces and 35 rolling mills. The rail trade accounted for a considerable proportion of total wrought-iron output and the industry received a major boost in the later 1860s as a result of booming export markets in Europe, India and North America. In 1871 the number of works had reached twenty-four, containing 1,178 puddling furnaces. Over the years the manufacture of pig-iron and wrought-iron was complemented by the growth of the shipbuilding and heavy engineering trades. In 1862, Teesside shipbuilders launched approximately 10,000 tons of iron shipping, double the tonnage of wooden vessels. By that time the district had begun to develop engineering specialisms in bridge and marine engine construction, metal tube and pipe making, in addition to the manufacture of railway locomotives and rolling stock.

The growth of the iron and engineering industries had major implications for the coal trade in south Durham. By the early 1860s the Teesside iron trade had an annual requirement of at least 3 million tons of coal. To service this need substantial investment in new collieries was undertaken in the later 1850s. In 1858 the *Colliery Guardian* drew attention to 'the opening

Table 24. *Coal shipments from Middlesbrough, 1851–69*

Year	Coastwise (tons)	To foreign ports (tons)	Total (tons)
1851	388,646	88,808	477,454
1852	336,821	74,936	411,757
1853	289,135	89,334	378,469
1854	212,526	86,312	298,838
1855	142,205	92,505	234,710
1856	153,341	106,937	260,278
1857	158,367	117,390	275,757
1858	191,744	112,915	304,259
1859	197,526	103,606	301,132
1860	217,712	120,941	338,653
1861	202,444	142,392	344,836
1862	175,504	135,372	310,876
1863	178,493	128,116	306,609
1864	212,993	110,696	323,689
1865	193,935	145,373	339,308
1866	151,772	123,395	275,167
1867	138,309	107,142	245,451
1868	93,005	81,883	174,888
1869	76,198	67,662	143,860

Note: the figures up to 1860 incorporate shipments from Middlesbrough.
Source: Jeans, *Jubilee Memorial*, pp. 177–8.

out of thousands of acres of coal belonging to Lord Boyne and other owners on the line of the Auckland branch railway'.[17] Other recent developments included the sinking of new collieries at Oakenshaw and Brandon by Messrs Straker and Love, at Waterhouses and New Brancepeth by the Pease family, and also at the latter location by the Elswick Coal company. Further to the west, new pits were being opened out at Coundon, St Helens' Auckland, Hunswick, West Stanley, and Newton Cap.[18] So great was the industrial demand for coal on Teesside itself that the hitherto dominant export trade began to fall off significantly in the 1850s. Table 24 sets out the volume of coal shipments from Middlesbrough after 1851. Although there was some recovery towards the end of the decade, the downward trend continued into the 1860s. By 1873 total shipments from Middlesbrough had dwindled to 71,127 tons.

A further raw material source to be stimulated by the growth of the iron trade was the quarrying of limestone. In 1849 limestone shipments on the Stockton and Darlington Railway amounted to 139,632 tons. By 1855 they had reached 249,000 tons, with a further advance to 310,706 tons by 1860.

At the end of the 1860s the limestone traffic of Weardale, principally from quarries in the neighbourhood of Stanhope and Frosterley, was in excess of 500,000 tons per annum. Up to 1850 the sole users of raw materials for iron making were the Derwent Company and Bolckow and Vaughan at their Witton Park works. Twenty-five years later, Weardale limestone, ideally suited to the fluxing of Cleveland ironstone, was being utilised in nearly thirty ironworks possessing in excess of 150 blast furnaces.[19]

In his analysis of capital investment in the north-east of England in the nineteenth century A. G. Kenwood pointed out that in the years up to 1850 the expanding railway network acted as the pacemaker of regional economic growth primarily because it determined the rate at which the coal measures could be exploited. As Kenwood concluded, 'Through the familiar multiplier process, the initial impetus in railway construction led in widening arcs to increments of economic activity throughout the region far exceeding in their total volume the original outlay of investment.'[20] After 1850, however, the railways ceased to fulfil their former 'leading sector' role. Capital investment in the regional network continued to be significant, especially in south Durham and north-east Yorkshire, but the level was set by the rate of expansion of the iron and related industries. Thus, in the mid-Victorian decades, when the railways had moved from a 'constructive' to an 'operational' phase, 'Railway directors no longer justified further capital investment to their shareholders on the ground of estimated future receipts, but on the ground of its necessity to cope with a growing traffic. Existing railway facilities were being outgrown continually by the demands made on them by local industrialists.'[21] The last chapter is consistent with Kenwood's view that the initial impulse to economic growth in north-east England had run its course by 1850. For the Stockton and Darlington Company in particular, the commercial crisis of the later 1840s served only to highlight this fact, especially in view of the growth of intense rail and port competition on the north bank of the Tees. Thereafter, however, the company moved decisively into a new phase of development at a time when the industrialisation of Britain as a whole was proceeding to a new and more complex stage.[22] The effect of John Vaughan's discovery at Eston on the finances of the company was dramatic. By the end of 1851 it had not only resumed the payment of the guaranteed rental to the Wear Valley and Middlesbrough and Redcar Railways, but had also discharged the whole of the arrears.[23] Although the traffic revenues accruing from Bolckow and Vaughan's Witton Park works were reduced by the iron company's decision to construct new blast furnace capacity on Teesside, the link with the Derwent Iron company at Consett was especially lucrative in view of the firm's Cleveland iron ore and Weardale limestone requirements. As Tomlinson observed:

Table 25. *Report to the directors of the Stockton and Darlington Railway from the secretary, increase of traffic, 1849–53*

Number of tons taken over 1 mile in the year ending	30 June 1849 =	21,266,991
	31 Dec. 1853 =	48,158,208
	INCREASE	26,158,208
Number of locomotive engines	1849	64
	1853	68
Number of chaldron waggons	1849	6,350
	1853	8,397
Gross revenue in the year ending	30 June 1849	£147,367 7s 4d
	31 Dec. 1853	£241,314 19s 4d
	INCREASE	£93,947 12s 0d
Amount expended on capital up to	31 June 1849	£974,166 5s 8d
	31 Dec. 1853	£1,049,276 11s 1½d
	INCREASE	£75,109 5s 5½d
Total coal and coke shipments	1849	1,181,392 tons
	1853	1,469,672 tons
	INCREASE	282,280 tons
Total ironstone shipments	half-year ending 31 Dec. 1849	27,712 tons
	half-year ending 31 Dec. 1852	230,873 tons
	INCREASE	203,161 tons
Total merchandise shipments	half-year ending 31 Dec. 1849	95,273 tons
	half-year ending 31 Dec. 1852	148,759 tons
	INCREASE	53,486 tons

Source: PRO RAIL 667/180.

The Stockton and Darlington Railway Company had reason to congratulate themselves on the quite fortuitous circumstances that their system at one point touched the very edge of the ironstone field and at another, 54 miles away, was in contact with the principal ironworks of Co. Durham. It practically put £10,000 a year into the hands of the fortunate company. Dividends rose from 4 to 10 per cent and the holders of Stockton and Darlington stock became, as at an earlier period in the history of the company, the most envied of all railway proprietors.[24]

That Tomlinson grossly underestimated the traffic revenues from Teesside to the Wear valley is confirmed by the contract negotiated between the Stockton and Darlington and Derwent Companies in September 1851 for mineral shipments. This was to be of seven years' duration with charges of 4s per ton for ironstone and limestone and 3s per ton for coal.[25] According to an estimate prepared by John Dixon in 1857 the annual contract revenue from ironstone traffic alone (running at approximately 300,000 tons per annum at that date) was well in excess of £14,000.[26] So dramatic was the upturn in the Stockton and Darlington Company's fortunes after the uncertainties and anxieties of the late 1840s that the company secretary,

Table 26. *Tons of minerals and goods conveyed on the Stockton and Darlington Railway, 1850–60*

	1850	1851	1852	1853	1854	1855	1860
Coal and coke exported	491,734	441,352	372,065	329,663	249,624	186,448	
Coal and coke for landsale (excl. York junction)	514,814	548,951	515,969	611,100	800,096	960,314	2,045,596
Coal and coke to York junction	323,796	407,960	427,177	528,909	529,236	481,550	
Lime	35,645	40,748	36,060	39,535	48,499	46,988	
Limestone	67,706	79,856	77,566	92,315	154,763	249,660	1,484,409
Cleveland ironstone	—	181,909	275,119	372,346	420,186	533,910	
Goods	171,455	216,302	216,478	256,738	388,137	451,214	587,765
Sundries	249,920	154,431	61,753	116,235	164,197	116,639	
Total	1,905,070	2,075,509	1,979,195	2,346,841	2,754,738	3,026,723	

Sources: PRO RAIL 667/396 (1850–5); Jeans, *Jubilee Memorial*, p. 125 (1860).

Table 27. *Collieries, ironstone mines, and limestone quarries served by the Stockton and Darlington Railway, 1855*

Collieries	Shildon Lodge, St Helens, Woodhouse Close, West Auckland, Norwood, Evenwood, Cragwood, West Tees, West Hartley, East Butterknowle, Rowntree, Copley Bent, Adelaide, South Durham, Black Boy, Old Etherley, Witton Park, Marshall Green, North Bitchburn, Howden, Bitchburn, Low Bitchburn, Constantine, Woodfield, Cold Knote, White Lee, Peases West, Black Prince, Inkerman, Thornley.
Ironstone mines/limestone quarries	Upleatham, Eston, Hutton, Normanby, Belmont, Rookhope, Constantine, Frosterley, Bishopley, Broadwood, Stanhope, Middridge, Eldon, Old Tom, Aycliffe.

Source: PRO RAIL 667/739.

Thomas MacNay, drew up the statistical summary, reproduced in table 25, for the directorate early in 1854. The composite figures in table 26 confirm the statistical trend after 1850 of substantially rising traffic volumes in all categories except coal and coke exports, lime and sundries. Particularly noteworthy is the rapid growth of ironstone shipments. These had reached well over half a million tons in 1855 by which time this category of traffic was accounting for 22 per cent of gross revenues. By 1855 the Stockton and Darlington Company was meeting the whole of the traffic needs of thirty collieries, mainly in the Auckland coalfield, and fifteen ironstone mines and limestone quarries (see table 27). With a mineral and freight locomotive fleet in excess of fifty, the traffic was shipped in more than 15,000 waggons.[27]

The physical expansion of the Stockton and Darlington network in the 1850s and early 1860s was funded by the conventional means of share issues and borrowing. The practice was also continued of establishing ostensibly independent undertakings which were then absorbed into the Stockton and Darlington Company after their lines were completed. In this respect, however, the developments of the 1850s facilitated far more than the expansion of traffic: by the end of the decade the company had acquired a position of major importance in the evolving railway network of northern England by virtue of its strategic location between the London and North Western Railway to the west of the Pennines, and the North Eastern Railway in north Yorkshire and Co. Durham. Table 28 describes the Stockton and Darlington Company's capital structure in May 1858, augmented by parliamentary Acts obtained in 1851, 1852, and 1855, and immediately before a major amalgamation with associated undertakings. From the outset of the decade the practice had been adopted of distributing

Table 28. *Capital structure of the Stockon and Darlington Railway Company, May 1858*

Ordinary shares	£1,000,000
Class A preference shares (5%)	450,000
Class B preference shares (6%)	849,950
Class C preference shares (6%)	178,000
Total	£2,477,950

Source: PRO RAIL 667/1645, Stockton and Darlington Railway half-yearly report, 30 June 1858.

Table 29. *Authorised loan structure of the Stockton and Darlington Railway Company, 1858*

Stockton and Darlington loans	£497,390	19s	9d
Branch line loans	78,939	2s	10d
Total	£576,330	2s	7d

Source: PRO RAIL 667/1645, Stockton and Darlington Railway half-yearly report, 10 August 1860.

additional capital 'rateably amongst the Proprietors' with calls spread over a five-year period. This applied equally to ordinary and preference shares. Revenue obtained from calls on the former was used primarily for infrastructure purposes and additions to the locomotive and rolling stock fleets. Thus, the ordinary share capital raised under the Act of 1854 provided funding for the construction of a tunnel branch from St Helens' Auckland to the northern end of the existing Shildon Tunnel. This was an important milestone in the Stockton and Darlington Company's history since it facilitated the elimination of the Brusselton inclines and stationary engines, and hence the spread of locomotive working in the Gaunless Valley and beyond.[28] With strongly rising traffic volumes after 1850 the inclines had developed into a major bottleneck, all the more so since the network to the west of Shildon contained the last vestiges of horse-drawn operations on the part of the Stockton and Darlington Company. The preference shares were used to build up a fund for the repayment of loans, with the additional objective of reducing the average interest payable at any point in time. Under the company's Act of 1858 a clause was inserted providing for the extinction of the authorised loans indicated in table 29 over a thirteen-year period ending in 1872.

Table 30. *Dividend warrant received by Henry Pease, 15 February 1855 (for the half-year ending 31 December 1854)*

Shares		£	s	d	£	s	d
Stockton and Darlington Railway shares							
Preference A shares paid up at	12s 6d						
Preference A shares calls paid	5s 6d						
Preference B shares paid up	10s 0d						
40 ordinary shares paid up	22s 6d	45	0	0			
418 ordinary shares calls paid	16s 10d	351	16	4			
410 ordinary shares calls paid	1s 6d	30	15	0			
(New shares under the Act of 1854)					427	11	4
Wear Valley shares							
26 £50 shares at	30s 0d	39	0	0			
12 £25 shares at	15s 0d	9	0	0	48	0	0
Middlesbrough and Redcar shares							
10 £50 shares at	30s 0d	15	0	0			
£25 shares paid up	15s 0d						
6 £25 shares calls paid	8s 11/2	2	8	9	17	8	9
					493	0	1
Income tax					28	15	2
Dividend payable					£464	4	11

Source: PRO RAIL 667/1401.

In terms of the pattern of share ownership the practice of pro rata distribution, together with prolonged share calls, ensured stability in what had come to be the hallmark of the Stockton and Darlington Company as a public joint stock enterprise. As before, the Peases continued to be the dominant family grouping with substantial holdings in all of the company's interests. An excellent example of this is provided by table 30 which reproduces the dividend warrant issued to Henry Pease for the half-year ending 31 December 1854.

It was Henry Pease who was to emerge as the Stockton and Darlington Company's principal strategist in the latter half of the 1850s, conducting relations with neighbouring undertakings and providing the driving force for an invaluable trans-Pennine railway link to the mineral-rich district of Furness in Cumberland. In the first half of the decade, however, before he succumbed to glaucoma, entrepreneurial initiative was demonstrated most forcefully by Joseph Pease.

In September 1851 the aged Edward Pease noted in his diary the recently announced proposal for 'a railway near Guisboro' south of the Eston hills.[29] This was the Middlesbrough and Guisborough Railway, a scheme which had been rejected by a majority within the Stockton and Darlington management committee 'who thought the whole thing ... chimerical'.[30] Although the new railway differed little from the mineral lines promoted by the Stockton and Darlington Company before 1850, owing its rationale to the discovery of Cleveland ironstone, the timing of the project in the aftermath of the financial difficulties of the late 1840s was no doubt a critical consideration. The company's recent experience with leased lines was a further factor encouraging caution. The Middlesbrough and Guisborough Railway was therefore projected by Joseph Pease and his oldest son Joseph Whitwell, as a demonstration of their own faith in the potential traffic revenues to be derived from ironstone shipments. The Peases subscribed £5,000 to the project and also took a lease of the Cod Hill ironstone royalty at Hutton Lowcross. Despite these confidence-boosting actions the subscription list filled up slowly, and even after the railway had received parliamentary authorisation in June 1852 further difficulties were encountered in raising sufficient capital for the construction of the line. Although Joseph was able to persuade his fellow Stockton and Darlington directors to subscribe £16,750 out of a total investment of £56,075, the funding shortfall was only closed by the Peases' offer of guaranteed consecutive annual dividends of 3, 4.5, 5, and 6 per cent. As a speculative enterprise the Middlesbrough and Guisborough Railway was an outstanding success. From its opening in November 1853 mineral traffic boomed and five years later the line was absorbed by the Stockton and Darlington Company on terms of a guaranteed income of 6 per cent on a capital of £96,000.[31]

In the same year that the Middlesbrough and Guisborough Railway received the Royal Assent a long-standing project was revived in south-west Durham for a rail link between Darlington and Barnard Castle, a small market town sixteen miles to the west of Darlington up the Tees valley. As the parliamentary member for the South Durham constituency Joseph Pease had undertaken surveys of a possible route at his own expense during the 1830s,[32] but it was not until 1844, when the carpet and shoe-lace manufacturers of Barnard Castle joined forces with the Stockton and Darlington Company that the project became a live issue. The stage was then set for a repetition of history since the main objector to the proposed line was Henry Vane, the second Duke of Cleveland. Vane's seat at Raby Castle stood in the way of the most convenient route and his considered response to a delegation of railway supporters was to point to the excellence of the turnpike road from Darlington to Barnard Castle. Since the proposed railway would interfere with his 'private comforts' the Duke concluded the interview with the warning that he would oppose the project 'whatever way it comes'.[33] As a member of the frustrated delegation Joseph Pease summed up the collective feeling: 'You see the man with whom you have to deal;

beyond his own private interests and comforts he has not a feeling. All argument with him is in vain.'[34] Perhaps hoping that the passage of time and the evident benefits of railways would mellow the Duke's opposition the Barnard Castle interest waited until 1852 before reviving the scheme. With Joseph's backing the Stockton and Darlington Company agreed to work the line on completion and charge only half of the costs of maintenance and haulage until the annual dividend on the new railway reached 4 per cent. The company also undertook to secure subscriptions to the value of £22,000 for the project. A bill of incorporation was drawn up and considered by a House of Commons committee in May 1853. The Duke of Cleveland, however, was still implacable in his opposition, having convinced himself that the project was 'the device of a scheming and Artful Individual to deceive the people of Barnard Castle for his own benefit' since it would reduce the cost of coal shipments along the Tees valley from the Peases' Auckland collieries.[35] Although Joseph rejected this charge by pointing out that an alternative route, north-east from Barnard Castle to Bishop Auckland, would be of greater advantage to his interest, the bill was rejected in June 1853. Ironically, when the promoters renewed their application in the autumn they were confronted by a rival scheme based upon the north-eastern route. The projected Barnard Castle and Bishop Auckland Railway was the focal point of an ambitious plan to link the ports of Liverpool and Sunderland. The product of an alliance between William Watson and his nephew, solicitors of Barnard Castle, and the West Hartlepool interests led by Ralph Ward Jackson, the scheme could not fail but to revive the kind of antagonism which had characterised the relationship between the Stockton and Darlington Company and Christopher Tennant. Feelings were heightened by Ward Jackson himself who used the occasion of his appearance before a parliamentary committee to launch a personal attack on Joseph Pease, accusing him of 'attempting to control, autocratically, the entire district'.[36] This was a reference not only to the Darlington–Barnard Castle link, but also to the Stockton and Darlington Company's Tunnel Branch bill then before Parliament. If authorised, the latter could only have detrimental effects on the volume of mineral traffic on Ward Jackson's West Hartlepool network. For Ward Jackson, therefore, the Liverpool–Sunderland link provided the opportunity to break the Stockton and Darlington Company's stranglehold over the greater part of the mineral traffic emanating from the Auckland coalfield.

By the autumn of 1853 the Duke of Cleveland was in the grip of 'Pease-phobia'[37] which could only have been intensified when a Commons committee approved the Darlington and Barnard Castle line in May 1854 on the grounds that it presented few engineering problems, and, in contrast to Ward Jackson's scheme, was strongly supported in Barnard Castle. When

24   Henry Pease (1807–81), chief promoter of the South Durham and Lancashsire Union Railway. Unenthusiastic about a merger between the Stockton and Darlington and the North Eastern Railway Companies, Pease eventually served as vice-chairman of the latter company's York board.

the line was opened in July 1856, however, the Duke attended the customary ceremony. He expressed the magnanimous hope that all past difficulties between his family and the Stockton and Darlington interest would be speedily forgotten. Cynics no doubt noted that he was to be permitted to appoint a director of the new railway for life.[38]

   The successful projection of the Darlington and Barnard Castle Railway was the catalyst for a new and vastly more ambitious scheme for a westwards extension into Lancashire and Westmorland. This was strongly canvassed in Barnard Castle, but the major impetus came from the Stockton and Darlington Company with Henry Pease taking the leading role. For the latter the point had been reached when a trans-Pennine line made sound commercial sense. Cleveland ironstone with its high silica content was not of the highest quality and by the mid-1850s the Derwent Iron Company was mixing Cleveland ore with richer hematite ores obtained from the Whitehaven district of Cumberland via the Newcastle and Carlisle Railway.[39] In order to adopt the same practice the Teesside ironworks were obliged to obtain their supplies of hematite ore from Ulverston in south Cumberland using a tortuous route to the south via Normanton and Leeds. Now, the completion of the Darlington and Barnard Castle Railway opened up the prospect of a far more direct link with Ulverston. The result of these considerations was the launching in August 1856 of the aptly named South Durham and Lancashire Union Railway to form a link between the Stockton and Darlington network and the Lancaster and Carlisle Railway at Tebay in Westmorland. The new line was also designed to link Barnard Castle with the Auckland coalfield via a terminus with the Stockton and Darlington Company's Hagger Leases branch. The chief promoter was Henry Pease in collaboration with banking interests in Kendal and several other long-standing members of the Stockton and Darlington directorate, including Henry Pascoe Smith, Isaac Wilson, W. R. I. Hopkins, and J. H. Stobart. The line was estimated to cost £375,000 to construct and the Pease family alone subscribed £15,000 to the project.[40]

The South Durham and Lancashire Union Railway Bill encountered little parliamentary opposition and received the Royal Assent on 13 July 1857. Capitalised at £400,000, the new line was completed in July 1861. It was one of the triumphs of mid-Victorian railway engineering. The Stainmoor summit was 1,374 feet above sea level and Robert Stephenson and Co. were invited to design a new and more powerful locomotive to cope with the severe gradients. Thomas Bouch, brother of the Stockton and Darlington Company's locomotive superintendent and designer of the ill-fated Tay Bridge, was the engineer of the line which possessed some of the most spectacular railway viaducts in Britain, the three longest constructed of wrought-iron girders from ironworks on Teesside.[41] In 1856, at the inception of the project, Joseph Pease had commented to his brother Henry, destined to be vice-chairman of the company, that if 'the busy, bustling, whistling railway ever traverse[s] Stainmoor's wintry wastes, or the industrialists beyond be supplied with cheapened and excellent fuel, they that profit thereby, and rejoice therein, will doubtless have much to thank thee for in thy exertions and perseverance'.[42] Such romantic sentiments should not be allowed to detract from the obvious commercial attractions of the project.

In July 1858, the Stockton and Darlington Company effected an amalgamation with all of its associated undertakings – the Wear Valley, Middlesbrough and Redcar, Middlesbrough and Guisborough, and Darlington and

Table 31. *Capital structure of the Stockton and Darlington Railway Company after the amalgamation of 1858*

	£
Class A, existing preference shares 5%	450,000
Class B, Wear Valley and Redcar shares, 6% preference	850,000
Class C. Guisborough and Barnard Castle, 6% preference	200,000
Ordinary shares	1,380,000
Total capital	2,880,000

Source: Stockton and Darlington Railway Amalgamation Act, 23 July 1858.

Barnard Castle Railways. Each shareholder in the absorbed companies received preference shares in the Stockton and Darlington Railway, thus creating the capital structure set out in table 31. The fact of the amalgamation, together with the working of the South Durham and Lancashire Union line by the Stockton and Darlington Company, served to confirm the latter's strategic position in the evolving railway network of northern England. When the trans-Pennine route opened for mineral traffic on 4 July 1861, six trains hauling 600 tons of Durham coal and coke left the Auckland coalfield for Tebay, whilst 150 tons of hematite ore reached Teesside from the west. A new pattern of mineral traffic was being established and the principal casualty was the North Eastern Railway (NER). Within weeks of its opening the South Durham and Lancashire Union Railway had severely reduced the NER's trans-Pennine mineral shipments, not least from the Peases' own collieries where the amount of fuel destined for north Lancashire and Ulverston fell from 20,000 tons in the last six months of 1860 to only 959 tons in the corresponding period of 1861.[43]

The NER had been formed in 1854 as a result of the merger of the York and North Midland, the Leeds Northern, and the York, Newcastle, and Berwick Railways. Following in the wake of the formation of the LNWR, it was one of several large-scale amalgamations in the British railway system at that time. Controlling 720 route miles extending through much of north Yorkshire, Durham, and Northumberland, the NER possessed the most extensive, yet geographically compact railway network in Britain,[44] a fact which had not escaped the notice of a select committee of the House of Commons appointed in 1852 under the chairmanship of Edward Cardwell to consider the likely effects of railway company amalgamations. The Cardwell Committee took a hostile view of amalgamations in principle, but its suspension of the NER merger was overridden in Parliament. The company was formed, moreover, when the Cleveland ore field was in the early stages of exploitation, and the new concern naturally wished to secure a portion of the resulting mineral traffic as well as to consolidate its position in the carriage of coal and freight in Northumberland and Durham. It might be thought, therefore, that as a direct rival to the Stockton and Darlington Company, relations between the two undertakings could hardly be harmonious. Almost from the date of the merger, however, a cooperative spirit was evident, even to the extent of merger discussions. Although the latter ultimately proved abortive, under an agreement of January 1854 the companies undertook to avoid competition in mineral traffic as far as practicable and to cooperate for their mutual benefit.[45] In 1855, for example, the Act for the incorporation of the Dearness Valley Railway, which had been promoted by Joseph Pease and Joseph Whitwell Pease to serve their new colliery on the royalty of Lord Boyne at Waterhouses to the west of Durham, provided for the working of the line by the NER, some of whose directors had taken shares to the value of £15,000 in the new railway.[46] A further indication of the close working relationship between the two companies was provided by their joint response to the collapse of the Derwent Iron Company in 1857 as a result of the failure of the Northumberland and Durham District Bank. This was one of several mid-Victorian banking calamities which were the product of overlending to industrial concerns. They were to reach a climax in 1878 with the failure of the City of Glasgow Bank, an event which presaged the withdrawal of the banking system from the long-term financing of industry.[47] The Derwent Iron Company had grown too rapidly for a banking concern which had been imprudent enough to lend £1 million on the security of £250,000 of promissory notes and a mortgage of £100,000 on the company's plant.[48]

The difficulty posed by the collapse of the iron company was that it generated a considerable mineral traffic in the north-east of England with an annual value in excess of £60,000 on the Stockton and Darlington network alone, and with so much capital sunk in local transport facilities there were pressing commercial reasons for preventing the break-up of such a large concern.[49] In 1858 the company was kept afloat by parties already connected with it and was also considerably aided by the joint action of the Stockton and Darlington Company and the NER, who, as major trade creditors, agreed to the suspension of traffic dues for a period of two years up to a combined total for both companies of £200,000.[50] The firm which eventually emerged in 1864 after a protracted process of reconstruction[51] was the Consett Iron Company, which, in marked contrast to its predecessor, proved to be technically efficient and ultimately highly profitable.[52] Throughout this period members of the Pease family, in particular Joseph Whitwell, were actively involved in financing the reconstruction[53] and it was due to Pease influence that their nominee, David Dale, was introduced to the management of the company. In 1846 Dale had begun his business

25   Ralph Ward Jackson, founder of West Hartlepool as a rival port to
Middlesbrough. Ward Jackson, like Christopher Tennant before him, was
an inveterate opponent of the Stockton and Darlington Railway Company.

career as a clerk in the Wear Valley Railway Company's office and in 1854
Joseph Pease had appointed him secretary to the Middlesbrough and Guis-
borough Railway. After the reconstruction of the Consett Iron Company,
Dale was appointed joint managing director (with Jonathan Priestman).[54]
   Other factors impelling the Stockton and Darlington Company and the

NER to greater cooperation were the threat to the former posed by the ambitious Ralph Ward Jackson and to the latter by attempted encroachments on its north-eastern traffic by other large railway companies. In Ward Jackson's case the successful merger in 1853 of his Hartlepool West Harbour and Dock Company with the Stockton and Hartlepool Railway inaugurated 'The Struggle for the Cleveland Ironstone District'.[55] Ward Jackson was intent upon securing access to the ironstone royalties leased by the Bell brothers at Normanby and Skelton. His major and obvious problem was how to link the ore field with a transport network centred on the north bank of the Tees. This he attempted to overcome in 1859 by projecting the Durham and Cleveland Union Railway with trains crossing the Tees on a steam ferry. The Stockton and Darlington response was aggressive in the extreme. As well as proposing to extend the recently absorbed Middlesbrough and Redcar Railway to Saltburn to increase mineral traffic from the Upleatham and Skelton ironstone royalties, the company proposed to connect its Middlesbrough and Guisborough line with Ward Jackson's own West Hartlepool system by means of a swing-bridge across the Tees.[56] At this point relations between Ward Jackson and the Stockton and Darlington interests had reached a low ebb. It is apparent from surviving correspondence that Ward Jackson was deeply aggrieved at 'personal abuse' and 'attacks on his credit' perpetrated by Stockton and Darlington directors in general and Joseph Whitwell Pease in particular. As Ward Jackson remarked, 'I consider it as inexcusable in a neighbouring Company to run down another by private accusation and scandal.'[57] Despite his injured feelings Ward Jackson was prepared to extend an olive branch, even to the extent of repeating an earlier offer for a fusion of interests. The Stockton and Darlington response, however, was deeply antagonistic, with John Pease accusing Ward Jackson of unacceptable poaching of coal traffic. In this respect Pease stated uncompromisingly,

Whilst I admit that the commerce of the kingdom is open to all and that *a fair and honourable competition* is not to be thoughtlessly deprecated, it would seem to me impossible that thy policy could be regarded as such ... thy movements have ever seemed to be a series of aggressions at once unprovoked and unreasoning. The Stockton and Darlington Railway has been most unblushingly assailed and in a way which they conceive has no parallel in the history of railway conflict; not one single stone would appear ever to have been unturned or opportunity missed to diminish the Stockton and Darlington Company's resources by abstraction of traffic. They are not aware on the other hand that upon any occasion they have intruded into your district or acted otherwise than strictly on the defensive.[58]

After an intense parliamentary struggle fought with 'consummate skill and self-possession' by Ward Jackson and Joseph Pease, the former was permitted to construct a railway from Guisborough to ironstone mines at

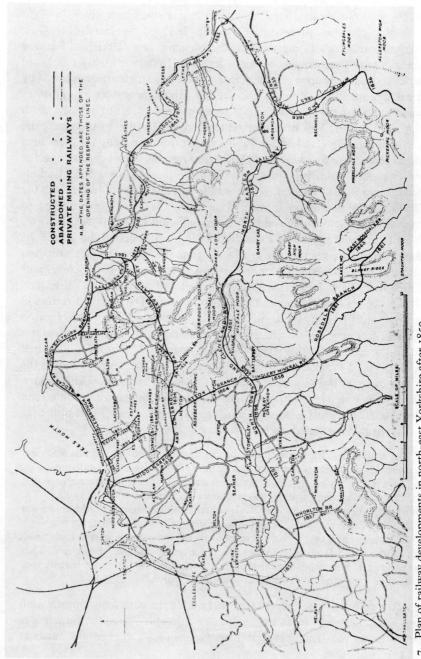

7 Plan of railway developments in north-east Yorkshire after 1850.

Skinningrove; there was to be no link to the Tees, thus placing the new line, to be known as the Cleveland Railway, at the mercy of the Stockton and Darlington Company. On the other hand, the latter was not permitted to bridge the Tees, although the Saltburn extension was sanctioned. As Tomlinson observed, it was something of a drawn battle.[59] Eventually, after further parliamentary struggles and much local obstruction emanating from the Pease-dominated Tees Conservancy Commission, Ward Jackson achieved his objective. In 1861 he received parliamentary sanction to extend the Cleveland Railway to a jetty on the Normanby estate from which loaded waggons of ironstone were to be transported across the Tees in open barges.[60] The price paid, however, was a high one: Ward Jackson was financially overstretched and in 1865 his West Hartlepool Company was absorbed by the NER.[61]

These events in Cleveland must be viewed in relation to the wider interests of the Stockton and Darlington Company. On the one hand competition for the Cleveland mineral traffic was intensifying and on the other the point had been reached by the end of the 1850s when a choice would have to be made between even greater cooperation with the NER or involvement in unwelcome competition with the larger company in west and south Durham. The eventual decision – for an amalgamation with the NER – was precipitated by an attempt launched in 1860 by the LNWR to link the Newcastle and Carlisle Railway with the Stockton and Darlington network via the projected Newcastle and Derwent Railway. This would have been the final link in a line of communication from Liverpool to Newcastle and would have enabled the predatory LNWR to penetrate the heart of the NER system with the possibility of a northern link to Edinburgh.[62] In the event, the Stockton and Darlington Company withheld its support and the Newcastle and Derwent scheme therefore lapsed. By the time the LNWR had devised a further scheme of invasion involving the construction of a new line of considerable length with running powers over part of the South Durham and Lancashire Union Railway, negotiations for an amalgamation between the Stockton and Darlington Company and the NER were all but complete.[63]

The negotiations began in December 1859 at the York headquarters of the NER.[64] They proceeded smoothly from the outset. The Stockton and Darlington delegation, led by John Pease, had as its main objective the establishment of full local control over the old Stockton and Darlington network, preferably by retaining the Darlington-based management committee intact for a period of twenty years. In view of the way in which the line had evolved – as a mineral railway serving local mines and quarries – this was not an unreasonable request. The NER response was that it would be simpler for designated Stockton and Darlington directors to join the NER board and that 'to them should be assigned for the specified period the

26   Joseph Pease, *c.* 1860.

management of Stockton and Darlington traffic'. Mutual good will was
evident in the inevitable compromise: following the amalgamation a 'Darlington Committee' would be established which would exist for ten years
with a possible extension of a further two years. Two NER directors would
sit on the committee whilst three members of the Stockton and Darlington
management committee would join the NER board.[65] By March 1860
agreement had been reached in principle and in July 1863 an amalgamation
bill received the Royal Assent after a smooth parliamentary passage. In 1862
the NER had absorbed the Newcastle and Carlisle Railway and, as noted
above, the Ward Jackson empire succumbed in 1865. By these three amalgamations the NER came to be acknowledged as 'the most complete monopoly
in the United Kingdom'.[66]

Table 32. *Capital structure of the Stockton and Darlington Railway Company, 1 January 1863*

	£	
Preference 'A' shares	450,000	
Preference 'B' and 'C' shares	1,050,000	
Preference 'D' shares	535,000	
		2,035,000
Ordinary shares		2,016,000
Loans		759,946
Total		£4,810,946

Source: PRO RAIL 667/1854.

Table 33. *Ordinary share dividends of the Stockton and Darlington Railway Company, 1852–62*

Half-year	Ordinary share dividend %
Jan. 1852 – June 1852	4
July 1852 – Dec. 1852	4
Jan. 1853 – June 1853	5
July 1853 – Dec. 1853	3½
Jan. 1854 – June 1854	7½
July 1854 – Dec. 1854	9
Jan. 1855 – June 1855	9
July 1855 – Dec. 1855	9
Jan. 1856 – June 1856	9
July 1856 – Dec. 1856	10
Jan. 1857 – June 1857	10
July 1857 – Dec. 1857	10
Jan. 1858 – June 1858	8½
July 1858 – Dec. 1858	9½
Jan. 1859 – June 1859	9½
July 1859 – Dec. 1859	9
Jan. 1860 – June 1860	9
July 1860 – Dec. 1860	9½
Jan. 1861 – June 1861	9½
July 1861 – Dec. 1861	9½
Jan. 1862 – June 1862	7½
July 1862 – Dec. 1862	8

Source: PRO RAIL 667/1633–1654, accountant's records.

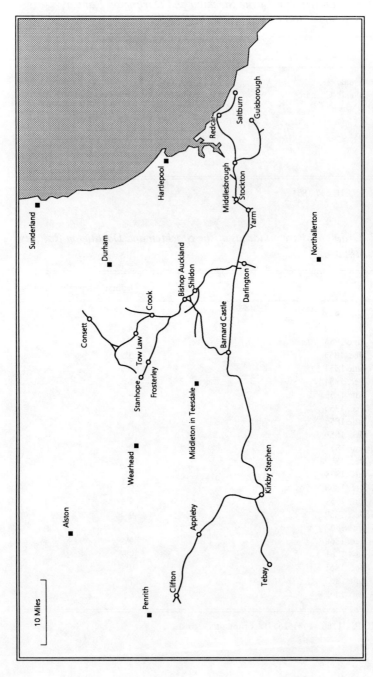

8   The Stockton and Darlington Railway network on the eve of the amalgamation with the North Eastern Railway, 1863.

Although failing health prevented Joseph Pease from taking an active part in the merger discussions, it is clear that the Stockton and Darlington negotiators acted in accordance with his wishes. Following the agreement of March 1860 Joseph noted in his diary that the decision in favour had been a unanimous one on the Stockton and Darlington board 'save my brother Henry who thinks we merge our usefulness and lose Caste'.[67] It may be assumed that Henry was appeased not only by his appointment as chairman of the Darlington Committee in 1863, an office which he held until the eventual winding up of the committee in 1879, but also by the liberal financial settlement whereby it was agreed that Stockton and Darlington shareholders should receive 15¼ per cent of the post-merger receipts, as well as the sum of £225 for every £100 of stock.[68]

For the NER the Stockton and Darlington merger represented a major strategic advance. Even at the time of the negotiations the latter company was continuing to expand its mineral traffic network. The Eden Valley Railway, projected by the Stockton and Darlington interests in 1858 provided a line from Clifton to the south of Penrith to Kirkby Stephen. It opened for traffic on 8 April 1862 when it began to feed hematite ore from Whitehaven through to Teesside via the South Durham and Lancashire Union Railway. A further Stockton and Darlington project which received parliamentary authorisation on 28 June 1861, was the Frosterley and Stanhope Railway. Opening for traffic seven months later than the Eden Valley line, it facilitated expansion in the supply of limestone to the Teesside iron industry. The final and logical development for the Stockton and Darlington company was to absorb the South Durham and Lancashire Union, the Eden Valley, and Frosterley and Stanhope Railways. This was accomplished on 30 June 1862, even before the Frosterley and Stanhope line had opened for traffic. In the meantime two further Stockton and Darlington Company Acts of Parliament had augmented the share capital. The first Act, passed on 15 May 1860, permitted the raising of £250,000 in ordinary shares, and £83,000 in loans, whilst the second, passed on 22 July 1861, authorised a further £287,000 in ordinary share capital. On the eve of the formal amalgamation in 1863 the capital structure of the Stockton and Darlington Company was as shown in table 32. By the standards of the 1860s a paid-up capital of less than £5 million was a modest total for a railway company. By 1870, the NER itself possessed a paid-up capital in excess of £40 million, whilst the LNWR was already capitalised at more than £29 million in 1851.[69] But this should not be permitted to downgrade the significance of the merger from the standpoint of the NER. Apart from the fact that the two companies had established cooperative working well before the merger, there were several key considerations of which the NER directorate was no doubt well aware. In the first instance there were considerable attractions in gaining control of an expanding route network which was strategically located in relation to the supply of abundant industrial raw materials. The fact that the whole of the 1850s had witnessed booming traffic in the transport of heavy minerals in the wake of the expansion of the iron trade had encouraged the NER itself to develop this aspect of its operations. Secondly, the east–west configuration of the Stockton and Darlington network was an ideal complement to the north–south orientation of the NER's own lines, all the more so since the Stockton and Darlington Company held the key to the entry of the LNWR into the north-east of England. A third consideration was the evident prosperity of the Stockton and Darlington Company, as indicated by the dividend record during the 1850s and early 1860s (see table 33). With a mean annual dividend of 9½ per cent on ordinary shares in the latter half of the 1850s the Stockton and Darlington Company's record compared extremely favourably with other railway companies. This is confirmed by table 34 which takes 1859 as a representative year for the decade as a whole. But not only was the Stockton and Darlington Company highly prosperous, it was also a well-managed concern. The expansion of the network in the 1850s, building on the Weardale and north Yorkshire extensions of previous decades, was extremely well conceived in relation to potential traffic flows. Indeed, it was Henry Pease's proud boast in 1863 that the Stockton and Darlington Company 'had never made a yard of railway in a district already accommodated by railways'.[70] The quality of strategic management was complemented by close internal surveillance of the company's cost structure. In this respect, the recruitment of John Dixon as the company's effectual 'chief civil engineer' in 1842 had proved invaluable. In the surviving records of the company one of the most extensive files is replete with Dixon's detailed calculations of working expenses in all categories of operations, based on ton and train per mile statistics. In addition, Dixon prepared annual surveys of the condition of the locomotive and rolling stock fleets and permanent way, as well as forecasts of expenditures necessary to sustain efficient operations. Depreciation charges were also calculated for locomotives and rolling stock.[71] It is clear, therefore, that within its admittedly narrower sphere of operations the Stockton and Darlington directorate was furnished with statistical information of high utility and quality. Dixon's contribution to the efficient functioning of the Stockton and Darlington Company was as valuable as that of Mark Huish to the LNWR (see above, p. 101).

Finally, from the perspective of the Stockton and Darlington interest, merger with the NER was an attractive entrepreneurial strategy by the later 1850s, especially so for the dominant Pease family. By that time the Peases' commercial and industrial interests were extremely diverse.[72] In addition to railway enterprise, they embraced private banking, coal and ironstone

Table 34. *Rate per cent realisable on railway company shares, August 1859*

Railway	Selling price of shares (£)	Amount of shares (£)	Rate per cent p.a. paid 30 June	Rate per cent selling price (£ s d)		
Stockton and Darlington	37	25	9½	6	8	4
Bristol and Exeter	98	100	5½	5	12	3
North British	57	100	3	5	5	3
Lancaster and Carlisle	28	50	9	5	2	3
Scottish North Eastern (Midland Stock)	20	25	4	5	0	0
Oxford, Worcester and Wolverhampton	125	100	6	4	16	0
Lancashire and Yorkshire	95	100	4½	4	14	8
North Eastern (Berwick Stock)	91	100	4¼	4	13	5
Midland 8 p.c. stock	174	100	8	4	12	0
Caledonian	41	50	3¾	4	11	6
London, Brighton, and South coast	110	100	5	4	10	10
London and North Western	94	100	4¼	4	10	5
Scottish Central	28	25	5	4	9	3
Edinburgh and Glasgow	73	100	3¼	4	9	0
East Lincolnshire	140	100	6	4	5	8
Eastern Counties	11	20	2⅛	3	16	3
Great Western	59	100	2	3	7	7
Midland	104	100	2¾	2	10	5
Manchester, Sheffield, and Lincolnshire	36	100	4s per share	0	11	1

Source: PRO RAIL 667/395, chronological record of important Stockton and Darlington Railway events.

mining, limestone quarrying, iron making, and locomotive construction. In this light an alliance with the NER was a sound proposition not only because of the identity of traffic interests between the two companies, but also because it would endow the family with an influential voice – as major traffic senders in their own right – in the managerial direction of the monopoly supplier of rail transport in the north-east of England. Far from the merger leading to the obliteration of the Stockton and Darlington legacy, it was one which the NER and its successors were at pains to acknowledge. This was exemplified in the jubilee celebrations of 1875 which were presided over by Henry Pease in his dual capacity as chairman of the Darlington section of the NER and vice-chairman of the York board. At a later date he was succeeded in the latter position by his nephew Joseph Whitwell Pease. As the foremost industrialist in the north-east of England, with political influence to match, Joseph Whitwell Pease was elected to the chairmanship of the NER in 1894, a position which he occupied until 1902.

Epilogue

The Darlington Committee of the NER survived until 1879 when it was merged with the Newcastle Committee to form a single 'Northern' entity. In the intervening period, following the amalgamation of 1863, there were two NER developments which were inspired by Stockton and Darlington interests. The first was the attempt to promote the fishing hamlet of Saltburn as a 'genteel' holiday resort on the coast of north-east Yorkshire. According to a family biographer the originator of the attempt to create a 'northern Brighton' was Henry Pease. After a walk along the coast to Saltburn in 1859 'he had seen in a sort of prophetic vision on the cliff before him, a town arise, and the quiet unfrequented glen, through which the brook made its way to the sea, turned into a lovely garden'.[1] The opportunity to fulfil this vision was provided by the Stockton and Darlington Company's decision to extend the railway from Redcar to Saltburn in order further to exploit the local mineral traffic. Following the opening of the Saltburn extension in 1861 Henry, borrowing from the precedent set by the owners of the Middlesbrough Estate, formed the Saltburn Improvement Company as the development agency for the proposed resort. The Darlington architect, George Dickinson, was commissioned to visit a range of existing holiday resorts in preparation for drawing up suitable plans. Dickinson's recommendations fully accorded with Pease's view that Saltburn should be developed as a watering place catering for a middle- and upper-class clientele conscious of the supposed benefits of spa resorts. As an attempt to construct a 'northern Brighton' Saltburn must be judged a notable failure. During the 1860s some imposing buildings were constructed, including the Italianate Zetland Hotel possessing 120 rooms with 'the facilities that some of its clientele would have expected in a country mansion'.[2] Valley gardens and a promenade were laid out, and in the best resort tradition, a pier constructed, 1,500 yards in length and equipped with a landing stage for excursion steamers. Although the resort was criticised at an early stage for the inadequacy of its water supply, by the end of the 1860s substantial progress had been made. By that time the Zetland Hotel had been joined by a further four hotels: the resort also possessed fifty-six

BOROUGH OF DARLINGTON.

RAILWAY JUBILEE,

SEPT. 27TH, 1875.

IN connection with the above, a PROCESSION will be formed. All Persons intending to take part in it are requested to assemble in the MARKET PLACE, at HALF-PAST ONE O'CLOCK. The Procession will start at Two o'clock, and proceed in the following order to the North Road Engine Works, where the Exhibition of Locomotive Engines will be opened by the Chairman of the Darlington Section of the North Eastern Railway.

Directors of the North Eastern Railway Company, their Guests and others connected with the Company.

Mayor and Corporation of Darlington.

Mayors and Town Clerks of Cities and Boroughs represented.

Members of the Pease Memorial Committee.

Friendly Societies, in the following order :—

1—Temperance Societies.
2—Free Gardeners.
3—Foresters.
4—Friendly Society.
5—Odd Fellows.
   1—Kingston Order.
   2—National Independent.
   3—Grand Unity.
   4—Independent Order.
6—Smiths.
7—Druids.
8—Stone Masons.

Immediately after the Exhibition of Locomotives is opened, the Corporation of Darlington, the Mayors of Cities and Boroughs, and some others, will proceed by train to Bank Top Station to meet the Lord Mayor of London. The other portion of the Procession will return down Northgate and along Victoria Road, where they will line the road until the Lord Mayor arrives, when they will accompany him to the Unveiling of the Statue of the late Mr. Joseph Pease, which will take place at Five o'clock. The Procession will be under the direction of Mr. Superintendent Rogers, and those taking part are requested to walk four abreast.

H. FELL PEASE,
MAYOR.

W. DRESSER, GAS PRINTING WORKS, HIGH ROW, DARLINGTON.

27 Notice of the Stockton and Darlington Railway jubilee, 1875.

lodging houses. Thereafter, Saltburn stagnated. By 1881 the resident population had only edged up to 2,232 and at no time did the number of visitors using overnight accommodation reach impressive figures. The ambitious building programme of the 1860s had long since ended, and although Saltburn's population continued to increase, albeit slowly, this was not in response to the town's role as a holiday resort.

In accounting for the failure of Pease's vision there are several short- and longer-term factors. In the former case the onset of a sustained price fall – in contemporary parlance the 'Great Depression' – in 1873 severely undermined the prosperity of local industry. In 1876 the periodical *Engineering* commented that 'Middlesbrough and the prosperous towns depending on the production and manufacture of iron will sink into insignificant places with grass grown streets, dilapidated houses and ruins of ironworks'.[3] This gloomy pronouncement was followed in 1879 by the 'Iron-smash' on Teesside, the product of overseas financial crises and the growth of competition from steel rails. Numerous iron making concerns went bankrupt, among them those belonging to Isaac Wilson, W. R. I. Hopkins and Edgar Gilkes – all of them Henry Pease's collaborators in the Saltburn Improvement Company. Pease himself died in 1881 and no subsequent member of his family betrayed any interest in fulfilling his plans. In a longer-term perspective the failure to develop indoor entertainment facilities, combined with an uncertain summer climate, weakened the resort's attractions compared with those more favourably located on the south coast. The approach to Saltburn, moreover, along the heavily industrialised Tees south bank was hardly calculated to impress the genteel visitor with its belching chimneys, noxious smells, and pervasive dirt. In any event, the local population preferred the brasher resort of Redcar further up the coast as a day-trip destination.

If the Saltburn project was a resounding failure, a second Pease-inspired initiative proved to be an outstanding success, setting precedents which were to stretch forward well into the twentieth century. This was the decision of the NER board of directors, following the suggestion of the vice-chairman, Henry Pease, to celebrate the jubilee of the railway system following on the opening of the Stockton and Darlington line in 1825.[4] Darlington was inevitably chosen as the location of the festivities to be held during the final week of September 1875. The entire proceedings, including a sumptuous banquet attended by representatives of government, the local aristocracy, and directors of the leading British and foreign railway companies, were orchestrated by members of the Pease family, 'all of them fine, stately men, blue-eyed, big-brained, of [as] comely features as commanding figures'.[5] It was perhaps just as well that the archetypal plain Quaker, Edward Pease, was long dead. In recognition of his undoubted services to railway development the most that he had been prepared to accept from his colleagues in the year before his death in 1857 was a rather effusive address which was read to him, to the embarrassment of all concerned, in the living room of his own home. The highlights of the jubilee, however, were the unveiling by Harry Vane, the fourth Duke of Cleveland, of a bronze statue of Joseph Pease in the centre of Darlington, followed by the gift of Joseph's portrait to the town's corporation.[6] Before he died in 1872 Joseph, like his brother Henry, had abandoned the plain lifestyle of his father's generation of Quakers but, as an inveterate opponent of all things martial, even he would have blanched at the unveiling ceremony when the band of the Grenadier Guards struck up 'God save the Queen' followed by 'Rule Britannia'.

The history of the NER after 1863 was that of a well-managed concern which consistently refused to exploit its position as the monopoly supplier of rail services in the north-east of England. As the company's most recent historian has remarked, although Quaker influence within the directorate persisted well into the 1890s, the company's restraint need not necessarily have been the product of Quaker views of business life. The fact remains that members of the directorate tended to possess interlocking industrial interests and in these circumstances it made sound commercial sense to integrate the railway company with localised traffic senders. To the extent that this took place, 'the North Eastern [Railway] might be regarded as a sort of holding company for the region as a whole, and to attempt to isolate its pricing policy in terms of the individual firm may not be fully relevant. It may have been attempting to maximize not just company profits but to some extent also the profits of local industry.'[7]

There was, however, one aspect of the company's activities which in all likelihood was influenced by Quaker religious impulses. In contrast to other railway undertakings the NER adopted a relatively liberal approach to labour relations. The later 1880s, for example, were marked by major procedural advances, even to the extent of the company permitting permanent trade union representatives to attend official meetings for determining wage levels. With the election of Edward Pease's grandson, Sir Joseph Whitwell Pease, to the chairmanship of the company in 1894 it was but a short step to the formal recognition of the Amalgamated Society of Railway Servants in 1897. As a leading Liberal politician Sir Joseph had long been concerned to accommodate the emergent labour interest within the Liberal Party, albeit in a subordinate position to organised capital. A voice for moderation in the Durham Coal Owners' Association, he was a leading advocate of conciliation and arbitration in industrial disputes, a cause which he espoused vigorously in collaboration with his fellow industrialist and partner, David Dale.[8] For Sir Joseph, trade unions were the co-guarantors

28 Sir Joseph Whitwell Pease (1828–1903), grandson of Edward Pease
and chairman of the North Eastern Railway Company, 1894–1902.

of industrial harmony and stability, helping to replicate in the industrial
domain a means of reconciling conflict which as a Quaker and president of
the Peace Society he earnestly wished to see established in the conduct of
international affairs. As Sir Joseph remarked in 1897, 'labour troubles will
be brought to an end by the quiet process of arbitration, rather than we
should be at daggers drawn, losing trade, losing wages, losing capital'.[9]

Religious impulses also played a role in precipitating the end of the Peases' status as the foremost industrial dynasty in the north-east of England. The price fall inaugurated by the Great Depression after 1873, together with the onset of managerial deficiencies, placed a number of Pease-related business concerns under severe financial pressure. Rather than preside over their liquidation Sir Joseph, responding to a strong sense of religious compassion, supported them both from his personal fortune and the resources of the family bank, J. and J. W. Pease. By the end of the 1890s his financial position had deteriorated to the point where the bank's ability to meet the bi-annual dividend payments of major public companies, including the NER and the Consett Iron Company, was endangered. The denouement came in 1902 when Barclay and Company, having agreed to take over J. and J. W. Pease as a going concern, issued a press announcement to the effect that they would not be honouring the Peases' banking liabilities amounting to more than £1 million. This statement destroyed the Peases' credit by depressing the value of the shares and properties which were the principal assets of Sir Joseph and his sons. They were technically bankrupt, but formal court proceedings were avoided as a result of generous financial support from within the wider Pease family, other business associates in the north-east of England, and from leading Quaker members of Barclay's own London board. This enabled the principal creditors, led by the NER, to acquiesce to an arrangement whereby the Peases' transferable assets were realised, except for a residue of personal effects.[10] It was a tragic end to a business dynasty which had fulfilled a critical role in the industrial economy of the north-east, propelling regional economic growth through a combination of shrewd commercial calculation and entrepreneurial flair. Personalised networks had provided much of the financial resources for the family's speculations, an aspect of the Peases' record which found reflection in an informed judgement on the causes of Sir Joseph's demise. In his draft autobiography, Henry Kitching, a descendant of the Kitching engineering partnership of the 1830s, commented that Sir Joseph, possessing 'an unbounded belief in himself', was 'open handed to a degree'. But then, 'He had been nursed and cradled in an atmosphere of borrowed capital, so a few thousand pounds more or less was neither here nor there.'[11] In retrospect, Sir Joseph's father, with his fortunes at a low ebb in the late 1840s, had been rescued by the timely discovery of Cleveland ironstone. It was simply unfortunate for Sir Joseph that by the end of the nineteenth century the dynamics of expansion of the heavy industries of the north-east economy had run their course.

Appendix 1 Financial and ordinary share dividend record of the Stockton and Darlington Railway Company, 1825–1862

Period	Receipts (£ s d)			Disbursements (£ s d)			Net profit (£ s d)			Dividend (%)
Sept. 1825 – June 1826	7,492	1	5	5,804	11	5	1,687	10	0	2½
Year ending 30 June 1827	18,305	15	9	15,146	15	7	3,159	0	2	5
Year ending 30 June 1828	23,176	4	5	18,650	1	2	3,091	7	7	5
Year ending 30 June 1829	20,772	4	10	18,859	3	8	1,913	1	2	5
Year ending 30 June 1830	23,727	4	11	17,974	15	6	5,775	11	5	5
Year ending 30 June 1831	35,104	12	1	27,509	12	5	7,594	9	8	6
Year ending 30 June 1832	57,140	9	8	44,032	10	8	13,107	19	0	8
Year ending 30 June 1833	62,150	16	1	54,282	13	6	7,868	2	7	8
Year ending 30 June 1834	44,275	13	8	43,492	15	11	782	17	9	6
Year ending 30 June 1835	62,207	10	1	52,794	4	6	9,413	5	7	6
Year ending 30 June 1836	68,795	6	4	56,294	12	0	12,500	14	4	11
Year ending 30 June 1837	72,609	4	10	52,509	6	7	20,099	18	3	11
Year ending 30 June 1838	85,651	17		62,648	13	4	23,003	4	4	14
Year ending 30 June 1839	96,388	1	3	70,773	1	5	25,614	19	10	14
Year ending 30 June 1840	120,286	12	7	93,349	19	2	26,936	13	5	15
Year ending 30 June 1841	118,925	0	11	85,065	5	4	33,859	15	7	15
Year ending 30 June 1842	115,321	1	0	82,335	0	2	32,986	0	10	12½
Year ending 30 June 1843	98,394	6	2	71,136	2	9	27,258	3	5	12½
Year ending 30 June 1844	86,250	1	10	65,798	2	9	20,451	19	1	12½
Year ending 30 June 1845	108,341	7	2	74,233	18	8	34,107	8	6	14

	£	s	d	£	s	d	£	s	d	
Year ending 30 June 1846	98,657	9	5	71,192	15	1	27,464	14	4	12½
Year ending 30 June 1847	114,235	13	9	86,259	8	1	27,976	8	8	12½
Year ending 30 June 1848	135,068	6	5	114,695	13	5	20,372	13	0	10½
Year ending 30 June 1849	147,367	7	4	133,124	9	1	14,242	18	3	
Year ending 30 June 1850	159,120	17	3	130,707	2	0	28,413	15	3	
Year ending 30 June 1851	165,340	18	9	134,747	6	2	30,590	12	7	
Jan. 1852 – June 1852	110,487	11	7	100,293	11	0	10,194	0	7	4
July 1852 – Dec. 1852	102,339	3	0	85,736	6	0	16,602	17	0	4
Jan. 1853 – June 1853	113,240	5	8½	69,618	8	10½	43,621	16	10	5
July 1853 – Dec. 1853	128,074	13	8	75,937	3	2½	52,137	10	5½	3½
Jan. 1854 – June 1854	126,465	3	6½	76,393	2	10½	50,072	0	8	7½
July 1854 – Dec. 1854	143,541	6	3	85,130	19	7½	58,410	6	7½	9
Jan. 1855 – June 1855	143,062	5	8	85,181	17	2½	57,880	6	7½	9
July 1855 – Dec. 1855	151,159	7	7	93,871	10	6	57,267	17	1	9
Jan. 1856 – June 1856	155,351	18	0	95,911	12	7	59,440	5	5	9
July 1856 – Dec. 1856	172,207	0	8	103,310	19	4	68,496	1	2	10
Jan. 1857 – June 1857	175,616	1	7	103,000	3	8½	72,615	17	10½	10
July 1857 – Dec. 1857	198,156	11	8	118,688	4	4	79,468	7	4	10
Jan. 1858 – June 1858	176,234	6	1	102,653	8	2½	73,580	17	10½	8½
July 1858 – Dec. 1858	193,697	5	3½	111,487	0	4	82,210	4	11½	9½
Jan. 1859 – June 1859	190,292	16	7½	108,511	12	5	81,781	4	2½	9½
July 1859 – Dec. 1859	187,806	5	1½	106,545	1	4	81,661	2	7½	9
Jan. 1860 – June 1860	190,340	11	7½	105,590	15	0	84,749	16	7½	9
July 1860 – Dec. 1860	200,351	13	5½	109,304	0	10	91,047	12	7½	9½
Jan. 1861 – June 1861	179,416	18	1½	109,787	9	6	69,629	8	7½	9½
July 1861 – Dec. 1861	215,342	5	0½	108,132	1	8	107,210	3	4½	9½
Jan. 1862 – June 1862	220,766	14	6	120,533	7	9	100,233	6	9	7½
July 1862 – Dec. 1862	247,556	19	7	133,628	0	0	113,928	19	7	8

Source: PRO RAIL 667/1633–1654, accountant's records.

Stockton and Darlington Railway: statement of quantities of coal and other traffic conveyed upon the railway from the commencement to 30 June 1851 (tons)

Period	Darlington	Yarm	Stockton	Middles-brough	Redcar	York Junction	Simpasture	Witton Park Works	Tow Law	Consett	Stanhope	Ballast	Sundries	Total landsale
29 Sept. 1825 – 30 June 1826	14,196	7,394	13,202										896	35,687
1826-7	26,386	10,561	21,867										3,045	61,858
1827-8	25,838	12,193	21,855										5,114	65,000
1828-9	25,212	11,745	22,300										4,566	63,821
1829-30	18,688	10,979	23,269			11,127							4,074	68,136
1830-1	16,431	11,362	25,173			17,555							7,703	78,224
1831-2	17,272	12,031	26,027	285		18,075							10,537	84,726
1832-3	15,566	13,201	26,762	799		18,788							13,898	88,214
1833-4	15,658	12,283	9,482	651		17,390	21,532						12,739	89,555
1834-5	16,364	14,047	13,798	2,886		15,689	21,365						14,764	98,913
1835-6	17,816	16,187	14,817	6,855		16,744	30,031						16,990	119,240
1836-7	21,457	16,170	12,913	9,554		23,423	112,243						17,016	221,776
1837-8	21,700	16,836	13,955	10,781		30,873	117,170						18,736	230,051
1838-9	25,980	17,900	15,875	12,279		34,104	96,775						21,024	223,937
1839-40	26,909	17,483	18,908	16,383		32,985	102,762						32,018	247,448
1840-1	26,992	15,114	21,629	22,950		56,506	104,506					54,957	24,752	327,406
1841-2	22,939	11,286	19,761	27,611		88,851	55,548						56,088	282,154
1842-3	19,400	11,255	16,298	28,179		88,768	40,681						29,909	234,490
1843-4	19,761	12,025	16,886	28,878		100,944	29,190						30,166	236,850
1844-5	23,646	14,125	23,106	37,674		182,393	26,176					3,660	34,727	345,509
1845-6	18,963	15,130	25,186	54,817		204,816	3,801					14,769	49,112	386,594
1846-7	18,001	16,582	27,262	58,772		232,640	2,577					10,829	105,103	471,746
1847-8	19,924	14,782	20,513	50,117	5,329	275,518	2,708					5,654	209,290	603,835
1848-9	20,324	16,824	20,871	45,658	5,914	322,845	2,663	63,706	31,154	86,268	36,404	2,373	58,621	714,125
31 Dec. 1849	9,811	9,898	10,279	23,389	2,618	171,682	1,319	34,595	17,385	66,355	17,010	631	31,692	396,664
30 Aug. 1850	10,925	7,800	11,131	30,570	2,620	190,283	1,287	35,280	17,528	80,944	13,510		33,134	435,012
31 Dec. 1850	10,455	7,759	10,567	38,145	2,838	183,477	1,473	27,404	18,691	75,185	15,380		43,963	435,337
30 June 1851	9,837	6,726	9,499	36,494	2,871	202,403	910	35,584	19,320	54,040	15,399		69,630	462,903

Period	Coastwise Middlesbrough	Coastwise Stockton	Coastwise Total	Foreign Middlesbrough	Foreign Stockton	Foreign Total	Total exports	Grand total	Lime and stones	Goods	Passengers
29 Sept. 1825 – 30 June 1826		7,296	7,296				7,296	42,983	4,161	4,408	
1826-7		18,589	18,589				18,589	80,447	8,246	12,847	
1827-8		54,290	54,290				54,290	119,290	9,954	12,404	
1828-9		46,216	46,216				46,216	110,037	9,145	10,849	
1829-30		79,434	79,434				79,434	147,570	12,681	11,590	
1830-1	31,951	119,312	151,263				151,262	229,487	45,387	13,844	
1831-2	183,824	98,136	281,960				281,960	366,686	69,567	13,852	
1832-3	239,994	96,066	336,060				336,060	424,274	70,213	12,965	
1833-4	218,123	67,642	285,765				285,765	375,320	32,996	12,429	
1834-5	286,378	71,348	357,726				357,726	456,639	27,606	12,555	
1835-6	286,659	73,162	354,731				359,731	478,971	19,405	15,653	
1836-7	243,926	82,855	326,781				326,781	538,537	13,717	14,296	
1837-8	326,999	78,661	405,660				405,660	635,711	20,027	26,915	
1838-9	364,403	101,389	465,792				465,792	689,729	29,750	34,345	
1839-40	447,904	110,213	558,117				558,117	805,565	26,960	40,816	
1840-1	404,703	93,389	448,092				498,092	825,498	37,724	48,435	
1841-2	336,375	81,982	418,357	55,735		55,735	474,092	756,246	29,336	41,822	
1842-3	325,538	68,609	394,147	44,642		44,642	438,789	673,279	30,104	39,411	
1843-4	258,573	63,659	322,632	57,872		57,872	380,504	617,354	35,707	46,207	
1844-5	425,964	57,367	483,331	79,522		79,522	562,853	908,360	22,991	57,497	
1845-6	416,880	56,531	473,411	44,353		44,353	517,764	904,358	55,907	84,084	
1846-7	360,222	42,014	402,236	37,653		37,653	439,889	911,635	89,540	127,296	441,183
1847-8	304,455	34,144	338,599	84,088	5,722	89,810	428,409	1,032,244	221,394	215,696	374,702
1848-9	270,856	24,908	295,764	57,223	1,982	59,205	354,969	1,069,094	283,229	205,949	198,685
31 Dec. 1849	188,624	15,556	204,185	44,907	1,623	46,530	250,315	647,379	139,362	95,273	173,503
30 June 1850	169,590	13,757	183,347	31,169	1,506	32,675	216,622	651,034	170,801	81,327	211,853
31 Dec. 1850	227,049	14,609	241,658	31,460	2,594	34,054	275,712	711,049	182,470	90,128	178,869
30 June 1851	176,474	12,693	189,157	29,973	2,393	32,366	221,573	684,246	221,466	101,495	

Source: PRO RAIL 667/509.

Appendix 2 Directors and senior salaried officials of the Stockton and Darlington Railway Company, 1825–1862

THE CHANGING COMPOSITION OF THE MANAGEMENT COMMITTEE (BOARD OF DIRECTORS FROM 1848)

SEPTEMBER 1825

John Backhouse*, Jonathan Backhouse*, Richard Blanshard, William Kitching*, Thomas Meynell (chairman), Rev. D. M. Peacock, Edward Pease Sr*, Edward Pease Jr*, Joseph Pease Jr*, Thomas Richardson*, John Wilkinson.

JULY 1832

John Backhouse*, Jonathan Backhouse*, William Kitching*, Thomas Meynell (chairman), Rev. D. M. Peacock, Edward Pease Sr*, Edward Pease Jr*, Henry Pease*, Joseph Pease Jr*, Thomas Richardson*, Henry Stobart.

OCTOBER 1841

John Flintoff, John Castell Hopkins, William Kitching*, Thomas Meynell Sr, Thomas Meynell Jr (chairman), Henry Pease*, John Pease*, Joseph Pease Jr*, Leonard Raisbeck, Thomas Richardson*, Henry Stobart.

AUGUST 1845

Francis Gibson*, John Castell Hopkins, Alfred Kitching*, Thomas Meynell Sr, Thomas Meynell Jr (chairman), Henry Pease*, Joseph Pease Jr*, Thomas Richardson*, Henry Pascoe Smith, Henry Stobart, Isaac Wilson*.

SEPTEMBER 1858

John Castell Hopkins, W. R. I. Hopkins, Alfred Kitching*, Thomas Meynell Jr (chairman), Henry Pease*, Joseph Whitwell Pease*, Henry Pascoe Smith, Col H. Stobart, William Thompson, Isaac Wilson*.

The above members remained in office until the official merger with the North Eastern Railway Company in January 1863.

SALARIED OFFICIALS

Locomotive superintendent: Timothy Hackworth, 1825–40 (subcontractor, 1833–40)

Resident civil engineer: Thomas Storey, 1825–39 (a former mining engineer in Northumberland; introduced to the company by George Stephenson)

Traffic superintendent: John Graham, 1831–49 (an orphaned pit lad, by 1822 he was the head underground overlooker at Hetton Colliery. In 1839 he was appointed chief mining engineer for the Peases' collieries, but retained his Stockton and Darlington appointment until 1849).

Chief civil engineer: John Dixon, 1842–65 (served as assistant to George Stephenson in the constructional phases of the Stockton and Darlington and Liverpool and Manchester Railways; subsequently served as engineer on the London and Birmingham and Grand Junction Railways; appointed to Stockton and Darlington Railway in 1842 to oversee permanent way contracts).

Secretaries: Richard Otley, 1826–34; Samuel Barnard, 1834–46; Oswald Gilkes, 1846–9; Thomas MacNay, 1849–59 (MacNay joined Timothy Hackworth as an assistant in 1832 having been employed by Messrs Hawthorn and Co. of Newcastle upon Tyne; he subsequently served as secretary to the Bishop Auckland and Weardale, Wear Valley, and Middlesbrough and Redcar Railways before his appointment as secretary to the Stockton and Darlington Company).

* Denotes Quakers.

Appendix 3 Principal Acts of the Stockton and Darlington Railway Company, 1821–63

Royal Assent	Purpose
19 April 1821 23 May 1823 17 May 1824 23 May 1828	Original founding Acts up to and including the Middlesbrough Extension Authorised capital: £244,300
13 July 1849	Consolidation of unauthorised capital (£500,000) and vesting of Middlesbrough Dock
19 May 1851	Conversion of loan to share capital
23 July 1858	Absorption of Wear Valley,[a] Middlesbrough and Redcar, Middlesbrough and Guisborough and Darlington and Barnard Castle Railways: Saltburn Extension
15 May 1860	Additional capital: shares £250,000; loans, £83,000
22 July 1861	Additional capital: £287,000
30 June 1862	Absorption of South Durham and Lancashire Union, Eden Valley and Frosterley and Stanhope Railways
13 July 1863	Merger with North Eastern Railway Company

[a] The Wear Valley Railway was founded in 1845. It was reconstituted in July 1847 to incorporate the Bishop Auckland and Weardale, Wear and Derwent, and Weardale Extension Railways.

Appendix 4 Associated undertakings of the Stockton and Darlington Railway Company

1 *The Great North of England Railway*: received Royal Assent 4 July 1836 (6 & 7 Will. IV c. 105)
  Authorised capital: £1,150,000.
  First directors: John Charles Backhouse, Robert Botcherby, Thomas Cargill, John Mellar Chapman, Charles Heneage Elsley, John Flintoff, William Losh, Thomas Meynell Jr, Edward Oxley, Henry Pease, Jonathan Priestman, William Shields, Henry Pascoe Smith, Josiah Smithson, Henry Stobart, George Wall, George Hutton Wilkinson. First chairman: George Hutton Wilkinson.

2 *The Bishop Auckland and Weardale Railway*: received Royal Assent 15 July 1837 (7 Will. IV c. 1; Vic. c. 122)
  Authorised capital: £96,000 (shares, £72,000; loans, £24,000).
  First directors: Sir William Chaytor Bt, Lowinger Hall, William Hepple, Peter Johnson, Newby Lowson, Thomas Meynell Jr, Henry Pease, John Pease, Henry Stobart, George Hutton Wilkinson, Thomas Wilkinson. Hall, Meynell, and John Pease were subsequently replaced by George Coates Jr, Joseph Pease, and Henry Pascoe Smith.

3 *The Middlesbrough and Redcar Railway*: received Royal Assent 21 July 1845 (8 & 9 Vic. c. 127)
  Authorised capital: £48,000.
  First directors: John Castell Hopkins, Thomas Meynell, Edward Oxley, Henry Pease, Joseph Pease, Nathaniel Plews, Thomas Richardson, Henry Stobart, George Hutton Wilkinson. First chairman: George Hutton Wilkinson.

4 *The Wear Valley Railway*: received Royal Assent 31 July 1845 (8 & 9 Vic. c. 152)
  Authorised capital: £109,300 (shares, £82,000; loans £27,300).
  First directors: John Dolphin, John Castell Hopkins, Thomas Meynell, Henry Pease, Joseph Pease, Thomas Richardson, Henry Stobart, George Hutton Wilkinson. First chairman: George Hutton Wilkinson.

5 *The Middlesbrough and Guisborough Railway*: received Royal Assent 17 June 1852 (15 & 16 Vic. c. 73)
  Authorised capital: £96,000 (shares, £76,000; loans £20,000).
  First directors: Thomas MacNay, Henry Pease, Joseph Pease, Isaac Wilson.

6 *The Darlington and Barnard Castle Railway*: received Royal Assent 3 July 1854 (17 & 18 Vic. c. 115)
  Authorised capital: £133,300 (shares, £100,000; loans £33,300).
  First directors: John Hardcastle Bowman, John Buckton, Isaac Cape Cust, John Dickinson Holmes, Alfred Kitching, Owen Longstaff, Thomas MacNay, Joshua Coke Monkhouse, Henry Pease, Robert Thompson, Rev. Thomas Witham. First chairman: Rev. Thomas Witham.

7 *The Dearness Valley Railway*: received Royal Assent 30 July 1855 (18 & 19 Vic. c. 180) (projected jointly with the North Eastern Railway Company)
   Authorised capital: £73,000
   First directors: William Charles Copperthwaite, George Dodsworth, George Leeman, Joseph Pease, Joseph Whitwell Pease, Nathaniel Plews, James Pulleine, Isaac Wilson. First chairman: James Pulleine.

8 *The South Durham and Lancashire Union Railway*: received Royal Assent 13 July 1857 (20 & 21, Vic. c. 40)
   Authorised capital: £533,000 (shares, £400,000; loans, £133,000).
   First directors: Robert Hannay, William Randolph Innes Hopkins, Thomas MacNay, Henry Pease, Henry Pascoe Smith, John Henry Stobart, James Thompson, Matthew Thompson, Robert Thompson, John Wakefield, William Henry Wakefield, John Whitwell, Rev. Thomas Witham, Isaac Wilson, John Jowitt Wilson. First chairman: John Wakefield.

9 *The Eden Valley Railway*: received Royal Assent 21 May 1858 (21 Vic. c. 14)
   Authorised capital: £180,000 (shares, £135,000; loans, £45,000).
   First directors: Robert Addison, James Atkinson, William Brougham, William Crackanthorpe, John Crosby, Rear-Admiral Russell Elliot, William Hopes, William Randolph Innes Hopkins, Henry Pease, Sir Richard Tufton Bt, John Whitwell, Isaac Wilson. First chairman: Rear-Admiral Russell Elliott.

10 *The Frosterley and Stanhope Railway*: received Royal Assent 28 June 1861 (23 & 24 Vic. c. 72)
    Authorised capital: £13,000 (shares, £10,000; loans, £3,000).
    First directors: Peregrine George Ellison, Alfred Kitching, Henry Pease, Archibald Gilchrist Potter, Robert Thomas, John Anthony Woods. First chairman: Henry Pease.

Notes

The following abbreviations are used in the notes.
DCRO   Durham County Record Office
NCL   Newcastle City Library
PRO   Public Record Office

I THE STOCKTON AND DARLINGTON RAILWAY IN ECONOMIC AND BUSINESS
HISTORY

1 W. W. Tomlinson, *The North Eastern Railway: Its Rise and Development* (first
  published 1915; reprinted with an introduction by Ken Hoole, Newton Abbot
  1967).
2 See, for example, H. J. Dyos and D. H. Aldcroft, *British Transport; An Economic
  Survey from the Seventeenth Century to the Twentieth Century* (Harmondsworth
  1974), pp. 121–4; P. S. Bagwell, *The Transport Revolution from 1770* (London
  1974), pp. 91–2. For a more sympathetic view of the early achievements see Jack
  Simmons, 'Rail 150: 1975 or 1980?', *Journal of Transport History*, vol. 7, no. 1
  (1980), pp. 1–8.
3 The Middleton Colliery Waggonway, authorised by Act of Parliament in 1758.
4 The Surrey Iron Railway in 1801.
5 The Middleton Colliery rack-railway, 1812.
6 Patrick O'Brien, *Railways and the Economic Development of Western Europe,
  1830–1914* (London 1983), pp. 12–13. The 'axiom of indispensibility', as applied
  to railways, is well expressed in Leland H. Jenks, 'Railroads as an economic force
  in American development', *Journal of Economic History*, vol. 4 (1944), pp. 1–20.
  For a critique see Robert W. Fogel, *Railroads and American Economic Growth:
  Essays in Econometric History* (London 1964), pp. 1–16.
7 For the application of social savings analysis, see G. R. Hawke, *Railways and
  Economic Growth in England and Wales, 1840–1870* (Oxford 1970), and T. R.
  Gourvish, *Railways and the British Economy 1830–1914* (London 1980),
  pp. 33–40.
8 For the regional approach, see Pat Hudson (ed.), *Regions and Industries: A
  Perspective on the Industrial Revolution in Britain* (Cambridge 1989), and by the
  same author, *Britain's Industrial Revolution* (London 1992). The foremost aggregative study is N. F. R. Crafts, *British Economic Growth during the Industrial
  Revolution* (Oxford 1985). For a critique, see Maxine Berg and Pat Hudson,
  'Rehabilitating the industrial revolution', *Economic History Review*, 2nd series,
  vol. 45, no. 1 (1992), pp. 24–50.

9 E. A. Wrigley, 'The supply of raw materials in the industrial revolution', *Economic History Review*, 2nd series, vol. 15, no. 1 (1962), p. 16.

10 Sidney Pollard, *Peaceful Conquest: The Industrialisation of Europe 1760–1970* (Oxford 1981), p. 23. See also Sidney Pollard, 'Regional markets and national development', in Maxine Berg (ed.), *Markets and Manufacturers in Early Industrial Europe* (London 1991), pp. 29–56, and John Langton, 'The industrial revolution and the regional geography of England', *Transactions of the Institute of British Geographers*, vol. 9 (1984), pp. 145–67.

11 Neil Evans, 'Two paths to economic development: Wales and the north-east of England', in Hudson (ed.), *Regions and Industries*, p. 207.

12 D. J. Rowe, 'The economy of the north-east in the nineteenth century: a survey', *Northern History*, vol. 6 (1971), p. 118: Norman McCord, *North East England: The Region's Development, 1760–1970* (London 1979), pp. 36–42.

13 Alfred Marshall, *Industry and Trade* (London 1919 and 1923), p. 784.

14 Michael W. Flinn, *The History of the British Coal Industry*, vol. II: *1700–1830: The Industrial Revolution* (Oxford 1984), pp. 26–7.

15 See, for example, R. H. Coase, 'The nature of the firm', *Economica*, vol. 4 (1937), pp. 386–405, and O. E. Williamson, *The Economic Institutions of Capitalism: Firms, Markets, Relational Contracting* (New York 1985).

16 M. C. Reed, *Investment in Railways in Britain, 1820–1844: A Study in the Development of the Capital Market* (Oxford 1975), pp. 169–78; M. W. Kirby, *Men of Business and Politics: The Rise and Fall of the Quaker Pease Dynasty of North-East England* (London 1984), pp. 12, 26–7.

17 For extended discussion of the importance of external networks see Mary B. Rose and Jonathan Brown (eds.), *Firms, Entrepreneurship and Networks* (Manchester 1992).

2 THE PRELUDE TO RAILWAYS

1 Flinn, *History of the British Coal Industry*, pp. 240–1.

2 Ibid., pp. 119–20.

3 Baron F. Duckham, 'Canals and river navigations', in Derek H. Aldcroft and Michael J. Freeman (eds.), *Transport in the Industrial Revolution* (Manchester 1983), pp. 100–41.

4 Gerard Turnbull, 'Canals, coal and regional growth during the industrial revolution', *Economic History Review*, 2nd series, vol. 40, no. 4 (1987), pp. 537–60.

5 For these early developments see J. U. Nef, *The Rise of the British Coal Industry*, vol. I (London 1932), pp. 244–5; Robert Galloway, *Annals of Coal Mining and the Coal Trade* (1898; reprinted Newton Abbot 1971), pp. 154–7; R. S. Smith, 'Huntingdon Beaumont: adventurer in coal mines', *Renaissance and Modern Studies*, vol. 1 (1957), pp. 115–53, and 'England's first rails: a reconsideration', ibid., vol. 4 (1960), pp. 119–34.

6 On the development of waggonways in the eighteenth century, see R. A. Mott, 'English waggonways of the eighteenth century', *Transactions of the Newcomen Society*, vol. 37 (1964–5), pp. 1–33; C. E. Lee, 'The waggonways of Tyneside', *Archeologia Aeliana*, 4th series, vol. 29 (1951), pp. 25–40. The most recent and penetrating study of waggonways in the north-east of England is contained in G. Bennett, E. Clavering, and A. Rounding, *A Fighting Trade; Rail Transport in*

Tyne Coal, 1600–1800 (Gateshead 1990). See also P. E. H. Hair (ed.), *Coals on Rails or The Reason of my Writing: The Autobiography of Anthony Errington from 1778 to around 1825* (Liverpool 1988), for a fascinating insight into the life and work of an eighteenth-century waggonwright in the north-east coalfield.

7 M. J. T. Lewis, *Early Wooden Railways* (London 1970), p. 299.

8 Tomlinson, *The North Eastern Railway*, p. 7.

9 Bennett *et al.*, *A Fighting Trade*, pp. 11–12; Flinn, *History of the British Coal Industry*, pp. 152–7.

10 Tomlinson, *The North Eastern Railway*, p. 13; Lewis, *Early Wooden Railways*, p. 292.

11 T. S. Ashton, *Iron and Steel in the Industrial Revolution* (Manchester 1963), pp. 142ff.

12 Tomlinson, *The North Eastern Railway*, pp. 13–14.

13 Ibid.

14 C. E. Lee, *The Evolution of Railways*, 2nd edition (London 1943), pp. 76ff; Lewis, *Early Wooden Railways*, p. 294.

15 Lewis, *Early Wooden Railways*, p. 245.

16 For details of early producers' associations see P. M. Sweezy, *Monopoly and Competition in the English Coal Trade, 1550–1850* (Cambridge, Mass., 1938), and D. J. Williams, *Capitalist Combination in the Coal Industry* (London 1924).

17 For discussion of wayleaves see Flinn, *History of the British Coal Industry*, pp. 160–3; Tomlinson, *The North Eastern Railway*, pp. 6–7ff.

18 Flinn, *History of the British Coal Industry*, pp. 159–60.

19 Cited in Tomlinson, *The North Eastern Railway*, p. 9.

20 Anon., *An Enquiry into the Reasons for the Advance of the Price of Coals within Seven Years Past* (1739). For further discussion of the Grand Allies and combination in the north-east coal industry, see Edward Hughes, *North Country Life in the Eighteenth Century: The North East, 1700–1750* (London 1952), pp. 151–250 *passim*; T. S. Ashton and J. Sykes, *The Coal Industry of the Eighteenth Century* (Manchester 1929), pp. 212ff; Sweezy, *Monopoly and Competition*, pp. 143ff; P. Cromar, 'Economic power and organisation: the development of the coal industry on Tyneside, 1700–1828' (PhD thesis, University of Cambridge, 1977).

21 Cromar, 'Economic power and organisation', pp. 119–23; Sweezy, *Monopoly and Competition*, p. 144; Bennett *et al.*, *A Fighting Trade*, p. 25. On the demise of the Vend, see below p. 122.

22 Flinn, *History of the British Coal Industry*, pp. 156–7.

23 Ibid.

24 For details of these early railways, see Henry Grote Lewin, *Early British Railways: A Short History of their Origin and Development, 1801–1844* (London 1925), pp. 18–30; C. E. Lee, 'Early railways in Surrey', *Transactions of the Newcomen Society*, vol. 21 (1940–1, 1943), pp. 49–79; C. E. Lee, *The Swansea and Mumbles Railway*, 2nd edition (London 1954); C. R. Clinker, *The Hay Railway* (London 1960).

25 Lewis, *Early Wooden Railways*, pp. 297–8.

26 Cited in Tomlinson, *The North Eastern Railway*, p. 31.

27 On Trevithick's career, see L. T. C. Rolt, *The Cornish Giant: The Story of Richard Trevithick, Father of the Steam Locomotive* (London 1960).

28 Stanley Mercer, 'Trevithick and the Merthyr tramroad', *Transactions of the Newcomen Society*, vol. 26 (1947–9), pp. 89–103. The Pen-y-Daren tramway was engineered by George Overton, subsequently engaged as surveyor to the Stockton and Darlington project in 1818.
29 Rolt, *The Cornish Giant*, pp. 84, 86.
30 Lewis, *Early Wooden Railways*, p. 295.
31 On the Middleton Colliery railway see W. G. Rimmer, 'Middleton Colliery near Leeds (1770–1830)', *Yorkshire Bulletin of Economic and Social Research*, vol. 7 (1955), pp. 41–57; C. E. Lee, 'The first steam railway: Brandling's colliery line between Leeds and Middleton', *Railway Magazine*, vol. 81 (1937), pp. 7–25.
32 Tomlinson, *The North Eastern Railway*, pp. 21–4.
33 G. N. Von Tunzelmann, *Steam Power and British Industrialization to 1860* (Oxford 1978), p. 121.
34 Flinn, *History of the British Coal Industry*, pp. 155–6.
35 Tomlinson, *The North Eastern Railway*, pp. 23–4.
36 Ibid., pp. 26–7.
37 See R. W. Kidner, *The Early History of the Locomotive, 1804–1876* (London 1956); C. F. Dendy Marshall, *A History of Railway Locomotives down to the End of the Year 1831* (London 1953).
38 Samuel Smiles, *Lives of the Engineers*, vol. V: *George and Robert Stephenson* (London 1862).
39 For good accounts of Stephenson's career, see L. T. C. Rolt, *George and Robert Stephenson: The Railway Revolution* (London 1960); Hunter Davies, *George Stephenson: A Biographical Study of the Father of the Railways* (London 1975 and 1977); Michael Robbins, *George and Robert Stephenson* (London 1981).
40 Tomlinson, *The North Eastern Railway*, pp. 28–9; L. T. C. Rolt, *George and Robert Stephenson*, pp. 55–7.
41 Lee, *The Evolution of Railways*, p. 89.
42 Davies, *George Stephenson*, p. 44.
43 Galloway, *Annals of Coal Mining*, p. 71.
44 Ibid., p. 452.
45 E. Pawson, *Transport and Economy: The Turnpike Roads of Eighteenth Century Britain* (Oxford 1977), pp. 122–44; William Albert, *The Turnpike Road System in England, 1663–1840* (Cambridge 1972), p. 205.
46 John Temple, *Darlington and the Turnpike Roads* (Darlington 1971), pp. 11–16.
47 For early canal schemes in the north-east, and Co. Durham in particular, see Tomlinson, *The North Eastern Railway*, pp. 33–9.
48 Ibid., p. 35.
49 Flinn, *History of the British Coal Industry*, p. 181.
50 John Phillips, *The General History of Inland Navigation*, 4th edition (London 1803), p. 598.
51 W. T. Jackman, *The Development of Transportation in Modern England*, 2nd edition (London 1962), pp. 357–8; T. C. Barker, 'The beginnings of the canal age in the British Isles', in L. S. Pressnell (ed.), *Studies in the Industrial Revolution* (London 1960), pp. 1–22.
52 Tomlinson, *The North Eastern Railway*, pp. 37–8.
53 Ibid., p. 38.
54 Ibid., p. 39.

3 THE FOUNDATION OF THE STOCKTON AND DARLINGTON RAILWAY
COMPANY, 1818–1825

1 A. E. Smailes, *North England* (London 1960), pp. 157–8.
2 Kirby, *Men of Business and Politics*, pp. 3–4.
3 On credit flows in the eighteenth century, see B. L. Anderson, 'Money and the structure of credit in the eighteenth century', *Business History*, vol. 12, no. 2 (1970), pp. 90–100; Pat Hudson, *The Genesis of Industrial Capital: A Study of the West Riding Wool Textile Industry, c. 1750–1850* (Cambridge 1986); Julian Hoppit, 'The use and abuse of credit in eighteenth century England', in N. McKendrick and R. B. Outhwaite (eds.), *Business Life and Public Policy: Essays in Honour of D. C. Coleman* (Cambridge 1986), pp. 64–78.
4 Smailes, *North England*, pp. 158–9.
5 C. A. McDougall, *The Stockton and Darlington Railway, 1821–1863* (Durham 1975), p. 2.
6 Tomlinson, *The North Eastern Railway*, p. 40.
7 Ibid.
8 NCL Tomlinson Collection, vol. 1: early letters and papers relating to the Stockton and Darlington Railway, 'Meeting of Gentlemen, Merchants and Others for the Purpose of Promoting a Canal or Railway from Stockton by Darlington Westwards, 17 January 1812'.
9 Tomlinson, *The North Eastern Railway*, p. 40.
10 Maberley Phillips, *A History of Banks, Bankers and Banking in Northumberland, Durham, and North Yorkshire* (London 1894), p. 232.
11 C. J. A. Robertson, *The Origins of the Scottish Railway System 1722–1844* (Edinburgh 1983), p. 43.
12 Tomlinson, *The North Eastern Railway*, p. 42.
13 Ibid.
14 PRO RAIL 667/851, Jonathan Backhouse Jr, to Richard Miles, 7 August 1818; ibid. 667/865, Jonathan Backhouse Jr to Leonard Raisbeck, 11 August 1818.
15 PRO RAIL 667/853, Matthew Plummer to Richard Miles, 24 August 1818.
16 PRO RAIL 667/856, Richard Miles to George Overton, 22 August 1818.
17 NCL Tomlinson Collection, vol. 1, Thomas Meynell to Richard Miles, 15 August 1818; PRO RAIL 667/854, Robert Botcherby to Richard Miles, 20 August 1818; ibid. 667/855, Thomas Meynell to Richard Miles, 21 August 1818; ibid. 667/856, Richard Miles to George Overton, 22 August 1818.
18 P. L. Cottrell and G. Ottley, 'The beginnings of the Stockton and Darlington Railway, 1813–25: a celebratory note', *Journal of Transport History*, new series, vol. 3, no. 2, (1975), p. 90.
19 On Overton's background as an engineer of tramways, see Rolt, *George and Robert Stephenson*, pp. 62–3.
20 PRO RAIL 667/150, resolutions of a meeting, 4 September 1818.
21 Tomlinson, *The North Eastern Railway*, p. 53.
22 DCRO 'A Report relative to the opening of a communication by a Canal or a Railway or Tramway from Stockton by Darlington to the collieries' (1818).
23 J. S. Jeans, *Jubilee Memorial of the Railway System: A History of the Stockton and Darlington Railway and a Record of its Results* (1875; reprinted Newcastle upon Tyne 1975), pp. 21–2.

24 DCRO Stockton and Darlington Railway Records, U415j, 'Observations on the Proposed Rail-Way or Tram-Road from Stockton to the collieries by way of Darlington' (Durham 1818).
25 *Durham County Advertiser*, 21 November 1818.
26 Estimates in the prospectus differed from those presented at the meeting on 13 November. The cost was projected at £113,600 and annual receipts at £16,500.
27 PRO RAIL 667/856, Richard Miles to George Overton, 20 November 1818.
28 Ibid.
29 PRO RAIL 667/866, Francis Mewburn to Richard Miles, 11 December 1818.
30 PRO RAIL 667/1, Stockton and Darlington Railway, *Minutes and Reports 1818–21*, resolutions of a meeting held on 19 December 1818.
31 Tomlinson, *The North Eastern Railway*, p. 57.
32 See, for example, J. R. Ward, *The Finance of Canal Building in Eighteenth Century England* (Oxford 1974); S. A. Broadbridge, 'The sources of railway share capital', in M. C. Reed (ed.), *Railways in the Victorian Economy: Studies in Finance and Economic Growth* (Newton Abbot 1969), pp. 184–211.
33 PRO RAIL 667/233, 'A List of Subscriptions of the Darlington Railway'.
34 DCRO Pease Family Records U 418e PEA, 46/19, Joseph Pease Jr to W. Aldam and T. B. Pease, 26 December 1818.
35 O'Brien, *Railways and Economic Development*, p. 183.
36 On Nonconformist kinship ties and the supply of capital, see Arthur Raistrick, *Quakers in Science and Industry* (Newton Abbot 1968), pp. 34, 45, 335.
37 Ward, *The Finance of Canal Building*, passim.
38 NCL Tomlinson Collection, vol. 1, Lord Darlington to George Overton, 12 July 1819.
39 PRO RAIL 667/870, Joseph Pease Jr to Jonathan Backhouse Jr, 6 December 1818.
40 Tomlinson, *The North Eastern Railway*, p. 58.
41 Cited in *Memoir of Fra: Mewburn, Chief Bailiff of Darlington and First Railway Solicitor, by his Son* (Darlington 1867), p. 53.
42 Francis Mewburn, *The Larchfield Diary: Extracts from the Diary of the Late Mr Mewburn, First Railway Solicitor* (London and Darlington, 1876), p. 8.
43 PRO RAIL 667/153, 'Report of Sub-Committee to the Committee of the Darlington and Stockton Railway' (1819).
44 PRO RAIL 667/879, Richard Storey to Edward Pease, 11 June 1819.
45 Phillips, *A History of Banks*, pp. 148–9; P. W. Matthews and A. W. Tuke, *A History of Barclays Bank Limited* (London 1926), p. 206.
46 PRO RAIL 667/1, meeting of subscribers at Yarm, 20 July 1819.
47 Ibid., Stockton and Darlington Railway, *Minutes and Reports*, 9 December 1819.
48 Tomlinson, *The North Eastern Railway*, p. 65.
49 PRO RAIL 667/891, John Cartwright to Stockton and Darlington management committee, 14 April 1820.
50 PRO RAIL 667/899, J. Rowntree to Edward Pease, 19 July 1821; ibid. 667/901, Leonard Raisbeck and Francis Mewburn to Messrs Clarke and Gray, 15 September 1821.
51 Jeans, *Jubilee Memorial*, pp. 35–6.
52 DCRO Stockton and Darlington Railway Records, U415j, Henry Pease, 'George and Dragon' (1823).

53 Tomlinson, *The North Eastern Railway*, p. 69.
54 PRO RAIL 667/897, Leonard Raisbeck to Richard Miles, 30 March 1821.
55 Stockton and Darlington Railway Act, 1821: 'An Act for making and maintaining a railway or tramroad from the River Tees at Stockton to Witton Park Colliery with several branches therefrom, all in the County of Durham'. Although authorised by Parliament the Berwick and Kelso line was never built.
56 DCRO Stockton and Darlington Railway Records, U415j, 37764, *Prospectus: Darlington and Stockton Rail-Way: Observations in Parliament* (Sess. 1821). See also U415j R. 23986, Thomas Meynell (chairman), *A Further Report of the intended Rail or Tram Road from Stockton by Darlington to the collieries with a branch to Yarm* (February 1821).
57 J. G. Lambton, cited in Tomlinson, *The North Eastern Railway*, p. 69.
58 Rolt, *George and Robert Stephenson*, pp. 62–5; Davies, *George Stephenson*, pp. 53–5.
59 *Newcastle Chronicle*, 2 June 1821.
60 DCRO Hodgkin Papers, D/140/C/63, 'Thomas Richardson', Edward Pease to Thomas Richardson, 10 October 1821.
61 PRO RAIL 667/8, Stockton and Darlington management committee minutes, 23 July 1821.
62 Tomlinson, *The North Eastern Railway*, pp. 75–6.
63 Rolt, *George and Robert Stephenson*, p. 71.
64 PRO RAIL 667/8, Stockton and Darlington management committee minutes, 18 January 1822.
65 DCRO Stockton and Darlington Railway Records, U415j, Michael Longridge and John Birkinshaw, 'Remarks on the Comparative Merits of Cast Metal, and Malleable Iron Rails', Bedlington Ironworks, 28 February 1821.
66 PRO RAIL 667/8, Stockton and Darlington Railway, sub-committee minutes, 1821–36, 29 December 1821.
67 Rolt, *George and Robert Stephenson*, p. 74.
68 Tomlinson, *The North Eastern Railway*, p. 79.
69 Ibid., p. 83.
70 Stockton and Darlington Railway Act, 1823: 'An Act to enable the Stockton and Darlington Railway Company to vary and alter the line of their railway ... '.
71 PRO RAIL 667/8, 'Report to the General Committee appointed by the Proprietors in the Stockton and Darlington Railway Company', 22 January 1822, 8 July 1823.
72 For details of tenders, see PRO RAIL 667/907/909/910/918/920/921/922/923/924/925.
73 P. J. Holmes, *The Stockton and Darlington Railway, 1825–1975* (Ayr 1975), p. 10; Rolt, *George and Robert Stephenson*, p. 76.
74 Ibid., p. 74; Tomlinson, *The North Eastern Railway*, p. 88.
75 PRO RAIL 667/8, Stockton and Darlington Railway sub-committee minutes, 1821–36, 9 April 1823.
76 For the early history of Robert Stephenson and Co., see J. G. H. Warren, *A Century of Locomotive Building by Robert Stephenson and Company, 1823–1923* (Newcastle upon Tyne 1923); Michael R. Bailey, 'Robert Stephenson and Co., 1823–1829', *Transactions of the Newcomen Society*, vol. 50 (1980), pp. 109–37.
77 Kirby, *Men of Business and Politics*, p. 17.

78 Ibid., p. 79.
79 DCRO D/HO/C/653, Edward Pease to Thomas Richardson, 10 October 1821.
80 See, for example, DCRO, Pease–Stephenson Papers, D/PS/2/23, Michael Longridge to Edward Pease, 18 January 1825.
81 Bailey, 'Robert Stephenson and Co.', p. 115.
82 Ibid.
83 DCRO Pease–Stephenson Papers, D/HO/C/63, Edward Pease to Thomas Richardson, 23 October 1824.
84 PRO RAIL 667/30, Stockton and Darlington Railway sub-committee minutes, 7 November 1823.
85 Ibid., 16 September 1824.
86 DCRO Hodgkin Papers, D/140/C/63/10, Edward Pease to Michael Longridge, December 1824.
87 DCRO Pease–Stephenson Papers, D/PS/2/68, resolution of a meeting at Newcastle, 31 December 1824. The distribution of shares in the business was as follows: George Stephenson (2); Robert Stephenson (2); Edward Pease (4); Michael Longridge (2).
88 DCRO, Pease Family Papers, U415j, vol. III, memoranda of a meeting held in Robert Stephenson and Co.'s Office, 31 December 1824. By 1844 Michael Longridge had withdrawn from the business.
89 PRO RAIL 667/939/40, Fenton and Murray to Richard Otley, 26 October 1825 and 14 November 1825.
90 PRO RAIL 667/3, Stockton and Darlington management committee minutes, 13 December 1822.
91 Ibid. 25 July 1823.
92 Ibid.
93 NCL Tomlinson Collection, vol. 1, George Stephenson to Edward Pease, 31 May 1822.
94 PRO RAIL 667/935, Michael Longridge to Edward Pease, 23 July 1824.
95 *Select Committee on Railways: Second Report*, Parliamentary Papers, vol. 10 (1839), p. 5.
96 Stockton and Darlington Railway Act, 1824: 'An Act to authorise the Company of Proprietors of the Stockton and Darlington Railway to relinquish one of their branch railways, and to enable them to make another branch railway in lieu thereof; and to enable the Said Company to raise a further sum of money'.
97 PRO RAIL 667/955 'Interrogation from the Exchequer Loan Board with answers from the Railway Company', July 1826.
98 PRO RAIL 667/935, Thomas Storey to executive sub-committee, 29 March 1824, 6 April 1824; ibid. 667/933, J. and J. Burrell to Stockton and Darlington management committee, 13 May 1824, 27 July 1824.
99 PRO RAIL 667/3, resolution of management committee meeting, 12 July 1825.
100 NCL Tomlinson Collection, vol. 1, Richardson Overend and Co. to Francis Mewburn, 29 August 1825.
101 PRO RAIL 667/3, resolution of management committee meeting, 9 September 1825.

102 William Lillie, *The History of Middlesbrough: An Illustration of the Evolution of English Industry* (Middlesbrough 1968), p. 47.

103 Max Weber, *The Protestant Ethic and the Spirit of Capitalism* (London 1930).

104 D. C. McClelland, *The Achieving Society* (Princeton 1961).

105 Allan Thompson, *The Dynamics of the Industrial Revolution* (London 1973), p. 134.

106 David H. Pratt, *English Quakers and the First Industrial Revolution: A Study of the Quaker Community in Four Industrial Counties – Lancashire, York, Warwick and Gloucester, 1750–1830* (New York and London 1985), p. 9.

107 Ibid.

108 Raistrick, *Quakers in Science and Industry*, p. 338; Peter Mathias, *The First Industrial Nation: An Economic History of Britain, 1700–1914*, 1st edition (London 1969), p. 158.

109 F. M. A. Voltaire, *Letters on England* (London 1733; reprinted Harmondsworth 1980), p. 35.

110 T. A. B. Corley, 'How Quakers coped with business success: Quaker industrialists, 1860–1914', in David J. Jeremy (ed.), *Business and Religion in Britain* (Aldershot 1988), p. 169.

111 Pratt, *English Quakers*, p. 18.

112 Raistrick, *Quakers in Science and Industry*, pp. 34, 45, 335.

113 Michael Mullett, *Radical Religious Movements in Early Modern Europe* (London 1980), pp. 41–6; John Sykes, *The Quakers: A New Look at their Place in Society* (London 1958), p. 171. On the interrelatedness of Quaker families, see, for example, Verity Anderson, *Friends and Relations: 3 Centuries of Quaker Families* (London 1980), and R. L. Brett (ed.), *Barclay Fox's Journal* (London 1979).

114 Coase, 'The nature of the firm', pp. 386–405.

115 See, for example, Williamson, *The Economic Institutions of Capitalism*, and P. J. Buckley and M. C. Casson, *The Economic Theory of the Multinational Enterprise* (London 1985).

116 C. H. Lee, 'Corporate behaviour in theory and history: I the evolution of theory', *Business History*, vol. 32, no. 1 (1990), p. 21.

117 A. D. Chandler, *The Visible Hand: The Managerial Revolution in American Business* (Cambridge, Mass., and London 1977).

118 See M. C. Casson, *The Economics of Business Culture: Game Theory, Transaction Costs, and Economic Performance* (Oxford 1991), ch. 1 *passim*. For further comment on the importance of external networks, see Hudson, *The Genesis of Industrial Capital*, ch. 8; S. Nenadic, 'The family and the small firm in late nineteenth century Britain', paper presented at the tenth International Economic History Congress, Leuven 1990; and L. Davidoff and C. Hall, *Family Fortunes: Men and Women in the English Middle Class, 1780–1850* (London 1989), pp. 99–103, 215–16.

4 HOPES FULFILLED, 1825–1833

1 *Newcastle Courant*, 1 October 1825.

2 Ibid.

3 Cited in McDougall, *The Stockton and Darlington Railway*, p. 19.

4 PRO RAIL 667/158, report of the management committee to shareholders, 10 July 1827.

5 DCRO Hodgkin Papers, D/HO/C/63, Edward Pease to Thomas Richardson, 26 February 1825.
6 Rolt, *George and Robert Stephenson*, pp. 119–27.
7 PRO RAIL 667/955, John Trotter to Francis Mewburn, 21 September 1825; NCL Tomlinson Collection, vol. 1, Richard Otley to Michael Longridge, 21 October 1825.
8 NCL Tomlinson Collection, vol. 1, Jonathon Backhouse to Edward Pease, 30 May 1826.
9 PRO RAIL 687/955, 'Interrogation from the Exchequer Loan Board with Answers from the Railway Company', July 1826.
10 T. E. Rounthwaite, 'An outline history of the Stockton and Darlington Railway', *Railway Observer*, vol. 26 (1956), p. 37.
11 NCL Tomlinson Collection, vol. 1, Jonathon Backhouse to Edward Pease, 30 May 1826.
12 PRO RAIL 667/951, Stockton and Darlington Railway letter file, John Flintoff (Etherley Colliery) to Richard Otley, 18 October 1825, 11 November 1825, 6 January 1826; Joshua Ianson (Black Boy Colliery) to railway committee, 27 October 1825.
13 PRO RAIL 667/945, Thomas Storey to management committee, 21 October 1825.
14 Ibid., Thomas Storey to Joseph Pease, 2 November 1825.
15 PRO RAIL 667/950. Matthew Scotson to management committee, 5 November 1825.
16 PRO RAIL 667/171, report of George Stephenson to the projectors of the Stockton and Darlington Railway, 1821.
17 See, for example, PRO RAIL 667/974, Bedlington Iron Company to management committee, 17 February 1826; ibid. 667/31, management committee to William Kitching of Darlington, not dated, *c.* March 1826. PRO RAIL 667/947 contains order enquiries for wheel and rails addressed to various iron companies at this time, including Lumley Forge, and Losh, Wilson, and Bell.
18 Tomlinson, *The North Eastern Railway*, pp. 158–9.
19 Reverend James Adamson, Cupar, Fife, 'Sketches of our information as to railroads', *Caledonian Mercury*, 1826.
20 PRO RAIL 667/31, minutes of the Stockton and Darlington Railway sub-committee, 11 November 1825.
21 Ibid., 18 November 1825.
22 Ibid., 25 November 1825.
23 Theodore West, *An Outline History of the Locomotive Engine* (London 1885), pp. 14–15. See also Joseph Tomlinson, 'Presidential address', *Proceedings of the Institution of Mechanical Engineers* (1890), p. 182.
24 Robert Young, *Timothy Hackworth and the Locomotive* (London 1923), p. 144: Tomlinson, *The North Eastern Railway*, pp. 142–3.
25 J. C. Jeaffreson, *Life of Robert Stephenson*, vol. I (London 1864), p. 115.
26 Anon., *Observations on the Comparative Merits of Fixed and Locomotive Engines* (1829).
27 Young, *Timothy Hackworth*, p. 146.
28 Holmes, *The Stockton and Darlington Railway*, p. 25.
29 *A Chapter in the History of Railway Locomotion, etc.*, appendix by John Wesley

Hackworth (1892), p. 25. Cited in Tomlinson, *The North Eastern Railway*, p. 141.

30 Ibid. Italics in original.

31 Tomlinson, *The North Eastern Railway*, p. 141; Warren, *A Century of Locomotive Building*.

32 PRO RAIL 667/31, minutes of the Stockton and Darlington Railway sub-committee, 1825–30, 22 June 1827.

33 PRO RAIL 667/158, report of the management committee to shareholders, 10 July 1827.

34 Cited in Smiles, *Lives of George and Robert Stephenson*, p. 250. See also Jeaffreson, *Life of Robert Stephenson*, p. 101.

35 Smiles, *Lives of George and Robert Stephenson*, pp. 253–4.

36 *The Civil Engineer and Architect's Journal*, vol. 12 (July 1849), p. 206. Cited in Young, *Timothy Hackworth*, p. 146.

37 Ibid., p. 145.

38 PRO RAIL 667/31, minutes of the Stockton and Darlington Railway sub-committee, 1825–30, 28 March 1827.

39 Young, *Timothy Hackworth*, p. 150.

40 PRO RAIL 667/1158, testimonial for Timothy Hackworth by William Patter, Walbottle Colliery, 3 February 1825.

41 Young, *Timothy Hackworth*, p. 103.

42 James Walker, *Report on the Comparative Merits of Locomotive and Fixed Engines* (1829): E. L. Ahrons, *The British Steam Railway Locomotive, 1825–1925* (London 1927), pp. 5–7.

43 Tomlinson, *The North Eastern Railway*, p. 145.

44 Warren, *A Century of Locomotive Building*, p. 129.

45 Simmons, 'Rail 150', pp. 2–3.

46 Ahrons, *The British Steam Railway Locomotive*, pp. 18–32.

47 Young, *Timothy Hackworth*, p. 161.

48 Ibid.

49 Ahrons, *The British Steam Railway Locomotive*, p. 4.

50 Ibid.

51 Tomlinson, *The North Eastern Railway*, p. 153.

52 Stockton and Darlington management committee to Timothy Hackworth, 18 July 1828, 5 September 1828. Cited in Young, *Timothy Hackworth*, p. 169.

53 PRO RAIL 667/3, Stockton and Darlington management committee minutes, 14 July 1829.

54 Henry Booth, *Account of the Liverpool and Manchester Railway* (1831), p. 69.

55 Tomlinson, *The North Eastern Railway*, pp. 149, 159–60.

56 PRO RAIL 667/466, 'Considerations Reflecting the Situation of Black Boy Colliery in the event of the Branch Railway not being laid to same', not dated, *c.* June 1826; ibid. 667/3 Stockton and Darlington management committee minutes, 26 January 1827, 28 June 1827.

57 Ibid., 25 October 1825.

58 Tomlinson, *The North Eastern Railway*, p. 138.

59 *The Two James's and the Two Stephensons* (1861), p. 47.

60 PRO RAIL 667/3, Stockton and Darlington management committee minutes, 26 January 1827. Loans outstanding at 1 July 1828 amounted to £90,570. They were

made up as follows: Gurney and Co., £20,000; Overend and Co., £10,000; Joseph Gurney, £2,000; William Death, £5,000; Thomas Richardson, £4,000; Charlotte Gill, £3,000. See PRO RAIL 667/1401, Stockton and Darlington miscellaneous statistics.

61 PRO RAIL 667/3, Stockton and Darlington management committee minutes, 26 January 1827.

62 Ibid., 16 February 1827, 23 March 1827.

63 Tomlinson, *The North Eastern Railway*, p. 139.

64 Lillie, *The History of Middlesbrough*, p. 47.

65 PRO RAIL 667/971, Thomas Storey to Edward Pease, 24 February 1826.

66 Tomlinson, *The North Eastern Railway*, p. 165.

67 PRO RAIL 667/971, Thomas Storey to Edward Pease, 24 February 1826.

68 Tomlinson, *The North Eastern Railway*, p. 165.

69 PRO RAIL 667/971, Henry Blanshard to Thomas Richardson, 11 June 1826.

70 PRO RAIL 667/973, Christopher Tennant to Richard Otley, 8 September 1826, 5 October 1826, 15 November 1826.

71 *Durham Country Advertiser*, 19 February 1828.

72 PRO RAIL 667/3, Stockton and Darlington management committee minutes, 27 October 1826, 24 November 1826.

73 Ibid., 5 January 1827.

74 PRO RAIL 667/158, report of management committee to shareholders, 10 June 1827.

75 Ibid.

76 Tomlinson, *The North Eastern Railway*, p. 172.

77 J. S. Jeans, *Pioneers of the Cleveland Iron Trade* (Middlesbrough 1875), p. 136.

78 Kirby, *Men of Business and Politics*, p. 21.

79 PRO RAIL 667/3, Stockton and Darlington management committee minutes, 8 July 1828.

80 NCL Tomlinson Collection, vol. 1, Leonard Raisbeck to Edward Pease, 14 March 1828.

81 Ibid., Joseph Pease to Leonard Raisbeck, 17 March 1828.

82 Warren, *A Century of Locomotive Building*, p. 50.

83 See Kirby, *Men of Business of Politics*, *passim*.

84 Joseph Pease Diary, 18 August 1828.

85 J. W. Leonard, 'Urban development and population growth in Middlesbrough, 1831–1871 (D Phil thesis, University of York, 1976).

86 Alfred Edward Pease Journal, 6 October 1881.

87 See, for example, H. G. Reid, *Middlesbrough and its Jubilee* (Middlesbrough 1881).

88 Ann Prior, 'The interaction of business and religion within the Society of Friends', unpublished paper, Department of Economics, Lancaster University 1990.

89 Sir Alfred E. Pease (ed.), *The Diaries of Edward Pease*.

90 PRO RAIL 667/3, Stockton and Darlington management committee minutes, 28 July 1832.

91 Elizabeth Isichei, *Victorian Quakers* (Oxford 1970), pp. 144–65.

92 M. W. Kirby, 'The failure of a Quaker business dynasty: the Peases of Darlington, 1830–1902' in David J. Jeremy (ed.), *Business and Religion in Britain* (Aldershot 1988), p. 144.

93 *Durham County Advertiser*, 19 January 1828.
94 Tomlinson, *The North Eastern Railway*, p. 176.
95 Ibid., p. 179.
96 PRO RAIL 667/4, annual report to general meeting of shareholders, 14 July 1829.
97 *Northern Year Book* (1829), p. 99. Cited in Tomlinson, *The North Eastern Railway*, p. 180.
98 A. G. Kenwood, 'Capital investment in north eastern England, 1800–1913' (PhD thesis, University of London, 1962), p. 84.
99 Mewburn, *The Larchfield Diary*, p. 25.
100 Tomlinson, *The North Eastern Railway*, p. 122.
101 DCRO Stockton and Darlington Railway Records, D/XD/35/1, report to shareholders, 1832–3.
102 For examples, see George Graham, 'Notes of incidents connected with the Stockton and Darlington Railway', Stockton Reference Library, NE/-385.24F, pp. 5–8.
103 From Henry Pease's speech at the Stockton and Darlington Railway jubilee banquet, 1875, *Newcastle Daily Chronicle*, 28 September 1875.
104 PRO RAIL 667/873, James Meadows to Benjamin Flounders, 15 January 1819.
105 PRO RAIL 667/290, memorandum of agreement between Joseph Pease and R. W. Hawthorn, 29 April 1831.
106 Tomlinson, *The North Eastern Railway*, p. 384.
107 PRO RAIL 667/32, Stockton and Darlington management committee sub-committee minutes, 30 August 1833.
108 Ibid., 20 April 1833, 4 October 1833.
109 Tomlinson, *The North Eastern Railway*, p. 385.
110 Holmes, *The Stockton and Darlington Railway*, p. 27.

5 GROWTH AND COMPETITION, 1834–1847

1 Sir John Clapham, *An Economic History of Modern Britain: The Early Railway Age, 1820–1850* (Cambridge 1926).
2 Michael Robbins, *The Railway Age* (Harmondsworth 1965), pp. 20–1; Simmons, 'Rail 150'.
3 Dyos and Aldcroft, *British Transport*, p. 130.
4 B. R. Mitchell, 'The coming of the railway and United Kingdom economic growth', *Journal of Economic History*, vol. 24 (1964), p. 322, reprinted in M. C. Reed (ed.), *Railways and the Victorian Economy: Studies in Finance and Economic Growth* (Newton Abbot 1969), pp. 13–32.
5 Harold Pollins, 'The marketing of railway shares in the first half of the nineteenth century', *Economic History Review*, 2nd series, vol. 7 (1954–5), pp. 230–9. See also M. C. Reed, 'Railways and the growth of the capital market', in Reed (ed.), *Railways and the Victorian Economy*, pp. 164–5.
6 Dyos and Aldcroft, *British Transport*, p. 138.
7 Cited in Robbins, *The Railway Age*, p. 35.
8 Tomlinson, *The North Eastern Railway*, p. 526.
9 T. R. Gourvish, *Mark Huish and the London and North Western Railway: A*

Study of Management (Leicester 1972). The following account of LNWR managerial practices is based on Gourvish's study.

10 M. W. Kirby, 'Product proliferation in the British locomotive building industry, 1850–1914: an engineers' paradise?', *Business History*, vol. 30, no. 3 (1988), pp. 290–1. See also M. W. Kirby, 'Technological innovation and structural division in the UK locomotive building industry, 1850–1914', in Colin Holmes and Alan Booth (eds.), *Economy and Society: European Industrialisation and Its Social Consequences* (Leicester 1991), p. 36.

11 Gourvish, *Mark Huish*, p. 262.

12 Ibid., p. 265.

13 R. A. Buchanan, *The Engineers: A History of the Engineering Profession in Britain 1750–1914* (London 1989), pp. 76–80.

14 Sidney Pollard, *The Genesis of Modern Management: A Study of the Industrial Revolution in Great Britain* (Harmondsworth 1968), p. 62.

15 Ibid., p. 52.

16 A. J. Taylor, 'The sub-contract system in the British coal industry', in L. S. Pressnell (ed.), *Studies in the Industrial Revolution: Essays Presented to T. S. Ashton* (London 1960), p. 216.

17 Jeans, *Jubilee Memorial*, p. 268.

18 Young, *Timothy Hackworth*, p. 258.

19 Ibid., pp. 258–9.

20 Ibid., pp. 312–21.

21 For details, see DCRO Kitching Papers, D/Ki/27.41.,42,43 (letter and engine books). At some stage in the 1830s the Kitching brothers and the local engineer William Lister joined Hackworth as locomotive contractors. See table 12 below.

22 *Newcastle Daily Chronicle*, 28 September 1875.

23 Nicholas Wood, *Treatise on Railways*, 3rd edition (*c.* 1833), p. 737.

24 Young, *Timothy Hackworth*, pp. 270–2.

25 Tomlinson, *The North Eastern Railway*, p. 397.

26 Ibid.

27 Edgar J. Larkin and John G. Larkin, *The Railway Workshops of Britain, 1823–1986* (London 1988), pp. 80–1.

28 PRO RAIL 667/427, first officials of the Stockton and Darlington Railway. See appendix 2 for details of the company's senior salaried officials.

29 DCRO Kitching Papers, D/Ki G, John Dixon's report to the directors of the Stockton and Darlington Railway, 24 October 1843.

30 Ibid.

31 DCRO Stockton and Darlington Railway Records, D/XD/35/11, report to shareholders, 1843–4.

32 DCRO Stockton and Darlington Railway Records, D/XD/35/4, report to shareholders, 1835–6.

33 PRO RAIL 667/33, Stockton and Darlington management committee minutes, 2 January 1835.

34 T. R. Gourvish, 'Railway enterprise', in Roy Church (ed.), *The Dynamics of Victorian Business: Problems and Perspectives to the 1870s* (London 1980), p. 138.

35 On the importance of such managers, see Chandler, *The Visible Hand*, pp. 145–8.

36 Tomlinson, *The North Eastern Railway*, p. 219.

37 Ibid., pp. 249–53.

38 DCRO Stockton and Darlington Railway Records, D/XD/35/4, report to share-holders, 1835–6.
39 PRO RAIL 667/4, Stockton and Darlington management committee minutes, 1 February 1836.
40 Tomlinson, *The North Eastern Railway*, p. 237.
41 Ibid.
42 Ibid., pp. 239–40.
43 DCRO Stockton and Darlington Railway Records, D/XD/35/4, report to share-holders, 1835–6.
44 *Tyne Mercury*, 10 May 1836.
45 Tomlinson, *The North Eastern Railway*, p. 289.
46 Ibid., p. 364.
47 DCRO Stockton and Darlington Railway Records, D/XD/35/11, report to share-holders, 1842–3.
48 Cited in Asa Briggs, *Victorian Cities* (Harmondsworth 1968), pp. 244–5.
49 DCRO Stockton and Darlington Railway Records, D/XD/35/6, report to share-holders, 7 August 1839.
50 PRO RAIL 667/11, Stockton and Darlington management committee minutes, 14 December 1838 and 15 December 1838.
51 Tomlinson, *The North Eastern Railway*, p. 437.
52 PRO RAIL 667/222, Middlesbrough Dock leasing agreement, 1841.
53 DCRO Pease–Stephenson papers, vol. 4, minutes of the annual general meeting of the Stockton and Darlington Railway, 11 August 1837.
54 See PRO RAIL 667/169, Shildon Works Committee.
55 PRO RAIL 667/11, Stockton and Darlington management committee minutes, 31 August 1838: resolution on Bishop Auckland and Weardale Railway.
56 PRO RAIL 667/4, Stockton and Darlington management committee minutes, 23 August 1844.
57 DCRO Stockton and Darlington Railway Records, D/XD/35/13, report to share-holders, August 1845.
58 T. E. Rounthwaite, *The Railways of Weardale* (Railway Corresponding and Travel Society 1965), p. 4.
59 *Report of the Committee Appointed to Inquire into the State of the Population in Mining Districts*, Parliamentary Papers, vol. 24, (1846), p. 210; Kenneth Warren, *Consett Iron 1840 to 1980: A Study in Industrial Location* (Oxford 1990), pp. 6–9.
60 PRO RAIL 667/4, Stockton and Darlington management committee minutes, 11 November 1846.
61 PRO RAIL 667/5, general meeting minutes of the Stockton and Darlington Railway, 29 September 1847.
62 Holmes, *The Stockton and Darlington Railway*, p. 33.
63 Jeans, *Jubilee Memorial*, p. 124.
64 Peter Barton, 'The port of Stockton on Tees and its creeks, 1825 to 1861', *Maritime History*, vol. 1, no. 2 (1971), p. 129.
65 McDougall, *The Stockton and Darlington Railway*, p. 31.
66 Kenwood, 'Capital investment in north eastern England', pp. 88, 90.
67 A. G. Kenwood, 'Transport capital formation and economic growth on Teesside, 1820–50', *Journal of Transport History*, vol. 11, pt 2 (1981), p. 59.

68 Cited in R. A. Church, *The History of the British Coal Industry*, vol. III: *1830–1913: Victorian Pre-eminence* (Oxford 1986), p. 68.

69 Ibid., pp. 68–9.

70 Tomlinson, *The North Eastern Railway*, p. 278.

71 Ibid.

72 DCRO Stockton and Darlington Railway Records, U415j, 33061, minutes of the Committee of the Stockton and Darlington Railway, 30 October 1835.

73 Cited in David Brooke, 'The promotion of four Yorkshire railways and the share capital market', *Transport History*, vol. 5, no. 3 (1972), p. 257.

74 The following account of the Great North of England Railway is based in part on Brooke, 'The promotion of four Yorkshire railways', and Reed, *Investment in Railways*, pp. 184–92.

75 Tomlinson, *The North Eastern Railway*, p. 280.

76 *Durham County Advertiser*, 1 January 1836, 15 January 1836.

77 Cited in Brooke, 'The promotion of four Yorkshire railways', p. 261.

78 Ibid., p. 263.

79 Tomlinson, *The North Eastern Railway*, p. 357.

80 PRO RAIL 667/234, Stockton and Darlington Railway share registers.

81 Ibid.

82 See DCRO Stockton and Darlington Railway Records, D/XD/35, reports to shareholders; Reed, *Investment in Railways*, pp. 178, 235–6; Tomlinson, *The North Eastern Railway*, p. 357.

83 *Railway Times*, vol. 5 (1842), p. 192.

84 Reed, *Investment in Railways*, p. 175.

85 Kirby, *Men of Business and Politics*, pp. 47–72.

86 Kenwood, 'Transport capital formation', p. 66.

6 CRISIS, 1847–50

1 Mary Williams, *The Pottery that Began Middlesbrough* (Redcar 1985).

2 Briggs, *Victorian Cities*, pp. 245–6.

3 Reid, *Middlesbrough and its Jubilee*, pp. 85–6; Lillie, *The History of Middlesbrough*, pp. 70–1.

4 Kenwood, 'Transport capital formation', p. 63; R. P. Hastings, 'Middlesbrough: a new Victorian boom town in 1840–41', *Cleveland and Teesside Local History Society Bulletin*, no. 30 (Winter 1975–6), 1–26.

5 J. W. Ord, *The History and Antiquities of Cleveland* (1846), p. 107.

6 The failure of Middlesbrough as an exercise in idealistic town planning is analysed in Leonard, 'Urban development and population growth'. See also Norman McCord and D. J. Rowe, 'Industrialisation and urban growth in northeast England', *International Review of Social History*, vol. 22 (1977), pp. 48–50.

7 T. R. Pearce, 'The Tees Engine Works – Gilkes, Wilson and their successors, 1844–1896', unpublished paper 1990, pp. 2–4.

8 J. K. Harrison, 'The production of pig iron in north east England, 1577–1865', in C. A. Hempstead (ed.), *Cleveland Iron and Steel: Background and Nineteenth Century History* (British Steel Corporation 1979), p. 58.

9 I. Bullock, 'The origins of economic growth on Teesside, 1851–81', *Northern History*, vol. 9 (1974), pp. 83–4.

10 C. N. Ward-Perkins, 'The commercial crisis of 1847', *Oxford Economic Papers*, vol. 2 (1950), pp. 78–9.

11 Statement before the Select Committee on Commercial Distress, cited in ibid., p. 85.

12 David Brooke, 'The North Eastern Railway, 1854–80: a study in railway consolidation and competition' (PhD thesis, University of Leeds, 1971), p. 57.

13 Charles Postgate, *Middlesbrough: Its History, Environs and Trade* (Middlesbrough 1899), pp. 15–16.

14 Joseph Albert Pease and Alfred Edward Pease, *An Historical Outline of the Association of Edward Pease, Joseph Pease and Sir Jos. W. Pease with the Industrial Development of South Durham and North Yorkshire and with the Creation of the Railway System* (privately published *c.* 1903), p. 8; Kenwood, 'Capital investment in north eastern England', pp. 139–40.

15 DCRO Stockton and Darlington Railway Records, D/XD/35/14, report to shareholders, 1846–7.

16 Ibid., D/XD/35/15, report to shareholders, 1847–8.

17 Ibid., D/XD/36/16, report to shareholders, 1848–9.

18 See PRO RAIL 557/1122/1150.

19 PRO RAIL 667/521, Stockton and Darlington Railway Board of Directors: copy minute, 7 January 1848.

20 DCRO Stockton and Darlington Railway Records, D/XD/36/16, report to shareholders, 1847–8.

21 Ibid., D/XD/35/17, report to shareholders, 1848–9.

22 Joseph Pease Diary, preface for 1851.

23 PRO RAIL 667/6, report of the directors of the Stockton and Darlington Railway Company to the half-yearly general meeting, 27 February 1850.

24 Brooke, 'The North Eastern Railway', pp. 58–9.

25 Tomlinson, *The North Eastern Railway*, pp. 508–9.

26 PRO RAIL 667/20, Stockton and Darlington management committee minutes, 17 August 1849.

27 Pease (ed.), *The Diaries of Edward Pease*, pp. 230, 250.

28 Ibid., p. 248.

29 Ibid., pp. 275, 292.

30 Kirby, *Men of Business and Politics*, p. 31.

31 DCRO Stockton and Darlington Railway Records, D/XD/35/18, report to shareholders, 1849–50.

32 Kenwood, 'Capital investment in north eastern England', pp. 43–7.

33 Kirby, *Men of Business and Politics*, p. 31.

34 Aileen Smiles, *Samuel Smiles and his Surroundings* (London 1956), p. 107.

35 Church (ed.), *The Dynamics of Victorian Business*, p. 43.

36 *First Report from the Select (Secret) Committee on Commercial Distress*, Parliamentary Papers, vol. 8 (1847–8), Q.4690, p. 395.

37 Joseph Pease Diary, concluding remarks, December 1850.

7 THE MATURE COMPANY, 1850–1863

1 Marshall, *Industry and Trade*, p. 89.

2 Ibid., p. 87.

3 Ibid., p. 91.
4 François Crouzet, *The Victorian Economy* (London 1982), p. 56.
5 R. A. Church, *The Great Victorian Boom, 1850–1873* (London 1975), pp. 36–7.
6 S. G. Checkland, *The Rise of Industrial Society in England, 1815–1885* (London 1964), p. 27.
7 Church, *The Great Victorian Boom*, p. 16.
8 Ibid., pp. 36–7.
9 Ibid., p. 51.
10 The following section is based on Bullock, 'The origins of economic growth'.
11 J. S. Owen, 'The Cleveland ironstone industry', in Hempstead (ed.), *Cleveland Iron and Steel*, p. 21.
12 Kirby, *Men of Business and Politics*, p. 34.
13 M. W. Kirby, 'Quakerism, entrepreneurship and the "family firm" in railway development: the north-east of England in the eighteenth and nineteenth centures', in Rose and Brown (eds.), *Firms, Entrepreneurship and Networks*, pp. 105–26.
14 Cited in Briggs, *Victorian Cities*, p. 241.
15 Joseph Pease Diary, concluding remarks, December 1857.
16 J. K. Harrison, 'The development of a distinctive "Cleveland" blast furnace practice, 1866–1875', in C. A. Hampstead (ed.), *Cleveland Iron and Steel: Background and Nineteenth Century History* (British Steel Corporation 1979), pp. 81–115.
17 *Colliery Guardian*, 2 January 1858.
18 Kenwood, 'Capital investment in north eastern England', p. 232.
19 Jeans, *Jubilee Memorial*, p. 127.
20 Kenwood, 'Transport capital investment', pp. 292–3.
21 Ibid., p. 289.
22 T. R. Gourvish, *Railways and the British Economy*, pp. 32, 40.
23 Tomlinson, *The North Eastern Railway*, p. 509.
24 Ibid., p. 558.
25 PRO RAIL 667/21, traffic agreement with Derwent Iron Company, 12 September 1851.
26 PRO RAIL 667/172, estimate of revenue from Consett ironstone traffic by John Dixon, 3 November 1857.
27 PRO RAIL 667/739, waggon fleet statistics, August 1855.
28 Tomlinson, *The North Eastern Railway*, pp. 555–6.
29 Pease (ed.), *The Diaries of Edward Pease*, p. 300.
30 Evidence of J. W. Pease before the House of Commons Committee on the Cleveland Union Railway Bill, 15 May 1858.
31 Brooke, 'The North Eastern Railway', p. 72.
32 Ibid., p. 66.
33 'Recollections of John Steele of Barnard Castle of an interview with the Duke of Cleveland, 1844', cited in Brooke, 'The North Eastern Railway', p. 67.
34 Ibid.
35 Ibid., p. 72.
36 Tomlinson, *The North Eastern Railway*, p. 524.
37 G. Brown to T. MacNay, 15 November 1853, letters and papers on the construction of the Darlington and Barnard Castle Railway. Cited in Brooke, 'The North Eastern Railway', p. 72.

38 Anon., *Fortunes Made in Business*, vol. I, 'The Peases of Darlington' (1884), p. 334; Jeans, *Jubilee Memorial*, p. 117.

39 Kenwood, 'Transport capital investment', p. 269.

40 Brooke, 'The North Eastern Railway', p. 77.

41 McDougall, *The Stockton and Darlington Railway*, pp. 33–4.

42 Mary H. Pease, *Henry Pease: A Short Story of his Life* (1897), p. 72.

43 PRO RAIL 667/395, chronological record of the Stockton and Darlington Railway.

44 Tomlinson, *The North Eastern Railway*, p. 526.

45 Brooke, 'The North Eastern Railway', p. 88.

46 Kenwood, 'Transport capital investment', p. 232.

47 Michael Collins, 'The banking crisis of 1878', *Economic History Review*, 2nd series, vol. 421, no. 4 (1989), pp. 504–27.

48 Phillips, *A History of Banks*, pp. 333–45; P. L. Cottrell, *Industrial Finance, 1830–1914: The Finance and Organisation of English Manufacturing Industry* (London 1980), p. 11.

49 DCRO Stockton and Darlington Railway Records, U415j, 37744, Stockton and Darlington Railway: half-yearly meeting, 9 August 1861; statement by Joseph Whitwell Pease.

50 The greater portion – £160,000 – was advanced by the Stockton and Darlington Company. See PRO RAIL 667/1475A, T. MacNay to Official Liquidators of the Northumberland and Durham District Bank, 27 August 1858.

51 See A. S. Wilson, 'The Consett Iron Company Limited: a case study in Victorian business history' (MPhil thesis, University of Durham, 1973), pp. 26–34.

52 H. W. Richardson and J. M. Bass, 'The profitability of the Consett Iron Company before 1914', *Business History*, vol. 7, no. 2 (1965), pp. 71–93.

53 PRO RAIL 667/1475A, 'Derwent Affairs': note by J. W. Pease, 30 December 1857; Backhouse Papers, D9, agreement for financial assistance to Derwent and Consett Iron Company, August 1859.

54 For Dale's subsequent career as an industrialist see Sir Edward Grey, *Sir David Dale: Inaugural Address to the Dale Memorial Trust* (Darlington 1911).

55 Tomlinson, *The North Eastern Railway*, p. 560.

56 Ibid., pp. 563–4.

57 DCRO Stockton and Darlington Railway Records, U415j, 29644, Ralph Ward Jackson to John Pease, 10 December 1858.

58 Ibid., John Pease to Ralph Ward Jackson, 1 December 1858. Italics in original.

59 Tomlinson, *The North Eastern Railway*, p. 566.

60 Ibid., pp. 570–6.

61 Ibid., p. 621.

62 Ibid., p. 588.

63 Brooke, 'The North Eastern Railway', p. 90.

64 PRO RAIL 667/97, *Negotiations between the NER and S and DRCo*. The following account is based on this file.

65 The three Stockton and Darlington representatives who joined the NER board were Henry Stobart, Isaac Wilson, and Joseph Whitewell Pease.

66 *Joint Select Committee of the House of Lords and the House of Commons on Railway Companies Amalgamation: Proceedings of the Committee and Minutes of Evidence*, Parliamentary Papers, vol.13 (1872), p. 27.

67 Joseph Pease Diary, 26 March 1860; Mewburn, *The Larchfield Diary*, p. 186.
68 *Northern Echo*, 28 September 1895.
69 R. J. Irving, *The North Eastern Railway Company, 1870–1914: An Economic History* (Leicester 1976), p. 140; Gourvish, *Mark Huish*, p. 69.
70 *Darlington and Stockton Times*, 12 August 1863.
71 PRO RAIL 667/712, reports, letters etc. by John Dixon CE, mainly concerned with calculations of working expenses and efficiency of operations, 1845–64.
72 For full details, see Kirby, *Men of Business and Politics*, pp. 42–5.

EPILOGUE

1 Pease, *Henry Pease*, p. 89.
2 J. W. Leonard, 'Saltburn: the northern Brighton', paper delivered to the Conference of Regional History Tutors, Hull College of Higher Education, July 1980, p. 195. See also J. K. Harrison and A. Harrison, 'Saltburn-by-the-Sea: the early years of a Stockton and Darlington Railway Company venture', *Industrial Archaeology Review*, vol. 4, pt 2 (1980), pp. 135–59.
3 *Engineering*, 30 June 1876.
4 PRO RAIL 667/414, Railway jubilee celebration at Darlington, 27 September 1875.
5 *Railway Gazette Supplement*, 2 October 1875, p. 479.
6 *Northern Echo*, 28 September 1875.
7 Irving, *The North Eastern Railway*, p. 138.
8 For Sir Joseph's views on labour relations see M. W. Kirby 'The failure of a Quaker business dynasty', pp. 151–6.
9 Cited in Irving, *The North Eastern Railway*, p. 60.
10 For analysis of the end of the Pease dynasty see Kirby, *Men of Business and Politics*, pp. 73–116.
11 DCRO Kitching Papers, D/Ki/303.

Bibliography

MANUSCRIPT SOURCES

RECORD OFFICES AND LIBRARIES

Durham County Record Office
Durham: Hodgkin Papers
           Kitching Papers
Darlington: Pease Family Records
           Pease–Stephenson Papers
           Stockton and Darlington Railway Records

Public Record Office, Kew
Papers of the Stockton and Darlington Railway Company (RAIL 667); Papers of the
    North Eastern Railway Company (RAIL 527)

Newcastle City Library
Tomlinson Collection

Stockton Reference Library
Graham Papers

PRIVATE COLLECTIONS

Backhouse Papers, Barclays Bank, Darlington; Joseph Pease Diary and Alfred
    Edward Pease Journal (in the possession of Mr J. Gurney Pease)

PRINTED SOURCES

BOOKS AND ARTICLES PUBLISHED BEFORE 1900

Adamson, Reverend James, 'Sketches of our information as to railroads', *Caledonian
    Mercury*, 1826.
Anon., *An Enquiry into the Reasons for the Advance of the Price of Coals within Seven
    Years Past* (1739).
    Fortunes Made in Business, vol. I: 'The Peases of Darlington' (1884).
    Observations of the Comparative Merits of Fixed and Locomotive Engines (1829).

The Two James's and the Two Stephensons (1861).

Booth, Henry, *Account of the Liverpool and Manchester Railway* (1831).

A Chapter in the History of Railway Locomotion, etc., appendix by John Wesley Hackworth (1892).

Galloway, Robert, *Annals of Coal Mining and the Coal Trade* (1898; reprinted Newton Abbot 1971).

Jeaffreson, J. C., *Life of Robert Stephenson*, vol. I (London 1864).

Jeans, J. S., *Jubilee Memorial of the Railway System: A History of the Stockton and Darlington Railway and a Record of its Results* (1875; reprinted Newcastle upon Tyne 1975).

Pioneers of the Cleveland Iron Trade (Middlesbrough 1875).

Mewburn, Francis, *The Larchfield Diary: Extracts from the Diary of the Late Mr Mewburn, First Railway Solicitor* (London 1876).

Ord, J. W., *The History and Antiquities of Cleveland* (1846).

Pease, Mary H., *Henry Pease: A Short Story of his Life* (1897).

Phillips, John, *The General History of Inland Navigation*, 4th edition (London 1803).

Phillips, Maberley, *A History of Banks, Bankers and Banking in Northumberland, Durham and North Yorkshire* (London 1894).

Postgate, Charles, *Middlesbrough: Its History, Environs and Trade* (Middlesbrough 1899).

Reid, H. G., *Middlesbrough and its Jubilee* (Middlesbrough 1881).

Smiles, Samuel, *Lives of the Engineers*, vol. V: *George and Robert Stephenson* (London 1862).

Tomlinson, Joseph, 'Presidential address', *Proceedings of the Institution of Mechanical Engineers* (1890).

Voltaire, F. M. A., *Letters on England* (London 1733; reprinted Harmondsworth 1980).

Walker, James, *Report on the Comparative Merits of Locomotive and Fixed Engines* (1829).

West, Theodore, *An Outline History of the Locomotive Engine* (London 1885).

Wood, Nicholas, *Treatise on Railways*, 3rd edition (*c.* 1833).

BOOKS AND ARTICLES PRINTED SINCE 1900

Ahrons, E. L., *The British Steam Railway Locomotive, 1825–1925* (London 1927).

Albert, William, *The Turnpike Road System in England, 1663–1840* (Cambridge 1972).

Aldcroft, Derek H., and Freeman, Michael (eds.), *Transport in the Industrial Revolution* (Manchester 1983).

Anderson, B. L., 'Money and the structure of credit in the eighteenth century', *Business History*, vol. 12, no. 2 (1970), pp. 90–100.

Anderson, Verity, *Friends and Relations: 3 Centuries of Quaker Families* (London 1980).

Ashton, T. S., *Iron and Steel in the Industrial Revolution* (Manchester 1963).

Ashton, T. S., and Sykes, J., *The Coal Industry of the Eighteenth Century* (Manchester 1929).

Bagwell, P. S., *The Transport Revolution from 1770* (London 1974).

Bailey, Michael R., 'Robert Stephenson and Co., 1823–1829', *Transactions of the Newcomen Society*, vol. 50 (1980), pp. 109–37.

Barber, B., 'The concept of the railway town and the growth of Darlington: a note', *Transport History*, vol. 3 (1970), pp. 283–92.

Barker, T. C., 'The beginnings of the canal age in the British Isles', in L. S. Pressnell (ed.), *Studies in the Industrial Revolution* (London 1960), pp. 1–22.

Barton, Peter, 'The port of Stockton on Tees and its creeks, 1825 to 1861', *Maritime History*, vol. 1, no. 2 (1971), pp. 120–9.

Bennett, G., Clavering, E., and Rounding, A., *A Fighting Trade: Rail Transport in Tyne Coal, 1600–1800* (Gateshead 1990).

Berg, Maxine (ed.), *Markets and Manufactures in Early Industrial Europe* (London 1991).

Berg, Maxine, and Hudson, Pat, 'Rehabilitating the industrial revolution', *Economic History Review*, 2nd series, vol. 45, no. 1 (1992), pp. 24–52.

Brett, R. L. (ed.), *Barclay Fox's Journal* (London 1979).

Briggs, Asa, *Victorian Cities* (Harmondsworth 1968).

Broadbridge, S. A., 'The sources of railway share capital', in M. C. Reed (ed.), *Railways in the Victorian Economy: Studies in Finance and Economic Growth* (Newton Abbot 1969), pp. 184–211.

Brooke, David, 'The promotion of four Yorkshire railways and the share capital market', *Transport History*, vol. 5, no. 3 (1972), pp. 236–67.

Buchanan, R. A., *The Engineers: A History of the Engineering Profession in Britain, 1750–1914* (London 1989).

Buckley, P. J., and Casson, M. C., *The Economic Theory of the Multinational Enterprise* (London 1985).

Bullock, I., 'The origins of economic growth on Teesside, 1851–81', *Northern History*, vol. 9 (1974), pp. 79–95.

Casson, M. C., *The Economics of Business Culture: Game Theory, Transaction Costs, and Economic Performance* (Oxford, 1991).

Chandler, A. D., *The Visible Hand: The Managerial Revolution in American Business* (Cambridge, Mass., and London 1977).

Checkland, S. G., *The Rise of Industrial Society in England, 1815–1885* (London 1964).

Church, Roy, *The Great Victorian Boom, 1850–1973* (London 1975).
    The History of the British Coal Industry, vol. III: *1830–1913: Victorian Pre-eminence* (Oxford 1986).

Church, Roy (ed.), *The Dynamics of Victorian Business: Problems and Perspectives to the 1870s* (London 1980).

Clapham, Sir John, *An Economic History of Modern Britain: The Early Railway Age, 1820–1850* (Cambridge 1926).

Clinker, C. R., *The Hay Railway* (London 1960).

Coase, R. H., 'The nature of the firm', *Economica*, vol. 4 (1937) pp. 386–405.

Collins, Michael, 'The banking crisis of 1878', *Economic History Review*, 2nd series, vol. 42, no. 4 (1989), pp. 504–27.

Corley, T. A. B., 'How Quakers coped with business success: Quaker industrialists, 1860–1914', in David J. Jeremy (ed.), *Business and Religion in Britain* (Aldershot 1988), pp. 164–87.

Cottrell, P. L., *Industrial Finance, 1830–1914: The Finance and Organisation of English Manufacturing Industry* (London 1980).

Cottrell, P. L., and Ottley, G., 'The beginnings of the Stockton and Darlington Railway, 1813–25: a celebratory note', *Journal of Transport History*, new series, vol. 3, no. 2 (1975), pp. 86–93.

Crafts, N. F. R., *British Economic Growth during the Industrial Revolution* (Oxford 1985).

Crouzet, François, *The Victorian Economy* (London 1982).

Davidoff, L., and Hall, C., *Family Fortunes: Men and Women in the English Middle Class, 1780–1850* (London 1989).

Davies, Hunter, *George Stephenson: A Biographical Study of the Father of the Railways* (London 1975).

Dendy Marshall, C. F., *A History of Railway Locomotives down to the End of the Year 1831* (London 1953).

Duckham, Baron, F., 'Canals and river navigations', in Derek H. Aldcroft and Michael J. Freeman (eds.), *Transport in the Industrial Revolution* (Manchester 1983), pp. 100–41.

Dyos, H. J., and Aldcroft, D. H., *British Transport: An Economic Survey from the Seventeenth Century to the Twentieth* (Harmondsworth 1974).

Evans, Neil, 'Two paths to economic development: Wales and the north-east of England', in Pat Hudson (ed.), *Regions and Industries: A Perspective on the Industrial Revolution in Britain* (Cambridge, 1989), pp. 201–27.

Flinn, Michael W., *The History of the British Coal Industry* vol. II: *1700–1830: The Industrial Revolution* (Oxford 1984).

Fogel, Robert W., *Railroads and American Economic Growth: Essays in Econometric History* (London 1964).

Gourvish, T. R., *Mark Huish and the London and North Western Railway: A Study of Management* (Leicester 1972).

   'Railway enterprise', in Roy Church (ed.), *The Dynamics of Victorian Business: Problems and Perspectives to the 1870s* (London 1980), pp. 126–41.

   Railways and the British Economy, 1830–1914 (London 1980).

Grey, Sir Edward, *Sir David Dale: Inaugural Address to the Dale Memorial Trust* (Darlington 1911).

Hair, P. E. H. (ed.), *Coals on Rails or the Reason of my Writing: The Autobiography of Anthony Errington from 1778 to around 1825* (Liverpool 1988).

Harrison, J. K., 'The development of a distinctive "Cleveland" blast furnace practice, 1866–1875', in C. A. Hempstead (ed.), *Cleveland Iron and Steel: Background and Nineteenth Century History* (British Steel Corporation 1979), pp. 81–115.

   'The production of pig iron in north east England, 1577–1865', in C. A. Hempstead (ed.), *Cleveland Iron and Steel: Background and Nineteenth Century History* (British Steel Corporation 1979), pp. 49–79.

Harrison, J. K., and Harrison, A., 'Saltburn-by-the-Sea: the early years of a Stockton and Darlington Railway Company venture', *Industrial Archaeology Review*, vol. 4, pt 2 (1980), pp. 135–59.

Hastings, R. P., 'Middlesbrough: A new Victorian boom town in 1840–41', *Cleveland and Teesside Local History Society Bulletin*, no. 30 (Winter 1975–6), pp. 1–26.

Hawke, G. R., *Railways and Economic Growth in England and Wales, 1840–1870* (Oxford 1970).

Hempstead, C. A. (ed.), *Cleveland Iron and Steel: Background and Nineteenth Century History* (British Steel Corporation 1979).

Holmes, Colin, and Booth, Alan (eds.), *Economy and Society: European Industrialisation and its Social Consequences* (Leicester 1991).

Holmes, P. J., *The Stockton and Darlington Railway, 1825–1975* (Ayr 1975).

Hoole, Ken, *A Regional History of the Railways of Great Britain*, vol. IV: *North East England* (Dawlish 1965).

Hoppit, Julian, 'The use and abuse of credit in eighteenth century England', in N. McKendrick and R. B. Outhwaite (eds.), *Business Life and Public Policy: Essays in Honour of D. C. Coleman* (Cambridge 1986).

Hudson, Pat, *Britain's Industrial Revolution* (London 1992).

The Genesis of Industrial Capital: A Study of the West Riding Wool Textile Industry, c. 1750–1850 (Cambridge 1986).

Hudson, Pat (ed.), *Regions and Industries: A Perspective on the Industrial Revolution in Britain* (Cambridge 1989).

Hughes, Edward, *North Country Life in the Eighteenth Century: The North East, 1700–1750* (London 1952).

Irving, R. J., *The North Eastern Railway Company, 1870–1914: An Economic History* (Leicester 1976).

Isichei, Elizabeth, *Victorian Quakers* (Oxford 1970).

Jackman, W. T., *The Development of Transportation in Modern England*, 2nd edition (London 1962).

Jenks, Leland H., 'Railroads as an economic force in American development', *Journal of Economic History*, vol. 4 (1944), pp. 1–20.

Jeremy, David J. (ed.), *Business and Religion in Britain* (Aldershot 1988).

Kenwood, A. G., 'Transport capital formation and economic growth on Teesside, 1820–50', *Journal of Transport History*, vol. 11, pt 2 (1981), pp. 53–71.

Kidner, R. W., *The Early History of the Locomotive, 1804–1876* (London 1956).

Kirby, M. W., 'The failure of a Quaker business dynasty: the Peases of Darlington, 1830–1902', in David J. Jeremy (ed.), *Business and Religion in Britain* (Aldershot 1988), pp. 142–63.

Men of Business and Politics: The Rise and Fall of the Quaker Pease Dynasty of North-East England, 1700–1943 (London 1984).

'Product proliferation in the British locomotive building industry, 1850–1914: an engineer's paradise?', *Business History*, vol. 30, no. 3 (1988), pp. 287–305.

'Quakerism, entrepreneurship and the "family firm" in railway development: the north-east of England in the eighteenth and nineteenth centuries', in Mary Rose and Jonathan Brown (eds.), *Firms, Entrepreneurship and Networks* (Manchester 1993), pp. 105–26.

'Technological innovation and structural division in the UK locomotive building industry, 1850–1914', in Colin Holmes and Alan Booth (eds.), *Economy and Society: European Industrialisation and its Social Consequences* (Leicester 1991), pp. 24–42.

Langton, John, 'The industrial revolution and the regional geography of England', *Transactions of the Institute of British Geographers*, vol. 9 (1984), pp. 145–67.

Larkin, Edgar J., and Larkin, John G., *The Railway Workshops of Britain, 1823–1986* (London 1988).

Lee, C. E., 'Early railways in Surrey', *Transactions of the Newcomen Society*, vol. 21 (1940–1, 1943), pp. 49–79.

The Evolution of Railways, 2nd edition (London 1943).

'The first steam railway: Brandling's colliery line between Leeds and Middleton', *Railway Magazine*, vol. 81 (1937), pp. 7–25.

The Swansea and Mumbles Railway 2nd edition (London 1954).

'The waggonways of Tyneside', *Archeologia Aeliana*, 4th series, vol. 29 (1951), pp. 25–40.

Lee, C. H., 'Corporate behaviour in theory and history: I the evaluation of theory', *Business History*, vol. 32, no. 1 (1990), pp. 17–31.

Leonard, J. W., 'Saltburn: the northern Brighton', paper delivered to the Conference of Regional History Tutors, Hull College of Higher Education, July 1980.

Lewin, Henry Grote, *Early British Railways: A Short History of their Origin and Development, 1801–1844* (London 1925).

Lewis, M. J. T., *Early Wooden Railways* (London 1970).

Lillie, William, *The History of Middlesbrough: An Illustration of the Evolution of English Industry* (Middlesbrough 1968).

McClelland, D. C., *The Achieving Society* (Princeton 1961).

McCord, Norman, *North East England: The Region's Development, 1760–1970* (London 1979).

McCord, Norman, and Rowe, D. J., 'Industrialisation and urban growth in north-east England', *International Review of Social History*, vol. 22 (1977), pp. 48–50.

McDougall, C. A., *The Stockton and Darlington Railway, 1824–1863* (Darlington 1975).

McKendrick, N., and Outhwaite, R. B. (eds.), *Business Life and Public Policy: Essays in Honour of D. C. Coleman* (Cambridge 1986).

Marshall, Alfred, *Industry and Trade* (London 1919 and 1923).

Mathias, Peter, *The First Industrial Nation: An Economic History of Britain, 1700–1914*, 1st edition (London 1968).

Matthews, P. W., and Tuke, A. W., *A History of Barclays Bank Limited* (London 1926).

Mercer, Stanley, 'Trevithick and the Merthyr tramroad', *Transactions of the Newcomen Society*, vol. 26 (1947–9), pp. 89–103.

Mitchell, B. R., 'The coming of the railway and United Kingdom economic growth', *Journal of Economic History*, vol. 24 (1964), pp. 315–36.

Mott, R. A., 'English waggonways of the eighteenth century', *Transactions of the Newcomen Society*, vol. 37 (1964–5), pp. 1–33.

Mullett, Michael, *Radical Religious Movements in Early Modern Europe* (London 1980).

Nef, J. U., *The Rise of the British Coal Industry*, vol. I (London 1932).

Nenadic, S., 'The family and the small firm in late nineteenth century Britain', paper presented at the tenth International Economic History Congress, Leuven 1990.

O'Brien, Patrick, *Railways and the Economic Development of Western Europe, 1830–1914* (London 1983).

Owen, J. S., 'The Cleveland ironstone industry', in C. A. Hempstead (ed.), *Cleveland Iron and Steel: Background and Nineteenth Century History* (British Steel Corporation 1979), pp. 9–47.

Pawson, E., *Transport and Economy: The Turnpike Roads of Eighteenth Century Britain* (Oxford 1977).

Pearce, T. R., 'The Tees Engine Works – Gilkes, Wilson and their successors, 1844–1896', unpublished paper 1990.

Pease, Joseph Albert, and Pease, Alfred Edward, *An Historical Outline of the Association of Edward Pease, Joseph Pease and Sir Jos. W. Pease with the Industrial Development of South Durham and North Yorkshire and with the Creation of the Railway System* (privately published *c.* 1903).

Pollard, Sidney, 'Fixed capital in the Industrial Revolution in Britain', *Journal of Economic History*, vol. 24 (1964), pp. 299–314.

    The Genesis of Modern Management: A Study of the Industrial Revolution in Great Britain (Harmondsworth 1968).

    Peaceful Conquest: The Industrialisation of Europe 1760–1970 (Oxford 1981).

    'Regional markets and national development', in Maxine Berg (ed.), *Markets and Manufactures in Early Industrial Europe* (London 1991), pp. 29–56.

Pollins, Harold, 'The marketing of railway shares in the first half of the nineteenth century', *Economic History Review*, 2nd series, vol. 7 (1954–5), pp. 230–9.

Pratt, David H., *English Quakers and the First Industrial Revolution: A Study of the Quaker Community in Four Industrial Counties – Lancashire, York, Warwick and Gloucester, 1750–1830* (New York and London 1985).

Pressnell, L. S. (ed.), *Studies in the Industrial Revolution: Essays Presented to T. S. Ashton* (London 1960).

Prior, Ann, 'The interaction of business and religion within the Society of Friends', unpublished paper, Department of Economics, Lancaster University 1991.

Raistrick, Arthur, *Quakers in Science and Industry* (Newton Abbot 1968).

Reed, M. C., *Investment in Railways in Britain, 1820–1844: A Study in the Development of the Capital Market* (Oxford 1975).

    'Railways and the growth of the capital market', in M. C. Reed (ed.), *Railways and the Victorian Economy: Studies in Finance and Economic Growth* (Newton Abbot 1969), pp. 162–83.

Reed, M. C. (ed.), *Railways and the Victorian Economy: Studies in Finance and Economic Growth* (Newton Abbot 1969).

Richardson, H. W., and Bass, J. M., 'The profitability of the Consett Iron Company before 1914', *Business History*, vol. 7, no. 2 (1965), pp. 71–93.

Rimmer, W. G., 'Middleton Colliery near Leeds (1770–1830)', *Yorkshire Bulletin of Economic and Social Research*, vol. 7 (1955), pp. 41–57.

Robbins, Michael, *George and Robert Stephenson* (London 1981).

    The Railway Age (Harmondsworth 1965).

Robertson, C. J. A., *The Origins of the Scottish Railway System 1722–1844* (Edinburgh 1983).

Rolt, L. T. C., *The Cornish Giant: The Story of Richard Trevithick, Father of the Steam Locomotive* (London 1960).

    George and Robert Stephenson: The Railway Revolution (London 1960).

Rose, Mary B., and Brown, Jonathan (eds.), *Firms, Entrepreneurship and Networks* (Manchester 1993).

Rounthwaite, T. E., 'An outline history of the Stockton and Darlington Railway', *Railway Observer*, vol. 26 (1956), pp. 14–27.

    The Railways of Weardale (Railway Corresponding and Travel Society 1965).

Rowe, D. J., 'The economy of the north-east in the nineteenth century: a survey', *Northern History*, vol. 6 (1971), pp. 117–37.

Simmons, Jack, 'Rail 150: 1975 or 1980?', *Journal of Transport History*, vol. 7, no. 1 (1980), pp. 1–8.

Smailes, A. E., *North England* (London 1960).

Smiles, Aileen, *Samuel Smiles and his Surroundings* (London 1956).

Smith, R. S., 'England's first rails: a reconsideration', *Renaissance and Modern Studies*, vol. 4 (1960), pp. 119–34.

'Huntingdon Beaumont: adventurer in coal mines', *Renaissance and Modern Studies*, vol. 1 (1957), pp. 115–53.

Sturgess, R. W. (ed.), *The Great Age of Industry in the North East* (Durham 1981).

Sweezy, P. M., *Monopoly and Competition in the English Coal Trade, 1550–1850* (Cambridge, Mass., 1938).

Sykes, John, *The Quakers: A New Look at their Place in Society* (London 1958).

Taylor, A. J., 'The sub-contract system in the British coal industry', in L. S. Pressnell (ed.), *Studies in the Industrial Revolution: Essays Presented to T. S. Ashton* (London 1960), pp. 215–35.

Temple, John, *Darlington and the Turnpike Roads* (Darlington 1971).

Thompson, Allan, *The Dynamics of the Industrial Revolution* (London 1973).

Tomlinson, W. W., *The North Eastern Railway: Its Rise and Development* (first published 1915; reprinted with an introduction by Ken Hoole, Newton Abbot 1967).

Turnbull, Gerard, 'Canals, coal and regional growth during the industrial revolution', *Economic History Review*, 2nd series, vol. 40, no. 4 (1987), pp. 537–60.

Von Tunzelmann, G. N., *Steam Power and British Industrialization to 1860* (Oxford 1978).

Ward, J. R., *The Finance of Canal Building in Eighteenth Century England* (Oxford 1974).

Ward-Perkins, C. N., 'The commercial crisis of 1847', *Oxford Economic Papers*, vol. 2 (1950), pp. 75–94.

Warren, J. G. H., *A Century of Locomotive Building by Robert Stephenson and Company 1823–1923* (Newcastle upon Tyne 1923).

Warren, Kenneth, *Consett Iron, 1840 to 1980: A Study in Industrial Location* (Oxford 1990).

Weber, Max, *The Protestant Ethic and the Spirit of Capitalism* (London 1930).

Williams, D. J., *Capitalist Combination in the Coal Industry* (London 1924).

Williams, Mary, *The Pottery that Began Middlesbrough* (Redcar 1985).

Williamson, O. E., *The Economic Institutions of Capitalism: Firms, Markets, Relational Contracting* (New York 1985).

Wrigley, E. A., 'The supply of raw materials in the industrial revolution', *Economic History Review*, 2nd series, vol. 15, no. 1 (1962), pp. 1–16.

Young, Robert, *Timothy Hackworth and the Locomotive* (London 1923).

NEWSPAPERS

Colliery Guardian
Darlington and Stockton Times
Durham County Advertiser
Newcastle Chronicle
Newcastle Courant

Newcastle Daily Chronicle
Northern Echo
Railway Gazette
Tyne Mercury

PARLIAMENTARY PAPERS

Report of the Committee appointed to Inquire into the State of the Population in the Mining Districts, Parliamentary Papers, vol. 24 (1846).
First Report from the Select (Secret) Committee on Commercial Distress, Parliamentary Papers, vol. 8 (1847–8).
Joint Select Committee of the House of Lords and the House of Commons on Railway Companies Amalgamation: Proceedings of the Committee and Minutes of Evidence, Parliamentary Papers, vol. 13 (1872).

THESES

Brooke, David, 'The North Eastern Railway, 1854–80: a study in railway consolidation and competition (PhD thesis, University of Leeds, 1971).
Cromar, P., 'Economic power and organisation: the development of the coal industry on Tyneside, 1700–1828' (PhD thesis, University of Cambridge, 1977).
Kenwood, A. G., 'Capital investment in north eastern England, 1800–1913' (PhD thesis, University of London, 1962).
Leonard, J. W., 'Urban development and population growth in Middlesbrough, 1831–1871' (D Phil thesis, University of York, 1976).
Reed, M. C., 'Investment in railways in Britain, 1820–1844' (D Phil thesis, University of Oxford, 1970).
Wilson, A. S., 'The Consett Iron Company Limited: a case study in Victorian business history' (M Phil thesis, University of Durham, 1973).

Index

Ahrons, E. L., 67
Armstrong, Sir William, 12
Atkinson, George, 24
Auckland coalfield, 3, 21, 29, 86, 111, 155, 161, 162

Backhouse, J. and J., 26, 29
Backhouse, Jonathan: and Stockton and Darlington canal project, 29–31; treasurer to Stockton and Darlington Railway, 39; and coastal trade in coal, 50, 70–1; financing of Stockton and Darlington Railway, 56–7; resignation as treasurer, 80; and coal shipments, 139
Backhouse family, 26, 33, 139
Bank Charter Act (1844), 135
Bank of England, 97, 135–6
Barnard Castle, 153–9
Barnard Castle and Bishop Auckland Railway project, 159
Barrington, Lord, 36
Bedlington Iron Co., 12, 41, 44, 45
Bell, Isaac Lowthian, 147
Bell brothers, 147, 165
Bevan, David, 45
Birkbeck, Henry, 124, 129, 142
Birkinshaw, John, 41–2
Bishop Auckland and Weardale Railway, 117, 118–19, 120
Bishopley, 119
Black Boy Colliery, 57, 69, 70, 139
Blackett, Christopher, 17, 19
Blanshard, Henry, 72, 81
Blenkinsop, John, 18, 19
Blucher locomotive, 30
Bolckow, Henry, 133, 148
Bolckow and Vaughan, 133, 134–5, 136, 146, 147, 148, 152
Booth, Henry, 68
Botcherby, Robert, 30
Bouch, Thomas, 108, 161
Bouch, William, 108
Bowes, George, 13

Boyne, Lord, 151
Brandling, Charles, 18
Brandon, 151
Brandreth, Thomas Shaw, 67
Brassey, Thomas, 102
Bridgewater, Duke of, 10, 24
Brindley, James, 21, 23
Brown, Captain Samuel, 74
Brunton, William, 24
Brusselton Quarry, 48
Bubble Act, 1720, 34
Buddle, John, 12
Butterknowle Colliery, 21
Butterly Ironworks, 12
Byers Green, 83, 111

Cairns, Jeremiah, 31
canals: in eighteenth century, 9–10; in north-east England, 21–5, 143, 150–1; Stockton and Darlington project, 27–31 *passim.*
Cargo Fleet, 27, 147
Chandler, Alfred, 53
Chapman, William, 19
Chaytor, William Jr, 32, 33, 37
Church, R. A., 144, 146
City of Glasgow Bank, 163
Clapham, Sir John, 96
Clarence Railway: projected, 81; incorporated, 83; and Auckland coalfield, 85; competition with Stockton and Darlington Railway, 110–15; financial record, 112–13, 115; leased to Stockton and Hartlepool Railway, 114–15; coal shipments, 136; mentioned, 139
Cleveland, Duke of, 158–9
Cleveland Main Seam, 146–7
Cleveland Railway, 167
coal industry: in eighteenth century, 5, 9–25 *passim*; restrictive practices, 13–15; expansion in north-east England, 121–2, 143, 150–1
Coalbrookdale Iron Company, 11